What *Brown v. Board of Education* Should Have Said

What *Brown v. Board of Education* Should Have Said

The Nation's Top Legal Experts Rewrite America's Landmark Civil Rights Decision

EDITED WITH AN INTRODUCTION BY

Jack M. Balkin

Bruce Ackerman • Jack M. Balkin • Derrick A. Bell
Drew S. Days III • John Hart Ely • Catharine A. MacKinnon
Michael W. McConnell • Frank I. Michelman
Cass R. Sunstein

New York University Press
NEW YORK AND LONDON

NEW YORK UNIVERSITY PRESS
New York and London

First published in paperback in 2002.

Library of Congress Cataloging-in-Publication Data
What Brown v. Board of Education should have said : the nation's top
legal experts rewrite America's landmark civil rights decision / edited
with an introduction by Jack M. Balkin ; Bruce Ackerman . . . [et al.].
p. cm.
Includes bibliographical references and index.
ISBN 0-8147-9889-6 (cloth : acid-free paper)
ISBN 0-8147-9890-X (pbk. : acid-free paper)
1. Brown, Oliver, 1918– —Trials, litigation, etc.—History. 2. Topeka
(Kan.). Board of Education—Trials, litigation, etc.—History.
3. Segregation in education—Law and legislation—United States—
History. 4. Discrimination in education—Law and legislation—
United States—History. I. Title: What Brown versus Board of
Education should have said. II. Balkin, J. M. III. Ackerman, Bruce A.
KF228.B76 W48 2001
344.73'0798—dc21 2001001735

New York University Press books are printed on acid-free paper,
and their binding materials are chosen for strength and durability.

Manufactured in the United States of America
10 9 8 7 6 5 4 3 2 1

To Margret,
who always knows what to say

Contents

Preface

This is a book about America's most honored civil rights opinion, *Brown v. Board of Education*, and about what that opinion means for us today. For that reason, it is also a book about the modern law of race relations in the United States and the role that courts play in promoting racial equality.

For this book, I asked a group of distinguished constitutional scholars to rewrite the opinion in *Brown v. Board of Education*. I asked each one of them the same question: How would you have written the *Brown* opinion in 1954, if you knew then what you know now about the subsequent history of the country and the progress of race relations in the past half century? The results were staged at a session of the American Association of Law Schools in January of 2000, where the nine of us assumed the roles of a mock Supreme Court.

The rules were quite simple. Each person was asked to write an opinion using only materials available as of May 17, 1954, when the first opinion in *Brown* was handed down. The opinion could be structured as a majority opinion, a concurrence, or a dissent. The participants were allowed to predict events if they chose but they could not refer to anything in the future as fact. Thus, they could not cite a 1995 study on school desegregation or a law review article written in 1996, although they were free to make any arguments or predictions about the future they wanted. Although the opinions were to be written as of 1954, a few anachronisms remain. In 1954 the polite term for African Americans was "Negro." Some contributors retained that expression, while others used the (less appropriate then but more appropriate now) expression "black."

The contributors had to address three different sets of issues. The opinion we call *Brown* is actually three opinions. The first of these, usually called *Brown I*, was decided on May 17, 1954. It held that state-enforced racial segregation of public school children violated the Equal

Protection Clause of the Fourteenth Amendment. The second opinion, decided the same day, was *Bolling v. Sharpe*. While *Brown* concerned the states, *Bolling* concerned racial discrimination by the federal government. *Bolling* held that although the Fourteenth Amendment applied to the states, racial segregation by the federal government in the District of Columbia violated the Due Process Clause of the Fifth Amendment. A third opinion, usually called *Brown II*, was decided on May 31, 1955. It concerned the very thorny question of what, if anything, courts could do to remedy segregation, and it held that states should desegregate their schools "with all deliberate speed." I asked the participants to draft an opinion that addressed the legal issues raised by all three of these opinions: *Brown I* (the legality of segregation), *Brown II* (remedy), and *Bolling v. Sharpe* (applicability to the federal government).

It is important to be clear about the purpose of such an exercise. All of the participants well understand that simply changing the wording of the *Brown* opinion in 1954 probably would not have prevented the massive resistance to desegregation that occurred first in the South and later in the North. The goal is not to come up with the magic legal formula that would have made everything turn out right. Rather, the point is to rethink the meaning of America's constitutional commitment to equality in our own time.

Thus, rewriting the opinion today, almost fifty years after *Brown*, has three basic purposes. First, it is a good way to reexamine the premises of *Brown* and the American law of equality at the beginning of a new century. The meaning of *Brown v. Board of Education* is heavily contested today. Constitutional interpreters of all stripes find different things in it. Both proponents and opponents of race-conscious affirmative action, for example, claim that they are the true inheritors of *Brown* and its legacy. Thurgood Marshall and the NAACP pushed for *Brown* as part of a vision of a racially integrated society. Although *Brown* is revered today, many African American leaders, scholars, and intellectuals, including most prominently Justice Clarence Thomas, have attacked the integrative ideal that *Brown* seemed to represent. Many critics now argue that integration is a failed strategy and that it is better to push for equalization of facilities and equal educational opportunity.

Second, *Brown* has often been a litmus test for theories of constitutional interpretation. It is often said that no theory of constitutional interpretation is sound if it cannot explain and justify *Brown v. Board of Education*. Yet when it was first decided, many critics thought that *Brown* was inconsistent with sound principles of constitutional interpretation. Herbert Wechsler of Columbia Law School famously argued in 1959 that he could not come up with a neutral principle to justify the result in the case. Critics of the philosophy of original intention have pointed to *Brown* as a counterexample, arguing that the framers and ratifiers of the Fourteenth Amendment wanted only limited equality for blacks. That is one reason why a Fifteenth Amendment, explicitly granting blacks the right to vote, was thought necessary. Many of the contributors to this volume have distinctive theories about constitutional theory and constitutional interpretation. Rewriting *Brown* allows them to apply their theories to the difficult problems that *Brown* presents. It is an excellent test of what relatively abstract theories of constitutional interpretation mean in practice.

Finally, *Brown* has become a symbol of the role of courts in a democracy. It has been at the center of a continuing debate over the role of law in reshaping society, the extent to which courts can successfully push for lasting social change, and the legitimacy of their trying to do so. Many of the opinions in this book address the roles, abilities, and limitations of courts fifty years after *Brown*.

In Part I of the book, I have written three chapters introducing the reader to the *Brown* opinion. They explain the struggles over the meaning and legacy of *Brown*, outline the history of the *Brown* litigation, and explain the key issues that were at stake in the case. Part II features the contributors' revised opinions. Finally, as an appendix, I have included Chief Justice Warren's original opinions in *Brown I*, *Bolling*, and *Brown II* for comparison.

I am grateful to many colleagues and friends for their help in putting this volume together. First and foremost I would like to thank the contributors themselves for being willing to play along with this hypothetical exercise in a rare combination of intellectual seriousness and good humor. Derrick Bell, Bob Gordon, Mark Graber, Scot Powe, and Mark Tushnet read and commented on the three introductory chapters and offered excellent suggestions. Bruce Ackerman and Reva Siegel provided me with valuable advice about the project. And my former student, Cristina Rodríguez, offered exceptional research assistance.

Finally, as this project went through its inevitable ups and downs, I have always relied on the love and emotional support of my wife, Margret Wolfe, who remains the most important person in my life. Her generosity, and her love, make any task easy, and any burden light.

JACK M. BALKIN
New Haven, Connecticut
July 2000

Part I

Brown v. Board of Education
A Critical Introduction

Jack M. Balkin

Chapter 1

Brown as Icon

On May 17, 1954, the Supreme Court of the United States handed down one of its most famous opinions—*Brown v. Board of Education of Topeka, Kansas.*[1] The case called *Brown* was actually a collection of five cases, from Delaware (*Gebhart v. Belton*), Kansas (*Brown v. Board of Education*), South Carolina (*Briggs v. Elliott*), Virginia (*Davis v. County School Board of Prince Edward County*), and the District of Columbia (*Bolling v. Sharpe*). The Court heard them together because each raised the issue of the constitutionality of racially segregated public schools, albeit with slightly different facts and circumstances. In fact, Thurgood Marshall, the main architect of the NAACP's legal strategy to overturn Jim Crow, actually represented the plaintiffs in the South Carolina case, *Briggs v. Elliott*. The District of Columbia case, *Bolling v. Sharpe*,[2] was treated separately from the others because it raised distinct issues about the federal government's duty to respect racial equality. It was handed down on the same day. Finally, the Supreme Court decided to delay the issue of the proper remedy for segregated schools for another year. It issued a second opinion in *Brown v. Board of Education* on May 31, 1955,[3] to deal with remedial issues, concluding with the order to go forward "with all deliberate speed." This opinion is usually referred to as *Brown II*, to distinguish it from the first opinion, called *Brown I*. Together, the three opinions of *Brown I*, *Brown II*, and *Bolling* have come collectively to be known as "*Brown*" or "the *Brown* opinion" in the popular imagination, and in the discussion that follows I will refer to them in this way.

In the half century since the Supreme Court's decision, *Brown* has become a beloved legal and political icon. *Brown* is one of the most famous Supreme Court opinions, better known among the lay public than *Marbury v. Madison*,[4] which confirmed the Supreme Court's power of judicial review, or *McCulloch v. Maryland*,[5] which first offered an expansive interpretation of national powers under the Constitution. Indeed, in terms of sheer name recognition, *Brown* ranks with *Miranda v. Arizona*,[6] whose warnings delivered to criminal suspects appear on every police show, or the abortion case, *Roe v. Wade*,[7] which has been a continual source of political and legal controversy since it was handed down in 1973.

Even if *Brown* is less well known than *Miranda* or *Roe*, there is no doubt that it is the single most honored opinion in the Supreme Court's corpus. The civil rights policy of the United States in the last half century has been premised on the correctness of *Brown*, even if people often disagree (and disagree heatedly) about what the opinion stands for. No federal judicial nominee and no mainstream national politician today would dare suggest that *Brown* was wrongly decided. At most they might suggest that the opinion was inartfully written, that it depended too much on social science literature, that it did not go far enough, or that it has been misinterpreted by legal and political actors to promote an unjust political agenda. The use made of *Brown* is often criticized, but the idea of *Brown* remains largely sacred in American political culture.

It was not always thus. In the decade following 1954 the Supreme Court and its opinion in *Brown* were villified in terms far stronger than many of the attacks leveled against *Roe* and *Miranda*. Even many defenders of the result had little good to say about the opinion, arguing that its overruling of previous precedents was abrupt and unexplained and that its use of social science to demonstrate the harm that segregation imposed on black children was unconvincing. The day after the decision, May 18, 1954, James Reston wrote in the *New York Times* that the Court had rejected "history, philosophy, and custom" in basing its decision in "the primacy of the general welfare. . . . Relying more on the social scientists than on legal precedents—a procedure often in controversy in the past—the Court insisted on equality of the mind and heart rather than on equal school facilities. . . . The Court's opinion read more like an expert paper on sociology than a Supreme Court opinion."[8] If the defenders of *Brown* were uneasy, its opponents were positively incensed by the decision. People who accuse the contemporary Supreme Court of abusing its office may forget how deeply *Brown* was resented, especially in the South. In March of 1956, southern senators and congressmen issued a "Southern Manifesto" denouncing *Brown* as a "clear abuse of judicial power" that substituted the Justices' "personal political and social ideas for the established law of the land." This proved to be one of the more moderate reactions. Although congressional leaders pledged to "use all lawful means to bring about the reversal of this decision which is contrary to the Constitution,"[9] other opponents of the decision were less committed to peaceful legal methods. *Brown* gave rise to the era of "massive resistance" in the South, leading President Eisenhower at one point to call in federal troops to enforce a desegregation order in Arkansas. Yet, by the close of the twentieth century, *Brown* had achieved a special place of honor.

One reason for that special status is that *Brown* fits nicely into a widely held and often repeated story about America and its Constitution. This story has such deep resonance in American culture that we may justly regard it as the country's national narrative. I call this story the Great Progressive Narrative. The Great Progressive Narrative sees America as continually striving for democratic ideals from its founding and eventually realizing democracy through its historical development. According to the Great Progressive Narrative, the Constitution reflects America's deepest ideals, which are gradually realized through historical struggle and acts of great political courage. The basic ideals of America and the American people are good, even if America and Americans sometimes act unjustly, and even if people acting in the name of the Constitution sometimes perpetrate terrible injustices. The basic ideals of Americans and their Constitution are promises for the future, promises that the country eventually will live up to, and, in so doing, confirm the country's deep commitments to liberty and equality.

It is easy to see how *Brown* fits into this narrative and confirms its truth: Through years of struggle and a great Civil War, America gradually freed itself from an unjust regime of chattel slavery. The country's failures were redeemed by the Thirteenth, Fourteenth, and Fifteenth Amendments to the Constitution. To be sure, the Civil War was followed by retrenchment and the establishment of Jim Crow, which was given official sanction in the 1896 decision in *Plessy v. Ferguson*.[10] Nevertheless, eventually the country redeemed itself once again by overturning that unjust precedent and firmly establishing the principle of racial equality. Seen in this way, *Brown* represents the Good Constitution—the Constitution whose deeper principles and truths were only fitfully and imperfectly realized, rather than the Constitution that protected slavery and Jim Crow. By extension, *Brown* also symbolizes the Good America, rather than the country that slaughtered Native Americans, subordinated women, and enslaved blacks.

A. Brown *and the State of Education Today*

In many respects the honor *Brown* has received is ironic. *Brown* was a case about public school desegregation, but by the end of the twentieth century many public schools in the United States remained largely segregated by race. Indeed, the United States has been in a period of resegregation for some time now. The tendency is most pronounced in the South, which, during the 1970s and 1980s, was transformed from a region of virtually complete educational segregation to one of the most integrated parts of the country. The present tendency toward segregation of Latinos is, if anything, even more pronounced than that with respect to blacks.[11] Perhaps equally important, the increasing resegregation of schools is strongly correlated with class and with poverty. Although only 5 percent of segregated white schools are in areas of concentrated poverty, over 80 percent of segregated black and Latino schools are.[12] Schools in high poverty areas routinely result in lower levels of educational performance; even well-prepared students with stable family backgrounds are hurt academically by attending such schools.

The pace of desegregation has slowed since the middle of the 1970s, due in part to Supreme Court decisions that made it very difficult to implement desegregation orders that would encompass both increasingly white suburban and increasingly minority inner city school districts. The 1974 case of *Milliken v. Bradley*,[13] involving metropolitan Detroit, largely freed white suburban districts from any legal obligation to participate in metropolitan desegregation efforts. As a result, in metropolitan areas where minorities were concentrated in inner cities, significant desegregation became virtually impossible, because fewer and fewer white children lived in those school districts and fewer still attended public schools. Nevertheless, desegregation actually increased a bit during the 1980s, even though the Reagan Administration repeatedly tried to persuade courts to scale back their intervention in school districts.[14]

However, during the 1990s, the Supreme Court began to signal strongly to the lower federal courts to relax their supervision of school districts. In the 1991 case *of Board of Education of Oklahoma City v. Dowell*,[15] the Supreme Court held that courts could end desegregation orders in school districts that had attempted in good faith to comply, even if this would result in immediate resegregation. The replacement of Justice Thurgood Marshall by Justice Clarence Thomas in 1991 consolidated a general trend toward restricting court supervision. In 1992, in *Freeman v. Pitts*,[16] the Supreme Court held that courts could end some aspects of school desegregation orders even if other aspects had never been fully complied with. And in the 1995 case of *Missouri v. Jenkins*,[17] the Supreme Court overturned an ambitious plan for magnet schools in Kansas City designed to attract white students back into the inner city as unjustified and unnecessary to achieve desegregation. It also rejected the argument that increased spending on education could be justified in order to remedy reduced achievement by students in inner city schools. Justice Thomas, concurring, chastised those who thought of integration as a panacea for the problems of the black community, arguing that the theory that black children suffer psychological harms from segregation "rest[ed] on an assumption of black inferiority."[18]

The Supreme Court's decisions have accelerated the federal courts' drive to end existing desegregation orders. In other cases school districts have remained technically subject to court orders but now face virtually no enforcement activity. These districts have not even bothered to press for termination of existing court orders because the necessary litigation would impose new legal costs and subject them to renewed judicial scrutiny.[19] Both of these trends have enhanced the tendency toward resegregation in the 1990s.

Racial segregation today is the result of a complicated mix of social, political, legal, and economic factors, rather than the result of direct state commands ordering racial separation. Yet whatever the causes, it remains overwhelmingly the case that minority children in central cities are educated in virtually all-minority schools with decidedly inferior facilities and educational opportunities. Even when minorities in suburban and rural schools are included, a majority of black and Latino students around the country still attend predominantly minority schools.[20]

In a way, the subsequent history of school desegregation mirrors the Supreme Court's original separation of the principle of racial equality (*Brown I*) from the remedy for previous injustices (*Brown II*). *Brown I* is venerated for declaring segregation unconstitutional, but the desegregation remedies begun in *Brown II* have been honored in the breach more than the observance. The shift in attitudes over the past half century is well symbolized by the fact that the Supreme Court seat once held by Thurgood Marshall, the acolyte of integration as the path to equal opportunity for blacks, is now held by Clarence Thomas, who argues that integration will not help blacks, that one-race schools do not necessarily violate the Constitution, and that the only concern of the courts should be whether schools have deliberately classified students by race.

The effective compromise reached in the United States at the close of the twentieth century is that schools may be segregated by race as long as it is not due to direct government fiat. Furthermore, although *Brown I* emphasized that equal educational opportunity was a crucial component of citizenship, there is no federal constitutional requirement that pupils in predominantly minority school districts receive the same quality of education as students in wealthier, largely all-white suburban districts.[21] Although these suburban districts seem as healthy as ever, the public school system in many urban areas is on the brink of collapse. Increasing numbers of parents who live in these urban areas are pushing for charter schools, home schooling, or vouchers for private schools in order to avoid traditional public school education. By the end of the century, the principle of *Brown* seems as hallowed as ever, but its practical effect seems increasingly irrelevant to contemporary public schooling.

B. What Does Brown Mean?

As with all honored icons, *Brown* has come to mean different things to different people. In many ways, *Brown* functions as a sort of Rorschach test for politicians and legal theorists. Americans naturally invest the decision with the principles and philosophies they believe in.

A good example is the holding of the case. Stated in its narrowest terms, *Brown I* stood for the proposition that state laws could not require separate but equal facilities in public elementary and secondary schools. Although the Court based its opinion in *Brown I* in part on the effects of segregation on small children, it quickly extended the case to graduate and professional schools. This was hardly surprising. Supreme Court cases immediately preceding *Brown* involved challenges to segregation in law schools. Thus, in 1956, the Court held that blacks were entitled to prompt admission to all state-run graduate and professional programs under the authority of *Brown I*. Indeed, the Supreme Court actually distinguished *Brown II*, arguing that the latter opinion, "which contemplates some delay in the desegregation of public elementary and secondary schools, has no application."[22]

In the 1958 case of *Cooper v. Aaron*, which arose out of the Little Rock controversy, the Supreme Court described its holding in *Brown I* fairly narrowly: *Brown* stood for the proposition "that the Fourteenth Amendment forbids States to use their governmental powers to bar children on racial grounds from attending schools where there is state participation through any arrangement, management, funds or property."[23] Within a decade, however, the meaning of *Brown* began to change and expand, both within the larger political culture and in the opinions of the Supreme Court itself. Although the case was nominally about segregated schools and the educational harms to schoolchildren that flowed from them, the Supreme Court followed *Brown I* with a series of unsigned (*per curiam*, literally "by the court") orders affirming lower court decisions involving municipal golf courses, public buses, public beaches, and the like.[24] In most of these cases the Court did not give reasons for its orders; it simply summarily affirmed (or reversed) the decisions below. As a result many legal scholars criticized the per curiam opinions as an inappropriate exercise of judicial review.[25] Nevertheless, the per curiam orders clearly contemplated that *Brown* was about something more than educational opportunity. To its admirers, *Brown* seemed to point to a larger theory about racial equality and perhaps about equality as a whole. In 1963, the Court cited *Brown* for a considerably more general proposition: "[I]t is no longer open to question," the Court explained, "that a State may not constitutionally require segregation of public facilities."[26] That same Term the Court cited *Brown* as prohibiting federal or state discrimination in employment.[27] By 1964 Justice Goldberg could state confidently that *Brown* "affirmed the right of all Americans to public equality." The case stood for the general proposition that "the Fourteenth Amendment commands equality and that racial segregation by law is inequality."[28] Eventually, as these words suggest, *Brown* became recognized as a symbol, not only of racial equality, but of equality and equal opportunity generally.

As an honored icon, *Brown* has been invested with different and often conflicting meanings. People of different political persuasions have fought over its significance and over its legacy. There is no better example than contemporary debates over affirmative action. Opponents of affirmative action argue that *Brown* stands for the proposition that government may never make a person's race a condition for the receipt of any benefit or detriment, special treatment or special burden. Under this view, affirmative action programs violate the spirit of *Brown* because they bestow benefits through classifying individuals according to their race. Supporters of affirmative action argue, to the contrary, that *Brown* stands for the proposition that government may not subordinate one group of citizens to another or use formally equal rules to perpetuate the social inferiority of one group with respect to another. Because affirmative action programs do not subordinate whites but rather attempt to provide opportunities for subordinated groups, they are on a different moral and political footing than government actions that maintain white supremacy or help preserve greater opportunities for whites. According to this view, when governments try to remedy the effects of past discrimination and help minorities gain greater opportunities in education and employment, they are acting consistent with the spirit of *Brown*, because the real goal of *Brown* was genuine educational opportunity.

The meaning of *Brown* and the struggle over its legacy are intertwined with the meaning of the case that it effectively overruled, the 1896 case of *Plessy v. Ferguson*. In *Plessy*, the Supreme Court upheld a Louisiana statute that required segregation of railway carriages, a decision that was later extended to segregated facilities generally, including segregated public education. (The author of the opinion was, ironically, a Justice named Brown.) The Court argued that Louisiana's regulation was a reasonable one, "consistent with the established usages, customs and traditions of the people, and with a view to the promotion of their comfort, and the preservation of the public peace and good order." Without segregation, Justice Brown reasoned, individuals would be subjected to "enforced commingling" that would be unpleasant to both races. Confronted with the argument that separation of the races was inherently demeaning and oppressive to blacks, and that it "stamp[ed] the colored race with a badge of inferiority," the Court responded with one of the most disingenuous statements in its history: "If this be so," Justice Brown opined, "it is not by reason of anything found in the act, but solely because the colored race chooses to put that construction upon it."[29] With these words, the Supreme Court gave its official blessing to Jim Crow, and over the course of the next few decades, state legislatures throughout the South passed laws effectively disenfranchising blacks and mandating segregation of schools, churches, drinking fountains, places of public accommodation, and even funeral parlors.

Seven Justices of the Supreme Court joined in Brown's majority opinion, suggesting that to the generation of the 1890s *Plessy* was a supremely easy case. Only one Justice, John Marshall Harlan, dissented. Harlan argued that "[i]n view of the Constitution, in the eye of the law, there is in this country no superior, dominant, ruling class of citizens. There is no caste here. Our Constitution is color-blind, and neither knows nor tolerates classes among citizens."[30] Among legal scholars these words have been honored almost as much as the *Brown* opinion itself. Yet this famous passage contains two distinct claims: first, that the Constitution is opposed to the maintenance of racial caste, group subordination, or second-class citizenship, and second, that the Constitution is colorblind and prohibits racial classifications. As time went on, the potential differences between these two formulations—the "antisubordination" or "equal citizenship" principle and the "anticlassification" or "color-blindness" principle—would become increasingly important. Although these two principles reach identical results in many cases—state enforced segregation of schools being one of them—they tend to produce different results in many others. Two important contemporary examples are affirmative action policies and the creation of "majority minority" voting districts that increase opportunities for minority representation in state legislatures and the U.S. Congress.

When Harlan wrote in 1896, these two versions of the antidiscrimination principle—antisubordination versus anticlassification, or equal citizenship versus color-blindness—did not strongly conflict. Nor was their conflict apparent during the opening years of the civil rights movement. Much of Martin Luther King's rhetoric, for example, combines both elements. In his famous "I have a dream" speech, delivered at the Lincoln Memorial on August 28, 1963, King spoke of his dream that his "four little children will one day live in a nation where they will not be judged by the color of their skin but by content of their character."[31] Yet King's speech is also about the maintenance of social inferiority. That injustice is not redeemed simply by the elimination of formal barriers: "We cannot be satisfied as long as a colored person in Mississippi cannot vote and a colored person in New York believes he has nothing for which to vote."[32] Clearly King believed that the fact that New York did not practice Jim Crow did not mean that there were no problems of inequality there. After all, the official title of the March on Washington was the March for Jobs and Freedom—much more than a demand for formal equality before the law. Indeed, King's vision is even more radical than this, for it combines color-blindness with full social equality not only in civil society but in the private sphere of everyday interaction; he dreams of a world in which whites and blacks treat each other as family, as "sisters and brothers."[33]

In the half century since *Brown*, it is clear that although the elimination of Jim Crow has done much good, blacks as a group still lag behind whites in many of the most important social measures of well-being and success—household income, infant mortality, life expectancy, educational opportunity, and employment levels. Although mandated segregation is forbidden by law, many blacks are practically segregated from whites in both housing and educational opportunities. The promises and failures of black advancement in the second half of the twentieth century have brought the differences between the anticlassification and antisubordination approaches into starker contrast. And, in the process, the meaning and legacy of *Brown* have become a terrain of struggle and controversy.

If *Brown* is a canonical case, *Plessy* has become an anticanonical case, *Brown*'s evil twin. Its incorrectness must be demonstrated in each generation, in order to demonstrate one's devotion to *Brown* and to equality itself. Not surprisingly, people with different interpretations of *Brown* offer contrasting accounts of the evils of *Plessy*. Just as the proponents of the anticlassification and antisubordination models view themselves as the true inheritors of the mantle of *Brown* and its promise of equality for all Americans, each sees their opposite numbers as the misguided inheritors of the legacy of *Plessy*.

Those who support the color-blindness rationale understand the evil of Jim Crow and of *Plessy* to have been state classification of persons based on race. Hence whenever the state classifies by race, it risks returning to the racial division of society that characterized Jim Crow. According to the anticlassification view, racial classifications stigmatize blacks and deny them the ability to be considered as individuals. Those who support racial classifications or affirmative action to benefit blacks or other disadvantaged minorities—even for the best of reasons—are the inheritors of *Plessy*'s flawed reasoning about race. Like the majority in *Plessy*, they harbor the dangerous delusion that treating people differently because of their race can sometimes be "reasonable." So-called benign racial classifications not only are unfair to innocent whites, they inevitably stigmatize blacks in the eyes of whites, undermine black self-confidence, and foment racial division in society.

By contrast, those who support the equal citizenship rationale see the evil of Jim Crow and of *Plessy* quite differently. The evil of segregation lay in its meaning—that blacks were less worthy than whites—and in the role that separation played in a larger system of racial subordination. Racial classifications were simply one means by which society maintained the subordination of blacks to whites, established cumulative material disadvantages for blacks in many areas of social and economic life, and preserved the notion that it was better to be white than black. Racial classification was and is neither necessary nor sufficient to preserve racial stratification and subordination. As times changed, Jim Crow was abolished, and overt racial classifications disadvantaging blacks were largely eliminated from law. Even so, American law and society could and did employ quite different methods to preserve white advantage and black disadvantage. According to the antisubordination approach, the real question is not whether law classifies by race, but whether the law—whatever its form—is working to remedy subordination or to enhance it. Moreover, because few legislatures these days are likely to make classifications directly burdening blacks, the anti-classification principle now works largely to perpetuate black inequality. That is because the principle outlaws all race-conscious efforts to ameliorate the cumulative social and economic disadvantages that blacks have suffered. At the same time, the anticlassification model shields from scrutiny practices of subordination that cannot be explained as the result of direct racial classification or hidden racial animus. By helping to freeze cumulative black disadvantages in place, and by artificially limiting the reach of antidiscrimination law, the anticlassification model is the true heir of *Plessy*. It sanctifies and disguises the many forms of subordination that do not result from direct racial classification, and equates attempts to ameliorate subordination with attempts to preserve it. Finally, it encourages people to explain persistent black inequality as the result of private choices, cultural differences, or black inferiority rather than at least partially as the result of facially neutral legal policies that help preserve social stratification.

The controversy between color-blindness and equal citizenship conceptions extends through almost every part of antidiscrimination law. It is replicated in countless areas of social policy, ranging from voting rights to criminal justice, from affirmative action to welfare policy. Moreover both sides of this debate can and do see themselves as the rightful inheritors of *Brown* and the principles it stood for. No matter how much the two sides deride each other, each honors and worships *Brown*.

C. Brown *as a Symbol of Judicial Review—Judicial Heroism and Revisionist Appraisals*

Indeed, *Brown* has come to mean much more than an honored symbol of equality. It has also come to symbolize important beliefs about the U.S. Supreme Court and the role of courts generally in American democracy. For many Americans, and particularly American liberals, *Brown* became a symbol of what courts devoted to justice could achieve if they had the necessary will and courage. In this respect, *Brown* represented a sea change in attitudes about the proper role of the judiciary. For the generation before *Brown*, the most important constitutional event was surely the struggle over the constitutionality of the New Deal. Prior to the pivotal year of 1937, the Supreme Court had intermittently used its powers of judicial review to strike down what its critics believed was progressive social legislation. The Court argued that these social and economic regulations violated freedom of contract and went beyond the limited powers of the federal government. The Court's attitude was symbolized by two famous cases: *Lochner v. New York*, which struck down a sixty-hour maximum work week for the baking industry, and *Hammer v. Dagenhart*, which struck down a national child labor law. These cases symbolized the Court's commitment to use judicial review to protect states' rights and limited government. Indeed, the period from roughly 1897 to 1937 is sometimes called the *Lochner* era.

After years of struggle and controversy—including President Franklin D. Roosevelt's failed attempt to pack the Supreme Court with allies favorable to his New Deal policies—these cases were finally overruled in the late 1930s and early 1940s by a new Court staffed with Roosevelt appointees.[34] Many drew the lesson that the great problem of the *Lochner* era had been the Supreme Court's resistance to changing times and its hostility to democracy. Cases like *Lochner* and *Hammer* were incorrectly decided, so the standard account went, because courts did not recognize that they had only a limited role in a democracy. Judicial displacement of legislative prerogatives was antidemocratic, and, as Alexander Bickel would put it, the Supreme Court was a "countermajoritarian" institution that perpetually needed to restrain itself so as not to overstep its bounds.[35] The new jurisprudence that emerged from the New Deal struggle gave both the federal government and the states broad new powers over the economy; it seemed to vindicate the view that courts should exercise judicial restraint and show proper respect for democratic processes.

Against this background, *Brown* seemed to symbolize a very different set of values and a very different vision of the role of courts in a constitutional democracy. In *Brown* the Court held unconstitutional well-settled and long-established practices of many different states and thousands of localities. It struck down precedents that had stood for well over half a century, all in the name of higher constitutional values. For many members of the New Deal generation, *Brown* was worrisome because it seemed to abandon the new religion of judicial restraint all too easily. But for a later generation of thinkers *Brown*'s intervention into the stagnant racial politics of the South was precisely what the Constitution demanded. Judicial restraint under these circumstances was not respect for democracy; it was collaboration with evil and capitulation to moral cowardice. For these thinkers, and for their students as well, *Brown* symbolized the Supreme Court's proper role as the articulator and defender of America's fundamental constitutional values. In *Brown*, the story went, the Court took the lead in advancing justice in the face of injustice. It used law to promote and provoke progressive social change. It educated the public by articulating what Owen Fiss, one of the Warren Court's most distinguished academic defenders, has called America's "public values."[36] "[T]he truth of the matter," Fiss explained in a tribute to the great liberal Justice William Brennan, "is that it was the Court that spurred on the great changes to follow, and inspired and protected those who sought to implement them."[37]

Brown's rejection of laws enforcing segregation symbolized to many that democracy meant more than majority rule. The New Deal dictum that courts should defer to the considered judgments of democratically elected majorities rang particularly hollow when the laws in question were the result of centuries of racial prejudice, and when blacks as a group were effectively denied the right to vote throughout much of the South. The country's democratic ideals required more than formal majority rule: they also required enforceable guarantees of equality, fundamental rights, and legal safeguards for minorities. Thus, *Brown* stood as the key precedent for a responsible form of judicial activism; not the activism of *Lochner*, which protected the rich and powerful and gave constitutional sanction to an unjust status quo, but an enlightened judicial activism that protected fundamental rights and minority interests from the tyranny of majorities.

According to this hagiography, *Brown* showed that, despite the attempts of politicians to preserve long-standing injustices for selfish reasons, the Supreme Court, as a branch of government relatively isolated from day-to-day political struggle, could change society for the better. It could make important statements about the fundamental values enshrined in the Constitution, statements that had the force and effect of law. The Court's special status as interpreter and promulgator of the country's deepest values was enhanced because the Supreme Court was the final authority on the meaning of constitutional guarantees. As the Court explained in *Cooper v. Aaron*,[38] which arose out of the Little Rock controversy, other branches of government were duty bound to obey its orders and its interpretations of the Constitution regardless of their personal disagreements.

In short, *Brown* crystallized in a single example the importance of the United States Supreme Court as a central authority that interpreted the meaning of the Constitution and protected and preserved public values from contrary and conflicting private interests. *Brown* seemed to demonstrate that the Supreme Court could be a progressive institution that used reason and principle to improve society through the development of legal doctrine. It reminded all that courts could make a difference, and for the better—that society could be improved and reformed through law rather than violence, through briefs rather than bombs. The example of *Brown* refuted those who believed that Supreme Court should respect settled customs and local traditions when those customs and traditions oppressed minorities, the politically unpopular, and the weak. It represented the key counterexample to Bickel's "countermajoritarian difficulty": The Court had promoted democracy in *Brown* rather than detracting from it. If the Court had not acted to protect the rights of African Americans, they might have lived under Jim Crow for many years. Although the civil rights movement surely did more to change political attitudes than anything the Supreme Court did, *Brown* symbolized the positive role that courts could play in inspiring, encouraging, and supporting social movements for justice. Through decisions like *Brown*, courts could educate the public about the deepest commitments of the Constitution. Through decisions like *Brown*, the Justices could light a path that others could and would follow.

It was inevitable that these sentiments—and *Brown*'s elevated status—would undergo considerable reassessment over the years. Worship of *Brown* coincided with a period when American progressives believed that the Supreme Court was a general force for good in society. Just as the Supreme Court desegregated the schools in *Brown*, so too the development of constitutional and civil rights law could help solve many other social problems. Yet over the next half century, some would become disenchanted with the claims of a special role for the courts, others with the ability of courts to effect lasting social change, and still others with the integrative ideals of *Brown* itself.

Chief Justice Warren's tenure ended in 1969. His successor, Warren Burger, presided over a much less liberal court, with a complicated and mixed record on issues of social reform. By the time that William Rehnquist ascended to the Chief Justiceship in 1986, it was quite clear that the heady days of the Warren Court were not returning anytime soon. In the intervening two decades, the country had witnessed continual battles over busing, which was unpopular with many parents, both white and black. Lower federal courts inspired by the example of *Brown* had attempted to reform institutions like schools, prisons, mental institutions, and hospitals. They met with mixed results, partly because of political and bureaucratic resistance to court intervention and implementation of court orders, partly because of the limited abilities and competencies of courts, and partly because of the limited possible avenues of relief that courts could offer when social problems stemmed from larger social and economic forces.

The political mood of the country shifted considerably over the course of half a century. The Republican Party—which increasingly became the more conservative of the two major parties on questions of race relations and equality—occupied the White House for much of this period, and eventually took control of both houses of Congress in 1994. Perhaps equally important, the Republican Party dominated the composition of the federal judiciary, with important long-term effects. To give only one example, the Democratic Party did not appoint a single Justice to the Supreme Court between 1967 and 1994.

The Supreme Court of the 1980s and 1990s was decidedly more conservative and more deferential to the states in civil rights matters than

its predecessor in the 1960s. It was most activist—in the sense of ener-
getically exercising judicial review—in striking down affirmative action
programs under the Equal Protection Clause, striking down regulations
on campaign finance and advertising under the First Amendment,
voiding environmental regulations under the Just Compensation
Clause of the Fifth Amendment, and limiting federal regulatory power
under doctrines of federalism and states' rights. As the 1980s wore on,
it became clear that judicial review was not being exercised in the way
that progressives hoped it would be, and that the Rehnquist Court
could and would exercise judicial review to protect a very different set
of interests and concerns. By the end of the 1990s, the major beneficiaries of the emerging conservative judicial activism appeared to be
whites, state governments, advertisers, opponents of environmental
and land use regulation, and wealthy contributors to political cam-
paigns. And in December 2000, the Supreme Court's five person conservative majority used the power of judicial review to hand the Presidency to the Republican candidate, George W. Bush, in *Bush v. Gore*.[39]

Conservatives had long complained about the excesses of judicial review and judicial reform of institutions. But as the century ended, skeptical voices began to be heard from the middle and left as well. It is no
accident, then, that the romance with the Supreme Court and the special role of courts in promoting social change symbolized by *Brown*
slowly dissipated as the century came to a close. Indeed, many liberal
and left-leaning legal scholars began to sound like the conservatives of
previous decades—skeptical about the value of robust judicial review,
urging respect for democratic decision making. As Mark Tushnet wrote
in his aptly entitled 1999 book, *Taking the Constitution Away from the
Courts*, "[i]n getting the decisions we like, we run the risk of decisions
we despise. . . . [T]hose who celebrate *Brown* as the exemplar of judicial
review have to live with Supreme Court decisions restricting affirmative action and campaign finance reform."[40]

Brown's status as a symbol of judicial independence and courage also
came under attack in the last half century. Proponents of the courts' special role in fostering progressive social change argued that because
courts—and particularly the U.S. Supreme Court—are isolated from
day-to-day political struggle, they can preserve and defend principles
and policies that are in the long-term interest of the country whether or
not current majorities happen to favor them. *Brown* served as the clas-

sic example of this courageous practice. Critics have responded that, on the contrary, *Brown* demonstrates the Court's relative lack of political independence and its long-run congruence with existing political forces. For them, *Brown* is an example of Mr. Dooley's famous aphorism that "no matter whether th' Constitution follows th' flag or not, th' Supreme Coort follows th' iliction returns."[41] Political scientists like Robert Dahl and Martin Shapiro have articulated Mr. Dooley's aphorism more systematically: they have argued that the Supreme Court rarely strays for long from a sustained national political majority.[42]

Indeed, *Brown* was not so much an outlier as one might imagine. The Truman Administration had specifically asked the Court to overrule *Plessy* in 1950 in *Sweatt v. Painter*, a challenge to the University of Texas' whites-only law school.[43] Rather than taking the lead on the issue, the Court had deferred, ordering the integration of the University of Texas law school on the grounds that the separate law school for blacks was not substantially equal. By contrast, Harry Truman had run on a civil rights plank in 1948, and that same year ordered the desegregation of the armed forces. He was willing to stake his presidency on support for civil rights. In retrospect, Truman's actions seem much more courageous than the Court's. Nor was racial equality unheard of in popular culture. Major League Baseball had already begun a highly publicized process of desegregation well before the decision in *Brown*.

The work of courts also tends to respond to the consensus of elite policy makers. Historians have argued that the concerns of foreign policy elites were particularly important during the period leading up to *Brown*. Mary Dudziak, for example, has argued that *Brown* is the result of a "Cold War imperative."[44] In the years following World War II, the American foreign policy establishment was trying to gain allies in the newly emerging nations of the Third World and to head off Soviet influence by arguing that the American way of life was superior to Soviet communism. However, the Soviet Union repeatedly pointed to Jim Crow as proof of the hollowness of American promises of liberty and equality and the moral bankruptcy of the American way of life. These Soviet attacks on Jim Crow were an enormous embarrassment. The perceived need to counteract America's bad image abroad during the Cold War, Dudziak explains, "was one of the critical factors driving the federal government's postwar civil rights efforts." Thus, the Justice Department's brief in *Brown* quoted at length the views of Secretary of

State Dean Acheson emphasizing the threat to American interests that Jim Crow posed. Acheson noted that school desegregation in particular had been

> singled out for hostile foreign comment in the United Nations and else-where. Other peoples cannot understand how such a practice can exist in a country which professes to be a staunch supporter of freedom, jus-tice, and democracy. . . . [R]acial discrimination in the United States re-mains a source of constant embarrassment to this Government in the day-to-day conduct of its foreign relations; and it jeopardizes the effec-tive maintenance of our moral leadership of the free and democratic nations of the world.[45]

As Dudziak points out, *Brown* served international as well as do-mestic interests. It "laundered the principles of democracy in the eyes of the world," demonstrating "that racial segregation and American constitutional rights were inconsistent with each other." *Brown* allowed the American foreign policy establishment to "argue that the American Constitution provided for effective social change,"[46] and that although the country was by no means perfect, it was working to improve itself and live up to its most deeply held principles. It is perhaps no accident that "[w]ithin an hour of [Chief Justice] Warren's announcement, the Voice of America broadcast the decision to Eastern Europe in thirty-four different languages."[47] Nor was the connection between *Brown* and the Cold War lost on the public; the day after the decision the *New York Times* described *Brown* as a "blow to communism."[48]

Still other historians, like Lucas A. Powe Jr. in his recent study of the Warren Court,[49] have pointed out that *Brown* may reflect the imposition of the views of a national majority on a regional majority. After all, at the time *Brown* was decided, mandatory school segregation was largely a southern phenomenon. Segregation laws were concentrated in the seventeen southern and border states (plus the District of Columbia), although four states—including Kansas—permitted local choice on school segregation. Twenty-seven states either had no laws requiring school segregation or had laws actually prohibiting it.[50]

Thus, instead of a decision by a fearless Supreme Court standing up to an entrenched and powerful majority, it is also possible to see *Brown* as part of a general strategy of imposing northern values, and particu-larly the values of liberal northern elites, on the South, and particularly the rural South.[51] Under Powe's interpretation, *Brown* should be read together with the Warren Court's school prayer cases, which imposed northern liberal ideals of secularism on southern schools.[52] *Brown* should also be read together with the Court's criminal procedure opinions, like *Gideon v. Wainwright*,[53] which guaranteed the right to an attorney, and *Miranda v. Arizona*, which constrained police interrogation.[54] These decisions reformed southern criminal justice practices that, in the eyes of northern liberals, were tainted by racism and unfairness to the poor.

Mark Tushnet sounds a similar theme: By 1954 segregation was an embarrassment to the North, and, as Dudziak's work suggests, a real hindrance to national foreign policy. However, Congress could not easily act to change matters. Since Reconstruction the South had been effectively a one-party region, dominated by Democrats. The congressional seniority system gave these southern Democrats disproportionate legislative power, and they used it to block civil rights legislation. Southern Democrats also threatened to prevent other initiatives by northern and liberal Democrats and Republicans if they tried to push too hard for civil rights reforms.[55] Thus, argues Tushnet, "[t]he Court's decision in *Brown* might best be understood as enforcing a national political view against a regionally dominant one that happened to have excessive power in Congress."[56]

In short, many critics have argued that the widely held vision of the Supreme Court as a brave and progressive countermajoritarian institution is largely a myth: Indeed, they argue, there is little evidence that the Court consistently protects minority interests in the face of a national consensus to the contrary. For example, the Court did little to protect the First Amendment rights of Communists until well after McCarthyism had been discredited in the political process.[57] The Warren Court's protections of criminal defendants were watered down by later courts in the 1970s, 1980s, and 1990s, as the country became more conservative and more concerned about getting tough with crime and drug trafficking. In the area of race relations, Derrick Bell has argued that *Brown* demonstrates a similar pattern. *Brown* is not an example of courageous countermajoritarianism. Instead, Bell argues, *Brown* exemplifies what he calls the "interest convergence thesis."[58] The Supreme Court has typically acted to protect the interests of blacks and other racial minorities only when these interests converge with those of whites, and in particular the interests of powerful white elites. Bell sees *Brown* and the subsequent history of desegregation efforts as a key example: During the early 1950s, Bell argues, ending Jim Crow—at least formally—was in the interests of northern whites and the foreign policy establishment. However, the convergence of interests between blacks and white elites did not mean that whites had an interest in full social and economic equality for blacks, and the limited convergence of interests that did exist did not last. Actual desegregation remedies were a long time in coming and fell far short of providing genuinely equal educational opportunities for blacks.

While these critics have questioned the value of judicial review and the reality of judicial independence, still other scholars have questioned whether judicial review, and in particular the Supreme Court, is particularly efficacious in promoting lasting social reform. For these critics, *Brown* is an icon not of judicial success but of judicial failure; it is a symbol not of the power of courts but of their relative impotence in American society. What for one generation of thinkers had been the icon of progressive social change achieved through litigation and constitutional interpretation had become for another the most prominent symbol of the futility of trying to change society through judicial constructions of constitutional law. The separation of right from remedy symbolized by the separate opinions in *Brown I* and *Brown II*, *Brown II*'s decision to proceed with "all deliberate speed"—which effectively sanctioned years of delay—and the ultimate resegregation of American public schools in the 1990s, all seemed to demonstrate that *Brown*, and the institution of judicial review that it symbolized, were much less important, much less powerful, and much less influential than earlier generations wanted to believe. *Brown*, and particularly *Brown II*, was not a symbol of what courts could do, but a symbol of what they could not do.

In his 1991 book *The Hollow Hope: Can Courts Bring About Social Change?* Gerald Rosenberg argued that *Brown*'s importance in promoting equality in the United States has been vastly overstated. Between 1954 and 1964, Rosenberg argued, little desegregation occurred: The Supreme Court issued only three full opinions on primary and secondary school desegregation, and the lower federal courts were mired in endless litigation involving recalcitrant school boards, with little practical result. Only when the political process was energized to the cause of civil rights did any important reforms actually come about. The 1964 Civil Rights Act threatened to cut off funds to schools that discriminated on the basis of race, and after a slow start, the Department of Health, Education, and Welfare eventually decided to require complete desegregation as a condition of federal funds under Title VI of the act.[59] In 1965 Congress passed the Voting Rights Act, which changed the balance of power in southern politics and led local officials in the South to take desegregation efforts much more seriously. By 1970, blacks were an important element of the Democratic coalition and "had substantial influence on the development of national policy" regarding race.[60]

Rosenberg goes further, and rejects even the possibility that the Court had a substantial indirect influence on the political discourse of civil rights: He argues that there is no evidence, either in measurements of public opinion or amounts of media coverage, that "a major contribution of the courts in civil rights was to give the issue salience, press political elites to act, prick the consciences of whites, legitimate the grievances of blacks, and fire blacks up to act."[61] At most, Rosenberg, says, Brown "reinforc[ed] the belief in a legal strategy for change of those already committed to it."[62]

Michael Klarman has argued, in fact, that *Brown*'s most important effects were perverse.[63] The decision was less important as a means of changing the minds of Americans than in "crystallizing . . . southern white resistance to racial change." The Supreme Court's intervention infuriated a wide range of Southerners and thus gave renewed political power to racists like Bull Connor and political opportunists like George Wallace. It silenced southern moderates or pressured them to back increasingly segregationist policies. *Brown*, Klarman argues, "propell[ed] southern politics dramatically to the right on racial issues," and "created a political climate conducive to the brutal suppression of civil rights demonstrations." When this violence "was vividly transmitted through the medium of television to national audiences, previously indifferent northern whites were aroused from their apathy, leading to demands for national civil rights legislation which the Kennedy and Johnson administrations no longer deemed politically expedient to resist."[64]

Finally, scholars of social movements have questioned the claim that the Court either led or inspired the civil rights movement through its decision in *Brown*. The June 1953 boycott of segregated buses in Baton Rouge, Louisiana, which marks the beginning of the "direct action" phase of the civil rights movement, occurred before the Supreme Court's decision in *Brown*.[65] The famous 1956 Montgomery bus boycott—which is identified with Rosa Parks—did occur after *Brown*.

However, in his history of the origins of the civil rights movement, Aldon Morris emphasizes the importance of the earlier, less well known Baton Rouge boycott. It demonstrated for the first time that concerted action by blacks could succeed against the white establishment. The early civil rights movement, he argues, was spawned largely through grassroots organizing in local communities, whose results were conveyed through word of mouth and connections within organizations like the black church. It was not the result of inspiration created by successful court litigation. Indeed, Morris argues, one perverse effect of *Brown* was to overshadow the grassroots work, to "thrust the NAACP into the limelight and crystalliz[e] the emerging massive resistance movement dedicated to systematically destroying the NAACP across the South."[66]

As these examples indicate, *Brown*'s significance as a symbol of judicial review, and what is best about the practice of judicial review, have been significantly revised over the years. What *Brown* tells us about the importance of courts and constitutional law is probably something more complicated than either the heroic praise heaped on the opinion or the more skeptical dismissals of Rosenberg, Klarman, and other recent scholars. Law does matter, and one of the ways it matters is that it structures the basic shape of political contest. *Brown* changed the playing field between supporters and opponents of Jim Crow. Even though *Brown II* limited relief in school cases, the principle announced in *Brown I* had long-term effects in the kinds of arguments about race that American lawyers and politicians could plausibly make. Because of *Brown* racial segregation was presumptively unconstitutional, and supporters now had to expend legal and political resources to defend it. Moreover, law has expressive and symbolic effects that should not be underestimated. With the decision in *Brown*, the symbolic weight of federal law and the federal Constitution was now placed on the side of African Americans and the civil rights movement and against their opponents. *Brown* provided a symbol that tied the Constitution and the Rule of Law itself to civil rights and racial equality. The power of that linkage in the country's political imagination was significant and long lasting. A deep connection between the Constitution, the Rule of Law, and equal citizenship has become an article of faith in the American civic religion. If *Brown* was not the sole cause of that powerful association, it certainly helped further and foster it.

Thus, *Brown* undoubtedly had influence, even if that influence has been overstated by its greatest admirers. If it is true that courts are only one player among many in national politics, it still follows that the federal courts did play a role, even if it was not the central one. And there seems to be no doubt that *Brown* lifted the hearts of many members of the civil rights movement, and "allow[ed] many blacks to think for the first time about the possibility of social change."[67] In the words of Dr. Benjamin Mays, "people literally got out and danced in the streets. . . . The Negro was jubilant."[68]

Fifty years after *Brown*, much has changed. What has not changed is the iconic status of *Brown* itself. It remains a central symbol of American constitutional law and constitutional equality. Nowadays we no longer fight about whether it was correct. Instead we dispute its meaning and its effects. We use it to fight our present-day battles about race, judicial review, and democracy. Those disputes in no way diminish its significance—indeed they merely confirm it. For different reasons, and for different purposes, *Brown v. Board of Education* is as important to us now as it ever was.

NOTES

1. 347 U.S. 483 (1954).
2. 347 U.S. 497 (1954).
3. 349 U.S. 249 (1955).
4. 5 U.S. (1 Cranch) 137 (1803).
5. 17 U.S. (4 Wheat.) 316 (1819).
6. 384 U.S. 436 (1966).
7. 410 U.S. 113 (1973).
8. Quoted in Richard Kluger, *Simple Justice* 711 (1975).
9. Id. At 752 (quoting Southern Manifesto).
10. 163 U.S. 537 (1896).
11. See Gary A. Orfield, Mark D. Bachmeier, David R. James, and Tamela Eitle, "Deepening Segregation in American Public Schools," Harvard Project on School Desegregation (April 5, 1997); Gary A. Orfield and John T. Yun, "Resegregation in American Schools" (June 1999)(available at <http://www.law.harvard.edu/groups/civilrights/publications/ resegregation99.html>).
12. Orfield et al., "Deepening Segregation in American Public Schools," at 2, 16–19.
13. 418 U.S. 717 (1974).
14. Orfield et al., "Deepening Segregation in American Public Schools," at 4, 7.

15. 498 U.S. 237 (1991).

16. 503 U.S. 467 (1992).

17. 515 U.S. 70 (1995).

18. 515 U.S. at 114 (Thomas, J., concurring).

19. See Wendy Parker, The Future of School Desegregation, 94 Nw. L. Rev. 1157, 1160 (2000).

20. Orfield et al., "Deepening Segregation in American Public Schools," at 11. The figures for the 1994–95 school year indicate that 67.1 percent of blacks and 74.0 percent of Latinos attend predominantly minority schools.

21. *San Antonio Independent School District v. Rodriguez*, 411 U.S. 1 (1973). However, in the years since that decision, many states have found obligations to equal educational funding in their own constitutions. This has produced considerable litigation with some degree of improvement in equalizing school expenditures. On the whole, however, results have not been uniformly successful. This is due in part to the fact that (1) in many states schools have traditionally been funded out of local property tax revenues, so that reform requires a complete overhaul of taxation and funding mechanisms; (2) parents in wealthier school districts continue to use their affluence to guarantee their children greater educational opportunities than other children; and (3) mere equalization of expenditures is only one step toward achieving equal educational opportunity; it may leave many other sources of inequality and many other serious problems in school districts untouched.

22. *Florida ex rel. Hawkins v. Board of Control of Florida*, 350 U.S. 413 (1956).

23. 351 U.S. 1, 2 (1958).

24. These per curiam orders applied to public parks, *New Orleans City Park Improvement Ass'n v. Detiege*, 358 U.S. 54 (1958) (per curiam), aff'g 252 F.2d 122 (5th Cir.); public buses and public transportation, *Gayle v. Browder*, 352 U.S. 903 (1956) (per curiam) , aff'g 142 F. Supp. 707 (M.D. Ala.); public golf courses, *Holmes v. Atlanta*, 350 U.S. 879 (1955), rev'g 223 F.2d 93 (5th Cir.); and public bath houses and beaches, *Mayor & City Council of Baltimore v. Dawson*, 350 U.S. 877 (1955), aff'g 220 F.2d 386 (4th Cir.).

25. See, e.g., Henry M. Hart, "The Supreme Court, 1958—Foreword: The Time Chart of the Justices," 73 *Harv. L. Rev.* 84, 98 & n.32 (1959); Herbert Wechsler, "Toward Neutral Principles of Constitutional Law," 73 *Harv. L. Rev.* 1, 21–22 (1959); Alexander M. Bickel & Harry H. Wellington, "Legislative Purpose and the Judicial Process: The Lincoln Mills Case," 71 *Harv. L. Rev.* 1, 3, 4 (1957).

26. *Johnson v. Virginia*, 373 U.S. 61, 62 (1963).

27. *Colorado Anti-Discrimination Commn. v. Continental Air Lines, Inc.*, 372 U.S. 714 (1963).

28. *Bell v. Maryland*, 378 U.S. 226, 287–88 (1964)(Goldberg, J., concurring).

29. 163 U.S. at 551.

30. 163 U.S. at 559.

31. Martin Luther King Jr., "I Have a Dream" (1963), in *A Testament of Hope: The Essential Writings and Speeches of Martin Luther King, Jr.* 219 (James M. Washington ed., 1986).

32. Id. at 218.

33. Id. At 219

34. *Lochner v. New York* was never officially overruled, but later cases involving the Due Process Clause, like *United States v. Carolene Products*, 304 U.S. 144 (1938), *Olsen v. Nebraska*, 313 U.S. 236 (1941), and *United States v. Darby*, 312 U.S. 100 (1941), effectively overruled it. *Hammer* and its restrictive view of the federal commerce power were explicitly overruled in *United States v. Darby*. The changes in constitutional doctrine began with *West Coast Hotel v. Parrish*, 300 U.S. 379 (1937)(overruling *Adkins v. Children's Hospital*, 261 U.S. 525 (1923)), and *NLRB v. Jones & Laughlin Steel Corp.* 301 U.S. 1 (1937). Both cases were decided before Roosevelt began to appoint new Justices.

35. Alexander M. Bickel, *The Least Dangerous Branch: The Supreme Court at the Bar of Politics* 15–16 (1962).

36. Owen M. Fiss, The Supreme Court, 1978 Term, Foreword: The Forms of Justice, 93 *Harv. L. Rev.* 1, 2, 9, 14, 29–30 (1979).

37. Owen M. Fiss, "A Life Lived Twice," 100 *Yale L. J.* 1117, 1118 (1991).

38. 358 U.S. 1 (1958).

39. *Bush v. Gore*, 121 S.Ct. 512 (2000) (*Bush I*); *Bush v. Gore*, 121 S.Ct. 525 (2000) (*Bush II*).

40. Mark Tushnet, *Taking the Constitution Away from the Courts* 141 (1999).

41. Finley Peter Dunne, *Mr. Dooley at His Best* 77 (Elmer Ellis ed., 1938).

42. Robert Dahl, "Decision-Making in a Democracy: The Supreme Court as a National Policy-Maker," 6 *J. Pub. L.* 279, 294 (1957); Martin Shapiro, *Freedom of Speech: The Supreme Court and Judicial Review* (1966).

43. 339 U.S. 629 (1950).

44. Mary L. Dudziak, "Desegregation as a Cold War Imperative," 41 *Stan. L. Rev.* 61 (1988).

45. Quoted in id. at 111–12.

46. Id. at 118–119.

47. Lucas A. Powe Jr., *The Warren Court and American Politics* 35 (2000).

48. Id. (quoting *New York Times*, May 18, 1954, at 19).

49. Powe, *Warren Court and American Politics*.

50. Gerald Rosenberg, *The Hollow Hope: Can Courts Bring About Social Change?* 43 (1991).

51. Powe, *Warren Court and American Politics*, at 489–494.

52. See *Engle v. Vitale*, 370 U.S. 421 (1962); *Abingdon School District v. Schempp*, 374 U.S. 203 (1963). Interestingly, both of these cases involved northern school districts, in New York and Pennsylvania, respectively.

53. 372 U.S. 335 (1963).

54. 384 U.S. 436 (1966).

55. Tushnet, *Taking the Constitution Away from the Courts*, at 145.

56. Id.

57. Powe, *Warren Court and American Politics*, at 135, 154–56, 310–17, 491.

58. Derrick Bell, "*Brown v. Board of Education* and the Interest-Convergence Dilemma," 93 *Harv. L. Rev.* 518 (1980).

59. Rosenberg, *Hollow Hope*, at 46–49.

60. Tushnet, *Taking the Constitution Away from the Courts*, at 145.

61. Rosenberg, *Hollow Hope*, at 156.

62. Id.

63. Michael Klarman, "*Brown*, Racial Change, and the Civil Rights Movement," 80. *Va. L. Rev.* 7 (1994).

64. Id. at 10, 13.

65. Aldon D. Morris, *The Origins of the Civil Rights Movement: Black Communities Organizing for Change* 25 (1984).

66. Id. at 25.

67. Id. at 81.

68. Quoted in id. at 81.

Chapter 2

The History of the *Brown* Litigation

A. The NAACP's Strategy

The plaintiffs' victory in *Brown* was the result of a long and carefully orchestrated legal campaign by the NAACP Legal Defense and Education Fund.[1] The campaign began in 1935 and achieved a string of impressive victories. The original architect of the NAACP's strategy was Charles Hamilton Houston, dean of the Howard University Law School. However, by 1939 the leadership passed to his student and protégé Thurgood Marshall. Marshall was probably the most important American lawyer of the twentieth century. He devised the basic strategy for *Brown* and its companion cases, and for many years he was the NAACP's main advocate before the Supreme Court. Marshall would later become Solicitor General of the United States and the first African American Justice of the Supreme Court.

The NAACP brought a series of lawsuits in the 1930s, 1940s, and 1950s challenging segregation in transportation, residential housing, and the white primary system in the South. It also brought lawsuits to equalize the salaries of black teachers with those of their white counterparts. But its most famous strategy, and the one that led directly to *Brown*, was bringing a series of lawsuits forcing southern graduate and professional schools—and, in particular, law schools—to admit blacks.

Three considerations justified this strategy. First, most southern states reserved graduate and professional education exclusively for whites—often with only token efforts at providing such education for blacks. As a result, the NAACP believed that the argument that blacks were receiving "separate but equal" treatment would ring particularly hollow. Thus, in *Missouri ex rel. Gaines v. Canada*,[2] the NAACP successfully argued that Missouri did not provide equal protection by paying tuition for black students at out-of-state law schools while denying them admission to the state school. Facilities for legal education within

Missouri were hardly "separate but equal"—they did not exist at all. And in *Sweatt v. Painter*,[3] the Court rejected the claim of the University of Texas that a hastily established law school for black law students met the requirements of equal protection. *Sweatt* demonstrated the second idea behind the NAACP's strategy. Establishing graduate facilities for blacks that were genuinely "separate but equal" would be either impossible or prohibitively expensive. It would be much cheaper simply to admit the students to the formerly white law schools.

Finally, the NAACP tried to make use of a peculiarity of southern racism. Southerners were much more upset about racial mixing in elementary and secondary education than in graduate and professional schools. Apparently, it was believed that once people became adults, the appropriate social roles of whites and blacks were clear to them, but young children were particularly impressionable and might get inappropriate ideas if they were integrated with other races. Hence it was better to challenge southern education where it would offer the least resistance, in graduate and professional schools. As Thurgood Marshall expressed it: "Those racial supremacy boys somehow think that little kids of six or seven are going to get funny ideas about sex and marriage just from going to school together, but for some equally funny reason youngsters in law school aren't supposed to feel that way. We didn't get it but we decided that if that was what the South believed, then the best thing for the moment was to go along."[4]

Although today we think of Marshall's and the NAACP's strategy as an attack on segregation, much of Marshall's early work actually employed the "separate but equal" doctrine of *Plessy* to equalize facilities for blacks and whites. Indeed, Charles Hamilton Houston's original strategy was to use *Plessy* to make it too expensive for the South to maintain segregated schools: hence Hamilton's dual plan of attack was to raise black teachers' salaries to the level of comparably qualified whites and to force southern universities to admit blacks to graduate schools. Marshall gradually decided to push for the goal of desegregation rather than equalization before his victory in *Sweatt v. Painter* in 1950, "but even toward the end of the 1940s he was willing to devote resources to equalization suits."[5] Not all blacks were convinced that integration was the right answer: Many feared that the end of segregation would threaten the jobs of African American professionals and particularly African American schoolteachers; others feared that whites would resist desegregation with violence. Although Marshall was committed to desegregation and the integrative ideal, he repeatedly had to convince his constituents that desegregation was the best direction for blacks.[6]

The case that eventually became *Brown v. Board of Education* arose out of the political agitations of Esther Brown, a white Jewish woman who was no relation to Oliver and Linda Brown, the father and daughter who were named as lead plaintiffs. Esther Brown lived in Merriam, Kansas, a suburb of Kansas City, Missouri. One day, driving her black maid home to South Park, she was shocked by the conditions at the local black elementary school. She made speeches in front of the school board for improvements; they listened politely but did little more than offer to put new lightbulbs in the black school and to move used desks from the white school. Then Brown discovered that while the black school was literally falling apart, the community was planning a new bond issue to build a brand new school for white children. Brown was infuriated. She campaigned against the bond issue and urged the black community to join her. After the bond issue passed despite black opposition, Brown began to organize the black community in earnest and to search for legal representation to challenge the segregated schools. She organized a three-week boycott of the local black school; black parents set up private schools in homes and churches. She persuaded the local Kansas City, Kansas, NAACP to take the case and raised money for their legal expenses. She badgered Thurgood Marshall at the national headquarters of the NAACP in New York to send help. She suffered a miscarriage, her husband lost his job, and a cross was burned on their lawn. But the plaintiffs won the suit and the black children of South Park were admitted to the white school.[7]

Energized by her victory in South Park, Esther Brown sought to challenge segregation in Wichita and Topeka. The Wichita branch of the NAACP proved unenthusiastic. Local schoolteachers feared for their jobs and opposed a lawsuit. But the Topeka branch was ready for a fight. By October of 1948 they had raised money for litigation and had located potential plaintiffs. But organizing the lawsuit took years. Local black schoolteachers viewed the NAACP as a threat to their existence. They doubted that whites would let them teach white children in integrated schools. Many black groups in Topeka were openly hostile to challenging segregation.[8] Finally, on February 28, 1951, Elisha Scott, a local NAACP attorney who had handled the South Park litigation, filed suit. From the national office Marshall sent his right-hand man, Robert

Carter, to oversee the Kansas litigation while Marshall concentrated on *Briggs v. Elliott* in South Carolina.

Twelve families joined the lawsuit against the school board. The first plaintiff named in the complaint was Oliver Brown, a welder in the Santa Fe railway shops who was also an assistant pastor at a local church that the other plaintiffs attended. Brown also had the distinct advantage of being a union member, which helped safeguard his job. The most famous civil rights case in American history was brought on behalf of his daughter, Linda Brown.

At the trial, Oliver Brown testified that Linda had to walk across railroad tracks and Topeka's main industrial street to wait for the bus that would take her to her segregated school. Walking across the railroad switchyards was dangerous, and Linda sometimes had to wait in the rain and the snow for the bus to arrive; when the bus deposited her she had to wait another thirty minutes in front of the school until it opened. Linda later recalled that her father was so fed up with the long trip she had to take every day that he agreed to join the lawsuit.[9] At the close of the trial, the three-judge court unanimously held that the facilities at the black and white schools were substantially equal. The opinion also noted that the Supreme Court had not yet overruled *Plessy*. But the court also found as a matter of fact that segregation harmed black children, "especially when it has the force of law," and "deprive[d] them of benefits they would receive in a racially integrated school system."[10] This finding set the stage for the NAACP's final assault on school segregation.

Brown was not the only school desegregation case the NAACP pursued. During 1951 and 1952, the NAACP was simultaneously conducting school litigation in South Carolina, Virginia, and Delaware. Still another challenge was brewing in the District of Columbia. The appeals in all five cases finally reached the Supreme Court in 1952. Robert Carter argued the *Brown* case before the Justices, while Marshall argued *Briggs*.

The Supreme Court heard arguments in *Brown* and its companion cases three times. The first arguments were held in December of 1952. After Chief Justice Vinson's death, the Court asked for further briefing and reargument on the original intentions behind the Fourteenth Amendment. In the interim Earl Warren became Chief Justice. The rearguments were held in December of 1953. Finally, after the Court decided *Brown I*, it ordered yet another round of briefing and argument on the appropriate remedy. Those arguments were held in April 1955 and resulted in the *Brown II* opinion.

Marshall's opponent in the South Carolina case was John W. Davis, former solicitor general under Woodrow Wilson and the Democratic nominee for president in 1924. By 1952 he was seventy-nine years old and perhaps the most experienced and distinguished Supreme Court advocate in the country. Davis hailed from West Virginia; he believed in segregation as a way of life and was passionate in its defense. He handled the case on South Carolina's behalf pro bono.[11] The two opponents could not have been more different in style or approach. Davis was polished, eloquent, a master of elegant rhetoric. Marshall was blunt, folksy, matter-of-fact. Marshall shone particularly in the first argument in 1952; Davis was masterful in the 1953 reargument.

In his final appearance in the *Brown I* argument on December 7, 1953, Davis ended with a stirring defense of the principle of respecting prior precedent. *Plessy*, he reminded the Court, had been the law of the land for seventy years: "Somewhere, sometime to every principle comes a moment of repose when it has been so often announced, so confidently relied upon, so long continued, that it passes the limits of judicial discretion and disturbance."[12] If schools in Clarendon County, South Carolina, were desegregated, Davis asked, "[w]ould that make the children any happier? Would they learn any more quickly? Would their lives be more serene?" Davis doubted that pressing for integration would benefit blacks in the long run. "Here is equal education," Davis exclaimed, "not promised, not prophesied, but present. Shall it be thrown away on some fancied question of racial prestige?" Although the plaintiffs and their "supporters and sympathizers" were doubtless sincere and believed that what they were proposing was for the best, Davis concluded, "I entreat them to remember the age-old motto that the best is often the enemy of the good."[13]

In rebuttal, Marshall scoffed at the suggestion that ending segregation would have dire consequences: "I got the feeling on hearing the discussion yesterday that when you put a white child in a school with a whole lot of colored children, the child would fall apart or something. Everybody knows that is not true." "Those same kids in Virginia and South Carolina," Marshall continued, "play in the streets together . . . they separate to go to school, they come out of school and play ball together. They have to be separated in school."[14]

Earlier decisions, Marshall stressed, had steadily chipped away constitutional support for separation of the races. Blacks and whites voted together and lived together in neighborhoods that could no longer have racially restrictive covenants. "You can have them going to the same state university and the same college, but if they go to elementary and high school, the world will fall apart."[15]

Segregation of schools, Marshall argued, was a continuation of the infamous Black Codes that southern legislatures passed after the Civil War to keep blacks in an enslaved condition. The Fourteenth Amendment, he reminded the Justices, was passed in large measure in response to those laws. Segregation in the South applied only to blacks and singled them out. The only way to justify this distinction, Marshall argued, would be "to find that for some reason Negroes are inferior to all other human beings . . . and that the people who were formerly in slavery . . . shall be kept as near that stage as is possible." The time had come, Marshall concluded, for "this Court [to] make it clear that this is not what our Constitution stands for."[16]

At 2:40 P.M. on December 9, 1953, three days of reargument in what would become *Brown I* came to a close. It was now up to the Court to decide.

B. How the Opinion in Brown Was Written

Chief Justice Warren faced great difficulties in writing *Brown I*. He knew that the Court's opinion would be scrutinized closely in the press and among the general public. He also knew that many southern whites would likely feel accused and impugned by a decision that declared Jim Crow inconsistent with the American Constitution, and that many white Southerners would resist dismantling segregation. Thus, he chose to place the authority of the Court behind the opinion in three ways.

First, Warren chose to write the opinion himself. Often in the Supreme Court's history the Chief Justice speaks for the Court in its most important pronouncements. Chief Justice Burger's opinion twenty years later in the Nixon tapes case, *U.S. v. Nixon*,[17] is only one example.

Second, Warren decided to make the opinion short and immediately accessible. In his history of the Warren Court, Lucas A. Powe points out that *Brown I* is only eleven pages long; by contrast, Warren's opinions in *Miranda v. Arizona* (1966)[18] and the *Reapportionment Cases* (1964)[19] both take up well over fifty pages in the *United States Reports*. *Brown I* was tailor-made to be reprinted in newspapers in order to reach the widest possible audience.[20] No matter what Warren wrote, the South would not much like it, but in a short opinion he could take the high ground and avoid unduly inflaming their sensibilities. If the American public could see that the Court was engaged in a reasoned discussion of the Constitution rather than an attack on the South, the Court's legitimacy would be strengthened and enhanced. Thus, Warren wanted to write an opinion that was "short, readable by the lay public, nonrhetorical, unemotional and, above all, nonaccusatory."[21]

Third, and finally, Warren worked hard to make the opinion unanimous. He thought it essential that the Court speak with one voice on this most important of issues. He believed that if there was a single dissent, especially from a Southerner on the Court, it might give the South licence to disobey the opinion. In hindsight, this seems to have been an unnecessary precaution; even with a unanimous opinion southern politicians ridiculed the decision and resisted it in every imaginable way. Nevertheless, it is possible that an eloquent dissent by a southern Justice might have spurred on even greater violence and civil disobedience in the South, or might have allowed President Eisenhower to offer less support to the Court, thus throwing the Court and the country into an even more serious constitutional crisis.

Even so, a unanimous opinion seemed like an impossible dream until Warren became Chief Justice. When *Brown* was first argued in the fall of 1952, the Chief Justice was Fred Vinson—who did not think that segregation was unconstitutional—and the Court was badly split. Five Justices—Hugo Black (a Southerner and former Ku Klux Klan member from Alabama), William O. Douglas, Harold Burton, Felix Frankfurter, and Sherman Minton—wanted to overturn *Plessy*. They believed that segregation was unconstitutional per se, and not only if facilities for blacks and whites were unequal. Vinson, a Kentuckian, disagreed, pointing to the long history of the practice. His conclusion was supported by Stanley Reed, also from Kentucky, and (with somewhat less assurance) by Tom Clark from Texas. One might have expected Robert Jackson, the former attorney general and prosecutor during the Nuremberg trials, to join the liberals. He had seen the consequences of racial persecution firsthand. But Jackson was a moderate, with conflicted views about race. Although he believed that racial segregation was wrong, he also feared that striking it down would be too great an intrusion into politics. He saw the controversy over racial segregation in light of the constitutional struggles over the New Deal; the apparent lesson of history had been that the courts should defer to legislative judgment. Thus, he was not altogether certain that segregation was unconstitutional.

Among the Justices who leaned toward overturning *Plessy*, Felix Frankfurter was perhaps the most worried about the need for unanimity and the most concerned about how to fashion a gradual remedy. Frankfurter was also uncertain about how to reconcile his strong commitment to racial equality with his equally strong commitment to judicial restraint and the apparent lessons of the struggle over the New Deal. Thus, Frankfurter did not want the Court to act prematurely. Faced with a split among the Justices, and uncertain about his own position, Frankfurter played for time. He helped persuade the Court that it should hold the cases over and request further briefing and argument on the question of the original understanding of the framers and ratifiers of the Fourteenth Amendment. And he set his law clerk Alexander Bickel the task of combing through the documentary record to discover the best construction of the original understanding on school desegregation.

Mark Tushnet has argued that the standard story that Frankfurter saved the day through delaying matters until he could pick up a few extra votes for the majority overlooks the extent to which Frankfurter himself was undecided about the unconstitutionality of segregation.[22] Frankfurter's respect for precedent, his dislike of "sociological" objections to segregation, and his general annoyance at Hugo Black's certainty that the framers' basic purpose in drafting the Fourteenth Amendment was to abolish racial segregation "left Frankfurter with no ground on which to rest a conclusion that segregation in the states was unconstitutional."[23] Even after he had convinced himself that *Plessy* could be overruled if segregation were ended gradually, Frankfurter was genuinely uncertain for a time about whether to join the Court's opinion or to write a concurrence that would have diluted the opinion's impact. Whatever Frankfurter's ultimate reasons for pressing delay on his brethren, the Court agreed, and on June 8, 1953 it set the cases for reargument in December of 1953.[24]

Then, on September 8, 1953, just two months before reargument,

Fred Vinson died of a heart attack. Frankfurter is said to have confided to a clerk that this was "the first indication that I have ever had that there is a God."[25]

Congress was in recess at the time, and so, on September 30, 1953, President Eisenhower appointed Earl Warren, the former attorney general and governor of the state of California, as acting Chief Justice.[26] Eisenhower barely knew Warren—he had first met him at the 1952 Republican National Convention—but Warren had helped him gain the nomination by working to seat pro-Eisenhower delegates.[27] And Warren was a respected reform governor who seemed to be a conscientious, moderate Republican, much like Eisenhower himself. Eisenhower would later say that appointing Warren was one of the biggest mistakes he made as president. But few people today now think so.

Warren was a man of enormous personal warmth and charm. A superb politician, he had both the charisma and the gravitas to lead his often contentious and independent-minded colleagues on the Court. By all accounts he was hardworking and sensible, friendly and down-to-earth; and he carried himself and his office with enormous dignity. He had the natural assurance of a man who knew his own abilities and weaknesses and understood his own worth. He had the self-confidence not to be overawed by any of his colleagues, including Frankfurter, the prickly former Harvard Law professor. Rather, he was able to work with all of his brethren to persuade them gradually to coalesce around a single unanimous opinion. The need for unanimity made Warren's task in writing the opinion especially challenging. As Dennis Hutchinson reports, "[i]nstead of having carte blanche for whatever he wrote, Warren faced the difficult task of accommodating in one statement eight other views that had been far from harmonious at conference."[28]

The basic compromise that Warren reached with his colleagues was that the Court would declare segregation unconstitutional by the end of the 1953 Term (that is, in the spring of 1954), but that there would be no holding on remedy. Those questions would be held over for reargument in the 1954 Term. This would give the parties time to argue how the constitutional principle should be implemented, and it would also give the South an extra year to get used to the result. Declaring separate but equal facilities unequal appealed to Black, Douglas, Burton, and Minton; moving slowly on remedy appealed to Frankfurter's and Jackson's sense of gradualism. The compromise also appealed to Tom Clark, who revealed at the December 1953 conference following reargument that he could go along with the majority if the Court recognized that the problem of segregation had to be dealt with differently in different places around the country.[29]

But Warren was not out of the woods just yet. Jackson had considered more than once writing a concurring opinion, which would spoil the effect of the Court's speaking with one voice and might introduce unwelcome complexities into the litigation. Jackson even began drafts of his proposed concurrence and discussed it with his clerks.[30] However, on March 30 Jackson had a serious heart attack that kept him hospitalized and away from the Court for the rest of the Term. As a result, the concurrence was never finished.[31]

Warren personally delivered the draft of his majority opinion to Jackson in his hospital room. Jackson was relieved. He gave the draft to Barrett Prettyman, his clerk, and asked him what he thought of it. Prettyman's reply probably explains why Jackson was won over. "I wished that it had more law in it," Prettyman said, "but I didn't find anything glaringly unacceptable in it. The genius of the Warren opinion," Prettyman explained,

> was that it was so simple and unobtrusive. He had come from political life and had a keen sense of what you could say in this opinion without getting everybody's back up. His opinion took the sting off the decision, it wasn't accusatory, and it didn't pretend that the Fourteenth Amendment was more helpful than the history suggested—he didn't equivocate on that point.[32]

Jackson suggested a few changes to the draft. Warren rejected one of them on the grounds that it would be interpreted as a general attack on segregation, when he wanted the opinion to be quite narrow, reaching only segregation in the public schools.[33] This decision is particularly interesting given *Brown's* later status as a general symbol of equality. Warren accepted another minor suggested change that noted the progress blacks had achieved since Reconstruction. Jackson's suggestion reflected his belief that segregation might have been justified at a time when most blacks were still a backward and ignorant people hampered by the effects of slavery.[34] But Warren, ever the politician, inserted Jackson's idea in the opinion in a way that made it seem less like a backhanded compliment or a claim that white supremacy actually did make sense at one point in history.

With Jackson's consent, Warren had eight votes for his opinion. That left Reed.

At the December 1953 conference following reargument, Reed had argued that *Plessy* was correctly decided because segregation was "not done on inferiority but on racial differences." "[O]f course there is no inferior race," Reed insisted, but blacks had been "handicapped by lack of opportunity." Segregation, he argued, "protects people against [the] mixing of races."[35]

For all the casual racism these remarks betrayed, Reed did believe in racial progress. He thought that segregation would eventually disappear of its own accord. He also believed that the meaning of the Constitution was not fixed, but that it could change over time. However, he was worried that the Court might be moving too fast on race relations, so fast that all the good work it was doing would be undone.[36]

Warren lobbied Reed quietly but persistently. At the beginning of May, after all of the other votes fell into place, Warren put the matter to him directly. "Stan, you're all by yourself in this now. You've got to decide whether it's really the best thing for the country."[37] Reed still did not agree with his colleagues. He thought that *Plessy* was good law. But, as his law clerk George Mickum explained later, Reed feared that, because he was a Southerner, "even a lone dissent by him would give a lot of people a lot of grist for making trouble. For the good of the country, he put aside his own basis for dissent."[38] Assured by Warren that segregation would be dismantled gradually, Reed changed his vote.

Warren had his unanimous opinion.

Following the decision in *Brown I*, the cases were set for yet another round of briefing and reargument. Justice Jackson, who had suffered a heart attack in March, died on October 8, 1954, after the Term had begun. President Eisenhower nominated John Marshall Harlan, the grandson of the Justice Harlan who dissented in *Plessy*. The second Justice Harlan would turn out to be a conservative on many issues, but he joined in all of the Warren Court's opinions on school desegregation. Southern senators held up his confirmation until March of 1955 primarily to vent their dissatisfaction with *Brown I*. That meant that the arguments in *Brown II* would also be delayed, because Warren did not want the question of remedy heard before less than a full court. Finally, the cases were reargued for the last time in April 1955, and the Court sat down to write its second opinion in *Brown*.

Once again Warren had to deal with conflicting interests among his brethren. Hugo Black wanted a bare-bones order immediately granting the named plaintiffs admission to the all-white schools, but nothing more. Black strongly believed that *Plessy* should have been overruled, but he believed equally strongly that there would be massive resistance in the South. Therefore, he suggested, the less the Court said about remedies, the better. Both Black and Douglas believed that there was little the Court could do in the short run, and so a quick, limited, and symbolic gesture was sufficient. Frankfurter, on the other hand, believed in a gradual transition to desegregation, and precisely for this reason he thought the Court should offer advice about how to achieve it.[39] Frankfurter and Jackson thought that appeasement was especially important because "it was essential that whatever the Court ordered should be obeyed."[40] Black and Douglas, on the other hand, were considerably more jaundiced. The western states with local segregation options like Kansas would probably desegregate fairly quickly, and the border states like Missouri and Oklahoma would probably do so with considerable grumbling. But Black and Douglas both believed that nothing the Court did would matter much in the deep South. Black repeatedly told his colleagues so, much to Frankfurter's chagrin.[41] The irony was that the two Justices who were most committed to the correctness of *Brown I* were most dubious about the Court's ability to enforce it in the deep South, while their colleagues were more optimistic that the Court could make a difference if it wrote the right sort of opinion.

Warren asked his clerks to draft "a short opinion embodying the view that most of the details should be left to the district courts." Frankfurter, however, prevailed upon Warren to change the order to implement desegregation "at the earliest practicable date" to an order to desegregate with "all deliberate speed."[42] That expression reflected Frankfurter's desire to appease the South. Given that massive resistance was soon to follow, the choice of phrase probably made little difference to desegregation efforts in the long run, but it would haunt the Court for many years to come as a symbol of its lack of genuine commitment to civil rights for blacks.

The final opinion in *Brown II* made one other quite significant change. Instead of encouraging the district courts to treat the cases as modern-style class actions, which would extend relief to all black children similarly situated, the Court limited relief to "the parties to these cases."[43] In effect, the Court's opinion adopted the most limiting features of everyone's position—Frankfurter's gradualism was coupled with Black's and Douglas's rejection of a broad decree that went beyond the named parties. This had two important consequences. First, the rejection of a class action approach meant that civil rights lawyers would have to bring separate lawsuits in each individual school district across the South, a time-consuming and costly process that greatly hindered the progress of desegregation and gave southern school districts a distinct strategic advantage. Put another way, Black and Douglas's rejection of class actions on the grounds that the South would do nothing to desegregate only made it easier for the South to do nothing.

Second, Frankfurter's formula of "all deliberate speed" would be used repeatedly to justify intransigence and delay in those school districts that were sued, not to mention those that were not. Black and Douglas were probably correct that given the massive resistance that would follow, Frankfurter's insistence on gradualism and careful language designed to appease the South was wholly unnecessary and probably counterproductive, and "that all the Court could accomplish in the short run was a clear statement of fundamental principle."[44] Frankfurter's formula thus squandered some of the Court's moral authority and gained little in return.

NOTES

1. The Legal Defense Fund, to which Marshall was special counsel, was originally an arm of the NAACP, set up to preserve its tax status, but an IRS investigation in 1956 instigated by southern opponents of the NAACP forced the two organizations to become separate.

2. 305 U.S. 337 (1938).

3. 339 U.S. 629 (1950).

4. Quoted in Alfred Kelly, "The School Desegregation Case," in *Quarrels That Have Shaped the Constitution* 253 (John Garraty ed. 1964).

5. Mark Tushnet, *Making Civil Rights Law: Thurgood Marshall and the Supreme Court, 1936–1961* 151 (1994).

6. Id. at 152.

7. Id. at 153; Kluger, *Simple Justice*, at 388–90 (1975).

8. Kluger, *Simple Justice*, at 394.

9. Id. at 393, 409–10; Tushnet, *Making Civil Rights Law*, at 154.

10. *Brown v. Board of Education*, 98 F. Supp. 797 (D. Kansas 1951); Tushnet, *Making Civil Rights Law*, at 162; Kluger, *Simple Justice*, at 423–24.

11. Tushnet, *Making Civil Rights Law*, at 178.

12. *Argument: The Oral Argument before the Supreme Court in* Brown v. Board of Education of Topeka, *1952–55* (Leon Friedman, ed. 1969), at 215.

13. Id. at 216–17.

14. Id. at 239.

15. Id.

16. Id. at 240.

17. 418 U.S. 683 (1974).

18. 384 U.S. 436 (1966).

19. *Reynolds v. Sims*, 377 U.S. 533 (1964); *Lucas v. Colorado 44th General Assembly*, 377 U.S. 713 (1964).

20. Lucas A. Powe Jr., *The Warren Court and American Politics* 29 (2000).

21. Kluger, *Simple Justice*, at 711.

22. Mark Tushnet and Katya Lezin, "What Really Happened in Brown v. Board of Education," 91 *Colum. L. Rev.* 1867, 1906, 1929 (1991).

23. Id. at 1906.

24. See Kluger, *Simple Justice*, at 615; see *Brown v. Board of Education*, 345 U.S. 972 (1953). The cases were originally to be reargued on Monday, October 12, 1953, but on August 4, acting at the government's request, Vinson rescheduled them for December 7. Bernard Schwartz, *Super Chief* 82 (1983).

Mark Tushnet and Katya Lezin have argued that "[r]ather than contributing to the collective deliberative process on the Court . . . Frankfurter's activities were designed primarily to allow him to resolve his own difficulties, although in a way that allowed Frankfurter to explain to himself that what he was doing actually made a difference to his colleagues." Tushnet and Lezin, at 1875.

25. Schwartz, *Super Chief*, at 72.

26. Warren was subsequently confirmed on March 1, 1954.

27. Kluger, *Simple Justice*, at 663.

28. Dennis J. Hutchinson, "Unanimity and Desegregation: Decisionmaking in the Supreme Court, 1948–1958," 68 *Geo. L.J.* 1, 56 (1979).

29. Kluger, *Simple Justice*, at 682.

30. Id. at 688–691.

31. Id. at 695.

32. Id. at 697.

33. Id.

34. Id. at 688–691.

35. As quoted in Tushnet, *Making Civil Rights Law*, at 211.

36. Id. at 211; Kluger, *Simple Justice*, at 698; Tushnet and Lezin, "What Really Happened in *Brown*," at 1905.

37. Kluger, *Simple Justice*, at 698.

38. Id. at 698.

39. Tushnet, *Making Civil Rights Law*, at 229–30.

40. Powe, *Warren Court and American Politics*, at 53.

41. Id. at 52.

42. Tushnet, *Making Civil Rights Law*, at 230.

43. *Brown II*, 349 U.S. at 301; Hutchinson, "Unanimity and Desegregation," at 57; Tushnet, *Making Civil Rights Law*, at 225, 230.

44. Tushnet, *Making Civil Rights Law*, at 230–31.

Chapter 3

Rewriting *Brown*
A Guide to the Opinions

In this book, nine constitutional scholars have rewritten the *Brown* opinion. Acting as Chief Justice of this mock Supreme Court, I have issued an opinion announcing the judgment of the Court. It is joined by two other participants, Bruce Ackerman and Drew Days. Their concurrences do not mean that they agree with everything in the opinion, only that they do not object too strenuously to its general contours. The best evidence of their own views is their individual opinions, which differ in many interesting and important respects.

Five other participants, Frank Michelman, John Hart Ely, Catharine MacKinnon, Michael McConnell, and Cass Sunstein, concur in the judgment, meaning that although they agree with the basic holding that segregated schools are unconstitutional, they do so for different reasons. Their different approaches illuminate many of the tensions implicit in the original *Brown* decision.

Finally, Derrick Bell offers a dissenting opinion. He disagrees with the conclusion that the separate but equal doctrine of *Plessy v. Ferguson* should be overruled. Instead, he gives a provocative argument for why *Plessy* should be read strictly to require genuine equalization of facilities for blacks and whites. Strict enforcement of the "equal" strand of *Plessy*'s "separate but equal" doctrine, Bell believes, would put such severe economic pressures on school boards that they would have to disestablish their dual school systems owing to budgetary necessity rather than judicial mandate.

To understand the issues these opinions raise, it is helpful to go back to Warren's original work and see how he dealt with the issues in the five cases that became *Brown I*, *Brown II*, and *Bolling v. Sharpe*. These include the issues Warren specifically chose to address, the issues that he chose to gloss over or leave in the background, and the issues that were immanent in the case but whose importance only became apparent later on. By comparing Warren's opinions in *Brown I*, *Brown II*, and *Bolling v. Sharpe* with the opinions of our nine participants, we can see how difficult, complicated, and rich a case *Brown v. Board of Education* was in Warren's day and remains in our own.

A. The Problem of Writing for the Future

Writing an opinion like *Brown* is not simply a matter of declaring what the law is or should be. It also involves making prudential judgments about the likely effect of the opinion. These include, among other things, how other governmental actors will implement the opinion and to what extent they will resist it, attempt to circumvent it, or refuse to enforce it. The events immediately following *Brown* are a case in point. Southern politicians and school boards largely sat on their hands for a decade; when they did act it was to devise strategies of resistance to *Brown*. Some schools in Virginia simply closed their doors to all students; in other places officials adopted school choice programs that effectively preserved the racial status quo. When desegregation cases moved northward, northern politicians were sometimes no less crafty than their southern counterparts in finding artful ways around desegregation orders while stoking racial resentment among their constituents.

Popular reception also matters greatly. Individuals and groups can often undermine the desired effect of a Supreme Court opinion. Many southern whites moved their children to private schools in response to desegregation orders, and in the seventies and eighties, many northern whites did the same. An even more common response was to move to largely white suburban areas, which grew increasingly in the last half of the twentieth century. Demographic shifts and economic growth allowed many whites to vote with their feet, while black parents, often possessing fewer resources and facing greater social impediments (which included widespread housing discrimination), were increasingly trapped in central urban areas.

Finally, a court must try to imagine how future judges will apply its language. This includes not only lower federal courts and state courts, but future Justices of the Supreme Court.

Because a judge on a constitutional court cannot know the future with any degree of precision, the task of decision produces two equal and opposite tendencies: One tendency is to try to state with clarity the basic principles that the judge does not want to be undermined over time. By articulating these basic commitments when the right opportunity presents itself, judges can preserve democratic values and fundamental rights from later periods of retrenchment, which are virtually certain to come as the political winds change. One does this not simply to tie the hands of future generations but because these values are truly fundamental and should be part of the basic fabric of American democracy. To be sure, later actors may resist them and may even overthrow them in time. Yet even if particular doctrines are overruled, distinguished, or ignored—a common enough occurrence in the history of the American Constitution—something else of value will be preserved. What will be preserved is a clear statement of principle, a vision of constitutional rights that will remain as a resource for future generations. In this way a judge cannot control the future, but he or she can make a lasting contribution to the constitutional tradition that others may draw on.

The other tendency takes the uncertainty of the future in precisely the opposite direction: Because one cannot know how events will play out, or what unintended consequences a decision will have, the judge should try to decide as little as possible, and leave the contours of constitutional principle, the details of implementation, or both, to future generations. Doing too much might backfire: It may lead to resistance that undermines the authority of the courts in a constitutional system. It may produce clever attempts to outwit the law that have disastrous social consequences. It may spawn a political reaction that leads to the election of politicians who appoint new judges who will dismantle or undermine all the good work one has attempted to do. For these and other reasons, doing little may be the best advice, in the hope that minor innovations will spur the political process to good effect and that future generations will gradually achieve a just outcome.

Interestingly, even full hindsight of almost fifty years does not fundamentally change this dilemma, or the problems facing an opinion writer in a case like *Brown*. The participants in this exercise all knew how the story of school desegregation had turned out by the end of the century, but there was no consensus among them as to precisely how best to deal with what the future held, even when it was a future that they were privy to. Some of the authors opted for minimal statements of constitutional principle, leaving most of the difficult issues to another day. Others hoped to stake a claim by outlining basic theories about equality and fundamental rights that they hoped would do more good than harm in the hands of future judges and political actors. Some gave rather specific remedies, others offered more general principles for remedial relief to be implemented by future courts, and still others were largely silent about remedies, believing that there was little that one could say in 1954 that would have any useful bearing on the remedial struggles of later decades.

B. *Overruling* Plessy

The first question a judge must face in writing *Brown* is whether to overrule *Plessy v. Ferguson,* or simply retain the doctrine of equalization of facilities that had been applied in *Sweatt v. Painter* and other cases. Thurgood Marshall and the NAACP, of course, had been pushing to overturn *Plessy* since at least the 1940s. Marshall believed that integration of schools and other facilities was in the best interest not only of black Americans but of all Americans.

In their revisions of the *Brown* opinion, all of the legal scholars in this book except one agree that this is the best approach. The exception is Derrick Bell, who has thought and written about *Brown* and school desegregation his entire life. In this book he now offers a dissenting opinion. Bell argues that by overturning *Plessy,* the Court might make itself and the country feel good about their commitment to equality. Nevertheless, this symbolic act will not prevent sustained white resistance to full social equality for blacks. Whites will not give blacks that equality unless they believe that it is in their interest to do so. Therefore, it is better to keep *Plessy* and press for strict enforcement of equalization of facilities for whites and blacks. If the Court tries to force whites to desegregate, Bell argues, they will simply resist. Blacks will end up with inferior schools rather than integrated ones.

Bell's opinion is a dissent rather than a concurrence because he does not hold that separate is inherently unequal. Rather, he argues, the promise of equal facilities should be strictly enforced in order "to lay bare the simplistic hypocrisy" of *Plessy.* Holding separate facilities inherently unequal will only provoke defiant resistance; it will be a largely symbolic gesture that will do little to help schoolchildren of either race in the long run. Instead Bell would impose a series of orders requiring strict equalization of facilities. Implementing them will demonstrate that segregated schools deny white as well as black children the quality of education they might have received in a unitary school district. Bell's dissent is nominally aimed at the plurality opinion in this exercise, but much of his rhetoric is directed at the whole course of desegregation cases beginning with Warren's opinion in *Brown I*. Drawing on his "interest convergence" thesis, Bell argues that the Court's decision to overrule *Plessy* should be understood as part of a long line of civil rights policies going back to the Emancipation Proclamation that ultimately served the nation's interests far more than they benefited blacks. Eliminating *Plessy* might help America's foreign policy interests, but the relief it offers blacks, warns Bell, will prove more symbolic than real.

One curiosity of Warren's opinion is that it does not overrule *Plessy* directly. It merely rejects *Plessy*'s reasoning as applied to public education. Today, of course, most people believe that *Brown* did overrule *Plessy*, and certainly the Justices understood in 1954 that this was the consequence of their decision. Nevertheless, it was not until 1957 that a federal court held that *Plessy* was overruled.[1] And the first clear statement in the Supreme Court to that effect does not appear until Justice Black's 1970 opinion in *Oregon v. Mitchell*.[2] By 1992, in *Planned Parenthood of Southeastern Pennsylvania v. Casey*, the joint opinion of Justices O'Connor, Kennedy, and Souter devotes considerable efforts to explaining why the Court was justified in overruling *Plessy* in *Brown*.[3] But in 1954 at least, Warren avoided saying directly what the Court was doing.

C. How Much of Plessy to Overrule?

Even if one decides to overrule *Plessy*, one could overrule it in different degrees. Should *Plessy* and its doctrine of "separate but equal" be overturned completely and in all contexts, rejected only in the context of public education, or even more narrowly, rejected in the context of public elementary and secondary education? As noted previously, Chief Justice Warren rejected one of Justice Jackson's suggested changes to the draft opinion because it might be interpreted as a general attack on racial segregation. Warren deliberately hoped to keep the holding narrow, applying only to segregation in the public schools.[4] He argued that segregation damaged the "hearts and minds" of black schoolchildren, a theory that would not necessarily apply with equal force to other forms of segregation. Nevertheless, as noted above, the Court soon followed *Brown I* with a series of per curiam orders that applied to many other kinds of municipal facilities that segregated adults. Warren and the Court decided to edge the country toward ending Jim Crow without offering a general theory of why Jim Crow violated the Constitution. Only in light of these later per curiam orders did it become clear that *Plessy*'s "separate but equal" doctrine was effectively overruled in all circumstances.

Cass Sunstein, an advocate of judicial "minimalism," also takes a narrow approach in his concurrence in this volume. He focuses only on the question of school segregation, suggesting that "[i]f the historical record demonstrated that the ratifiers specifically intended to preserve school segregation, immediately after ratification and for the future as well, I would certainly hesitate to rule otherwise." But such evidence is lacking. Thus, he argues that the result in *Brown* is foreordained by the weight of previous precedents. Following the basic outlines of the argument that Thurgood Marshall presented in 1952, Sunstein argues that *Plessy* is in tension with both the Court's earliest cases, like *Strauder v. West Virginia*,[5] which struck down a policy of excluding blacks from juries, and later cases like *Sweatt v. Painter* and *McLaurin v. Oklahoma State Regents*,[6] which upheld challenges to segregated graduate programs. According to Sunstein, it is a short step from these cases to overruling *Plessy*, at least with respect to schools. "Underlying circumstances have dramatically changed" since 1868, so that education is now a central feature of citizenship. No "pressing public necessity" can justify segregated education other than capitulation to racial prejudice, which is an impermissible goal. Consistent with his minimalist philosophy, Sunstein refuses to extend the decision past schools, leaving the continuing viability of *Plessy* in other contexts to another day.

By contrast, my opinion directly overrules *Plessy* and its associated doctrine of separate but equal. In his concurrence, Drew Days criticizes other scholars—presumably Cass Sunstein and Michael McConnell— for limiting their opinions to the constitutionality of school segregation, but Days's target could equally be Warren. In Days's view "[t]here is . . . no justification for judicial timidity in this regard." *Plessy* should be overturned "not only with respect to public schools but also as to transportation—the context in which it was originally announced."

D. *The Rationale of* Brown I—*Social Science or Social Meaning?*

Once the Court decided to overrule *Plessy*, the next question to face was why. What, precisely, was wrong with *Plessy*? The scope of the *Brown* decision—which kinds of segregation it reached—was clearly related to the question of its justification. In *Plessy* Justice Brown had noted that if segregation offended blacks, it was because they chose to put that construction on it. Warren wanted to reject that conclusion without infuriating the South too much. He tried to do this by narrowing his focus to elementary and secondary education. Warren argued that *Plessy* did not adequately take into account the special harms that segregation caused schoolchildren.

The entire argument for overturning *Plessy* in *Brown I* is remarkably brief: Warren began by noting that the Court had previously held in *Sweatt* and *McLaurin* that education and educational opportunity had "intangible" elements "incapable of objective measurement." These "considerations," he argued, "apply with added force to children in grade and high schools." Warren now made his central argument: "To separate [children] from others of similar age and qualifications solely because of their race generates a feeling of inferiority as to their status in the community that may affect their hearts and minds in a way unlikely ever to be undone."[7]

Segregation, Warren argued, harms black schoolchildren psychologically. Warren pointed to the Kansas litigation where the trial court found that segregation by law "is usually interpreted as denoting the inferiority of the negro group" and that children internalize this message: "A sense of inferiority affects the motivation of a child to learn," and "has a tendency to [retard] the educational and mental development of Negro children."[8]

Warren then tried to clinch the argument by explaining that these findings had scientific authority. "Whatever may have been the extent of psychological knowledge at the time of Plessy v. Ferguson," Warren argued, "this finding is amply supported by modern authority."[9] He then included a footnote—footnote 11 of the opinion—that cited a list of social science sources. It ended with a general cite to the Swedish economist Gunnar Myrdal's 1944 book *An American Dilemma*, which had studied America's racial caste system in depth, noting its conflict with American ideals of democracy.

The first source cited in footnote 11—and the one that generated the most controversy—was Kenneth C. Clark's doll study. Clark gave black children in the North and South, aged six through nine, a white doll and a black doll. He then asked them to give him "the white doll," "the colored doll," and "the Negro doll," in order to test whether children understood the notion of race. He then asked each child to give him "the doll you like best," "the doll that is the nice doll," "the doll that looks bad," and "the doll that is a nice color."[10] When black children preferred the white doll, Clark concluded that this proved that segregation created feelings of inferiority.

As Lucas A. Powe has pointed out, Clark's studies reflected the relatively unsophisticated state of social science at the time. The doll studies had numerous flaws, including sample sizes that were too small and the lack of a control group. Perhaps most problematic was that black children in northern states without segregation were even more likely to prefer the white doll than black children in the segregated South.[11] Clark may have offered evidence—if any was necessary—that in white-dominated American society, minority children would quickly learn the social meanings of white superiority and black inferiority. But he had hardly demonstrated that legal segregation in schools was the sole or even the dominant cause of this understanding.

Marshall had included testimony on the doll studies in part because Robert Carter was particularly impressed by them. But not all of Marshall's lieutenants agreed. "The dolls were the source of considerable derision," Richard Kluger reports, "and the social-science approach itself was viewed as unlikely to sway the Justices."[12] William Coleman, a brilliant lawyer who had been the first black clerk on the Supreme Court (for Felix Frankfurter), was particularly dismissive: "Jesus Christ, those damned dolls!" Coleman exclaimed. "I thought it was a joke."[13]

Warren included footnote 11 as part of his general strategy of adopting a nonaccusatory tone. Apparently he believed that by grounding his decision in empirical social science, he would not appear to be engaging in moral condemnation of the South or of segregation, and he would strengthen the authority of his decision. The strategy backfired. If anything, footnote 11 gave critics of the decision more ammunition than if Warren had simply omitted any reference to the studies. Critics accused several of the authors of the studies cited in footnote 11 of having communist leanings. Myrdal was dismissed as a "foreign sociologist."[14] Clark's doll studies were attacked as bad social science.

Moreover, even without criticizing the studies, one could criticize the Court's reliance on them. Powe sums up the basic problem succinctly: By trying to place weight on psychological studies, the Court "opened itself up to charges that it went beyond its own competence and may have therefore misinterpreted the materials. Worse, it implicitly suggested that if the teachings of modern psychology were different, so would be the legal outcome."[15]

Many of the contributors to this book eschew Warren's tack of relying on social science evidence to prove the unconstitutionality of segregation. My own opinion says nothing about these studies, relying instead on the history of Jim Crow as evidence that segregation was a subordinating practice. Drew Days argues that "we have developed criteria for evaluating the constitutionality of racial classification that do not depend upon findings of psychic harm or social science evidence." Days's concurrence quotes *Hirabayashi v. United States* for the principle that "distinctions between citizens solely because of their ancestry are by their very nature odious to a free people."[16] Michael McConnell insists that the social science studies are irrelevant to the Court's decision because "[n]o one has elected us to make decisions about effective pedagogy."

John Hart Ely does rely on the notion of psychological harm, although he too does not rest his conclusion on the social science studies cited in the original *Brown* opinion. Whether or not those studies were valid, he argues, the conclusion that enforced racial segregation is psychologically harmful is correct. Separation of children based on race "is bound to generate feelings of insecurity, even inferiority," that impede their ability to learn and have other serious long-term consequences.

By contrast, Catharine MacKinnon accepts the social science evidence presented before the courts, but she interprets it quite differently than Warren did. Warren thought that segregation created psychological damage to children's "hearts and minds" that might never be erased. Ely makes a similar point in his opinion. In MacKinnon's view, however, the injuries to the children that the experts testified to are not merely psychological. The point is not what the children feel but that their feelings are a symptom of a wrong that was done to them. The damage to which the experts testified in these cases, MacKinnon argues, is a measure of the effects of subordination. Using the law to treat people as part of a lower order of humanity is harm in itself. The feelings of inferiority measured by the social scientists may be damage but they are only traces of the greater injury. It is as if one identified blood that flows from a cut as the injury rather than the cut itself.

E. Original Intention or Evolving Meanings?

Another way to argue that *Plessy* was wrong is to rely on original intention. This avoids basing the antidiscrimination principle on a showing of psychological harm to the affected group. However, since Alexander Bickel first studied the matter at the request of Justice Frankfurter, the general consensus has been that most of the framers and ratifiers of the Fourteenth Amendment did not expect that it would outlaw segregation of the public schools.[17] School segregation was common in the North at the time of the adoption of the amendment, and even the galleries of Congress were segregated.

Nevertheless, Michael McConnell argues that the specific result in *Brown I* can still be defended on originalist grounds. Drawing on historical work he did in a 1995 article,[18] McConnell points to a series of congressional votes concerning whether to desegregate the public schools as part of a proposed measure to ban segregation in places of public accommodation. A large majority of Congress, McConnell argues, believed that segregated schools were inherently unequal. The legislation outlawing school desegregation was not enacted because a two-thirds vote was necessary to overcome a filibuster, but many of the persons who voted for the measure were also members of the Congress that voted for the Fourteenth Amendment, and, McConnell insists, "the opinions of legislators regarding the meaning of the amendment, expressed so soon after its enactment, are entitled to great weight."

McConnell's argument does not necessarily establish that all racial classifications are suspect—for example, classifications in statutes banning miscegenation, classifications denying blacks the right to jury service, or, for that matter, classifications in affirmative action programs. That is one reason why McConnell's opinion goes no further than holding segregation unlawful in public schools run by the states.

My opinion takes a different approach to constitutional interpretation. It assumes that the meaning and application of the Fourteenth Amendment change over time, and that even if its framers and ratifiers had approved of segregated schools, we are not bound by their intentions. Indeed, the opinion starts with the proposition that many of the

framers and ratifiers of the Fourteenth Amendment were quite uncomfortable with full equality for blacks. In 1868, at least, they decidedly
did not want a "color-blind" Constitution, because that would have
given blacks the vote. They employed a distinction between civil, political, and social equality to preserve white privilege. Only civil equality—the right to make contracts, own property, sue and be sued—was
guaranteed by the Fourteenth Amendment (although court decisions
later expanded the meaning of the amendment to include elements of
political equality). However, nothing in the Constitution or in any other
part of the law could make blacks social equals of whites. In the view of
the framers and ratifiers, social equality was the result of patterns of
free private choice and voluntary association with which law should
not interfere. This tripartite division of citizenship rights would later
form part of the ideological basis for Jim Crow. Nevertheless, over time
these categories became increasingly incoherent and difficult to justify.
For example it was hard to argue that social inequality was the result of
purely private decisions when the states engaged in widespread systems of segregation to preserve white supremacy and even defined who
was white and black by law in order to preserve white racial purity.

The opinion thus argues that the meaning of the American Constitution evolves because the document is redemptive. Its language continually presses the American people to live up to the promises and ideals
contained within it, even if the framers and ratifiers of the document
would have disagreed with later understandings of what those promises and ideals meant.

John Hart Ely offers still another approach. He rejects McConnell's
inquiry into the concrete intentions of the framers of the Fourteenth
Amendment. He points to the text of the Constitution as well as the interpretive practices of the framers themselves. The Equal Protection
Clause, he argues, "is among the . . . clearest examples of a provision
whose exact content was understood not to be frozen in time. . . . It was
not intended to be tethered by any 1954 or other future attempt to guess
what particular instances of equality our 1868 forebears had at the forefront of their minds." The framers of the Fourteenth Amendment, Ely
argues, had a different view of how to interpret constitutional provisions than McConnell does; one is hardly being faithful to their intentions by ignoring their views about how the document should be interpreted. The generation of 1868 was "accustomed to reading the 1789
and 1791 documents in terms of the principles they set forth rather than

trying to read the minds of the founding generation for further specificity, and there is no convincing indication that they intended their
own unratified thoughts to be given any greater deference."

F. Antisubordination or Anticlassification?

An issue that appears more insistently in our time than in Warren's is
the theoretical basis of the antidiscrimination principle—the view that
it is wrong for the state (or, in some cases, for a private party) to discriminate on the basis of race. In *Brown I*, Warren was content simply
to insist that segregation was inherently unequal because it harmed
schoolchildren. In 1967 in *Loving v. Virginia*[19] the Court unanimously
held that racial classifications were subject to "strict scrutiny"—and
hence almost always unconstitutional—but *Brown I* offers no general
theory of why this might be so, and indeed does not even use the language of scrutiny.

The underlying theoretical justification of *Brown* is important fifty
years later because of the ongoing controversy over whether the underlying principle of constitutional equality is anticlassification or antisubordination. Is the real evil of *Plessy* the classification of persons by
race or is it the subordination of one race by another? Is the problem of
Jim Crow that it made racial distinctions that unfairly stereotyped individuals or that it employed racial distinctions as a means of oppressing
a group and confirming social meanings about its inferiority? As noted
earlier, both sides claim to be the rightful inheritors of *Brown*, and the
choice between these two interpretations matters greatly in any number
of areas ranging from voting rights to affirmative action. Although
when Warren wrote in 1954, the debate over "affirmative action" was a
long way off, the question hangs heavily over several of the opinions
written in 2000.

Michael McConnell's opinion makes the clearest case for the anticlassification principle: "The question in every case is whether the state
has classified or segregated pupils according to race, or employed ostensibly neutral criteria for the purpose of classifying or segregating
pupils according to race." McConnell's argument seems to foreclose affirmative action by state governments, although because of his originalist views about *Bolling v. Sharpe*, benign racial classifications by the
federal government might be treated differently.

By contrast, my opinion and most of the other opinions—including Bell's dissent—adopt an antisubordination approach. Many of these opinions—like Frank Michelman's and my own—explain antisubordination principles in terms of a guarantee of equal citizenship: The state may not create or condone different degrees of citizenship. This argument echoes ideas in Justice Harlan's dissents both in *Plessy* and in the 1883 *Civil Rights Cases*.[20] Among legal academics, the equal citizenship principle is most often identified with the work of Kenneth Karst.[21] Using antisubordination rather than anticlassification reasoning has obvious consequences for contemporary debates about racial equality: For example, my opinion holds that any practice that has the purpose or effect of subordinating a social group violates the principle of equal citizenship, leaving open the possibility that practices like affirmative action that do not subordinate are constitutionally permissible. Similarly, Cass Sunstein's concurrence is careful to note that "[w]e have never held that the ban on racial discrimination is absolute."

Catharine MacKinnon's concurrence is perhaps the most overt statement of the antisubordination principle, a view that also infuses her work on gender discrimination. "[T]he evil of segregation," she argues, ". . . is one not of mere differentiation but of hierarchy; not a categorization as such but an imposed inferiority; not an isolated event but an integral feature of a cumulative historical interlocking social and legal system." In her concurrence MacKinnon repeats her famous criticism that if legal equality is grounded in the principle of treating likes alike, the law will simply reinforce the inequalities produced by previous acts of social subordination. Practices of subordination, she argues, differentiate people, and law should not confirm that subordination by treating the difference so produced as a justification for unequal treatment.

G. Education as a Fundamental Right?

Up to this point, the discussion has focused on racial equality. But one might also approach *Brown* as a case about equal educational opportunity. In other words, instead of (or in addition to) a concern with racial separation, the case could also turn on whether black children were receiving an education comparable to that of white students. Indeed, focusing on the right to education would have also allowed poor whites to challenge their lack of educational opportunity in comparison with children in richer neighborhoods. Wide diversities in educational quality in the United States are the result of many different factors, but one of the most important has been the traditional method of funding schools from local property taxes. Parents often move to more affluent neighborhoods in part because the schools have better funding, and they expect that—all other things being equal—this means that their children will receive a better education. Put more simply, parents understand that real estate prices correlate with higher average test scores, superior educational facilities, and—for those children who go on to college—admission to better colleges and universities. Thus, one way of promoting equality for blacks—quite aside from a ban on segregation—would be legal obligations that promote equal educational opportunity. These could take a number of different forms: reforming school finance systems, equalizing school expenditures and facilities, reassigning good teachers to underperforming schools, investing heavily in remedial educational programs to increase average test scores in underperforming areas, or even shifting students in order to share the burden of educating students more equitably.

My opinion adopts both strategies. It holds that separate facilities for whites and blacks are inherently unequal, and it also holds that education is a "fundamental interest." A fundamental interest differs from a fundamental right in that it imposes no positive obligations on the state. States can forego public education completely, but once they provide public education they have constitutional duties of fairness and equality under the Equal Protection Clause. Because "education is an interest of the most fundamental nature in our society," states that offer public education to their children must provide equal educational opportunity for all. In effect this holding anticipates (and prevents) the decision two decades later in *San Antonio Independent School District v. Rodriguez*.[22] In that case, a 5-4 majority led by Justice Powell held that education was not a fundamental right or a fundamental interest, that the poor had no constitutional right to equal treatment on grounds of their poverty, and that states and municipalities had no constitutional obligation to equalize funding for education, or, for that matter, to guarantee equal educational opportunity for rich and poor.

As schools resegregated in the last years of the twentieth century, with largely white suburbs ringing mostly minority inner cities, it became increasingly clear that educational funding and educational quality were goals every bit as important as racial balance. Indeed, one reason for the NAACP's original decision to push for integration was the assumption that majority black schools would always be neglected and underfunded by majority white governments. If white parents had to send their children to the same schools as black parents did, this would go a long way toward guaranteeing that black children would receive quality education. However, because *Brown I* was premised on the harms of segregation, civil rights attorneys could not directly argue for equalization of resources—they could argue for equal resources only in the context of remedying the effects of past segregation. This left them with doctrinal tools ill suited for meeting the educational problems of the present.

In *Bolling v. Sharpe*, Chief Justice Warren came close to holding that education was a fundamental liberty guaranteed under the Due Process Clause, but he left this language out at the urging of Hugo Black in order to ensure a unanimous decision.[23] Even so, both *Brown I* and *Bolling* contain language that emphasizes the importance of education to citizenship. Indeed, in *Brown I* Warren retained language that looks very much like a constitutional obligation: Warren proclaimed "the importance of education to our democratic society" and argued that "[i]n these days, it is doubtful that any child may reasonably be expected to succeed in life if he is denied the opportunity of an education." He concluded that "[s]uch an opportunity, where the state has undertaken to provide it, is a right which must be made available to all on equal terms."[24] Reading these lines today, one could be forgiven for thinking that the Court *did* hold that education was a fundamental interest in 1954, even if later courts came to a contrary conclusion.

Bruce Ackerman's concurrence argues that education is a fundamental right, and he reaches that result in a particularly interesting and original way. In 1868, guarantees of equal citizenship were generally understood to flow not from the Equal Protection Clause of the Fourteenth Amendment—which was regarded as having comparatively little importance at the time—but from the Privileges or Immunities Clause. No state, that clause held, could deny any citizen the privileges or immunities of national citizenship. However, by 1873, the Supreme Court had read this clause out of existence in the *Slaughterhouse Cases*.[25] It sharply distinguished between the privileges and immunities of state citizenship and those of national citizenship; and it held that the latter were virtually nonexistent. Ackerman argues that the Court should overturn the *Slaughterhouse Cases*. There is no reason, he argues, why an interest could not be a privilege of both state and federal citizenship. Moreover, he argues, education is a fundamental privilege of both state and national citizenship because it is so central to democracy. Ackerman points to the 1943 case *of West Virginia State Board of Education v. Barnette*,[26] which held that Jehovah's Witness schoolchildren could not be forced to salute the flag as a condition of attending public schools. Although *Barnette* is usually understood as holding that citizens have a First Amendment right not to be forced to state beliefs they do not hold, Ackerman argues that the real reasoning behind *Barnette* was that, by 1943, free public education was "fundamental to the framework of national life." "The democratic republic contemplated by our Reconstruction Constitution," Ackerman concludes, "cannot survive under modern conditions without *all* Americans receiving an education worthy of free and equal citizens."

Not all participants were so eager to overrule *Rodriguez* prospectively. Cass Sunstein objects to the dual holding of my opinion. In his view, the opinion "decide[s] too many complex questions, many of them not properly presented here." And Michael McConnell argues that "craft[ing] special rules of constitutional law appropriate to so vital an institution" as education "is . . . beyond our authority."

H. Discrimination by the Federal Government: The Special Problem of Bolling v. Sharpe

Bolling v. Sharpe—which involved the segregation of the District of Columbia schools—presents a more difficult case. The text of the Fourteenth Amendment seems to bind only the states. The Due Process Clause of the Fifth Amendment does apply to the federal government, but it says nothing on its face about equality. In *Bolling*, Warren solved this problem by holding that the purposes of the Equal Protection and Due Process Clauses were related: Although the concept of "'equal protection of the laws' is a more explicit safeguard of prohibited unfairness than 'due process of law,'" Warren argued, the two concepts were "not mutually exclusive," and "discrimination may be so unjustifiable as to be violative of due process."[27] Warren insisted that school segregation "is not reasonably related to any proper governmental objective" and was "an arbitrary deprivation of . . . liberty in violation of the Due Process Clause."[28] He then offered a structural argument: "In view of our decision that the Constitution prohibits the states from maintaining racially segregated public schools, it would be unthinkable that the same Constitution would impose a lesser duty on the Federal Government."[29] Later cases would expand these ideas, holding that the concept of due process in the Fifth Amendment contained a guarantee of basic equality similar to that of the Equal Protection Clause of the Fourteenth Amendment, or, as it is often expressed today, that the Due Process Clause has an "equal protection component."[30]

Bolling has proved to be a problem case for countless constitutional theorists. Many constitutional textualists and advocates of "strict construction" find the lack of a specific equality provision particularly troubling. Originalists who believe that the meaning of the Fifth Amendment depends on the understandings of the date of its ratification in 1791 also find *Bolling* problematic. As Frank Michelman points out in his concurring opinion, most blacks were held in slavery in 1791, so that it is unlikely that the framers and ratifiers of that amendment believed that the Due Process Clause guaranteed equality of treatment based on race.

At his 1987 confirmation hearings, Judge Robert Bork, a noted originalist, admitted that he had not thought of a way of justifying the case, much to the chagrin of his supporters and the delight of his opponents.[31] In his subsequent book, *The Tempting of America*, Bork stated outright that the case had been wrongly decided: Congress did have the power to segregate the D.C. public schools. Indeed, he dismissed the *Bolling* opinion as "social engineering from the bench,"[32] putting it in the same category as *Dred Scott* and *Lochner*. Not surprisingly, people have often pointed to *Bolling* as the key counterexample to originalism as well as a key rejoinder to those who deny the existence of fundamental rights not explicitly mentioned in the text of the Constitution: If originalism and textualism mean that Congress is not bound by principles of racial equality, the argument goes, that shows that there is something wrong with originalism and textualism, not the Constitution.

As a distinguished originalist himself, Michael McConnell well understands the challenge that *Bolling* presents. He argues that the Due Process Clause "is fundamentally a guarantee of procedural regularity [and] [i]f the Clause could be expanded to cover [segregation in the District of Columbia schools], it would lose any determinate meaning." Moreover, McConnell argues, it made perfect sense for the Equal Protection Clause to apply only to the states. The framers might well have thought that racist policies at the national level were less likely than at the state level. Hence there was less need for a constitutional guarantee of equality against the federal government. Moreover, through its powers under section 5 of the Fourteenth Amendment, Congress was expected to enforce the amendment's guarantees against the states.

McConnell's reading of due process as limited to procedural regularity not only undermines the decision in *Bolling*; it also throws into serious doubt cases like *Griswold v. Connecticut*,[33] which protected the right of married persons to purchase contraceptives, and *Roe v. Wade*,[34] which guaranteed women's right to abortion. Both of these decisions assumed that guarantees of due process imposed substantive limitations on governments. Given that McConnell is a noted critic of *Roe*, it is possible that he would not much mind this result. Critics of McConnell might insist, as Cass Sunstein does, that the Due Process Clause has always protected more than procedural regularity, and that there is abundant history suggesting that it had a more capacious meaning, at least in the nineteenth century. Nevertheless, McConnell's originalist objection to *Bolling* remains quite powerful.

If McConnell is right that *Bolling* cannot be justified by original intention, and if he is committed to a jurisprudence of originalism, does this mean that he would leave the District of Columbia schools segregated? Although the D.C. schools had been segregated for generations, McConnell argues that as of 1954, Congress had not explicitly authorized segregation of the schools. As a matter of statutory interpretation, courts should interpret "the silences and ambiguities of federal legislation" to guarantee a parity of rights against federal and state governments. Hence, McConnell argues, "[f]ederal courts should not presume that Congress has delegated the authority to depart from general principles of equal protection of the laws to subordinate agencies without a clear statement to that effect." Hence, because Congress did not explicitly give the D.C. school board the power to segregate by race, the board's decision to do so is beyond its authority.

Cass Sunstein agrees with McConnell that the Equal Protection Clause does not bind the national government. But he insists that federal action, like all economic and social legislation, must pass the test of having a rational basis; it must "be reasonably related to some legitimate state interest." School segregation, Sunstein concludes, has no legitimate purpose. It is merely a desire to accommodate prejudices that are themselves illegitimate, or to preserve white supremacy and a system of racial caste, which cannot be regarded as legitimate functions of government. Implicit in Sunstein's argument is that any asserted legitimate purposes the federal government might offer for continuing segregation—for example, the prevention of violence, or the administrative costs of changing to a unitary system—cannot be taken seriously, or, when analyzed sufficiently, will prove to be illegitimate goals. Normally courts give great deference to social and economic legislation and to the government's asserted interests under the test of rational basis, but because of historic understandings about race and racism, Sunstein would apparently apply the test differently when racial segregation was involved.

Frank Michelman argues that McConnell's solution begs the question. Why impose a rule of judicial construction requiring a clear statement if the federal government is not bound by principles of equal protection? And why insist that the District of Columbia school district acts beyond its legal authority only when it segregates students when there are dozens of other policies it has pursued without express congressional approval? Michelman thinks that if *Bolling* is correctly decided, it is because of "an attribution of national purpose and commitment" to equal citizenship and the elimination of caste, "for which no internal legal-textual or textual-historical demonstration can be found." If we attribute this commitment to our Declaration of Independence, Michelman adds, we must regard the first seventy-five years of the country's history as inconsistent with that commitment, or in his words, "as a visionary eclipse or occlusion."

Similarly, Michelman argues, Sunstein's use of a "rational basis" test in *Bolling* begs the question why the same test is not sufficient to overturn *state* segregation of schools. Obviously Sunstein must think that the antidiscrimination principle has more bite than a test of mere rationality. Indeed, Michelman argues, if the test is really whether the law has any rational basis, the Court should remand for further proceedings to assess the costs and benefits of segregation in the specific context of the District of Columbia. "Of course," Michelman notes, "we could cut [that process] short by announcing today that no pragmatic reason could ever be *sufficiently weighty* to provide a 'rational' justification" for racial segregation, but "to do so would obviously be to rely on some constitutional principle beyond that of a rational-basis due process requirement."

By contrast, John Hart Ely believes that the matter can be resolved simply. The framers of the Fourteenth Amendment, he argues, assumed that the federal government was already bound by a general principle of equality. Ely points to a number of sources for this conclusion, including the Declaration of Independence, the Federalist Papers, and the Ninth Amendment. The only issue, Ely thinks, was whether the equality principle that bound the federal government extended to race, and by 1868 it was clear that it did. Finally, Ely argues as a doctrinal matter that the Supreme Court had settled the issue in 1944 in *Korematsu v. United States*.[35] *Korematsu* upheld the internment of Japanese Americans and Japanese resident aliens during World War II. The opinion is now widely criticized as capitulating to the country's racist fears during wartime. However, the same opinion held that "all legal restrictions which curtail the civil rights of a single racial group are immediately suspect" and that "courts must subject them to the most rigid scrutiny."[36] This is the basis of the modern view that racial classifications are subject to strict scrutiny—i.e., presumptively unconstitutional. Equally important, Ely points out, *Korematsu* applied this test to a decision of the federal government, thus settling that "the demands of the Equal Protection Clause were fully applicable."

My own opinion uses a combination of structural, historical, and textual arguments to justify the result in *Bolling*. The structural argument is quite simple: America's commitment to equality, arising out of the Civil War, was a national one; this commitment would be fatally undermined if the federal government could sabotage or weaken the guarantees of racial equality that bound the states. The obvious analogy to this argument is the principle of freedom of speech: By its terms, the First Amendment binds only Congress, but it has long been held to apply to the executive and the judicial branches, because they could successfully destroy freedom of speech even if Congress could not.

The textual argument emphasizes the special role of the Citizenship Clause that begins the Fourteenth Amendment: "All persons born or naturalized in the United States, and subject to the jurisdiction thereof, are citizens of the United States and of the State wherein they reside." This clause applies to both the states and the federal government. It overrules *Dred Scott v. Sandford*,[37] which held that blacks could not be citizens because of their race. It stands for the proposition that neither the states nor the federal government can create more than one class of citizens. Segregation treats blacks as second-class citizens and therefore violates the amendment whether it is practiced by the states or the federal government.

The historical argument for *Bolling* is tied to the text of the Privileges or Immunities Clause, which prohibits the states from abridging the privileges or immunities of national citizenship. The framers of the Fourteenth Amendment assumed that the federal government was bound by guarantees of civil equality. That was why they spoke of the privileges and immunities of national citizenship. If states may not violate the privileges and immunities of national citizenship, a fortiori neither can the national government. The Court limited the list of privileges and immunities of national citizenship in the *Slaughterhouse Cases* of 1873,[38] but it nevertheless specifically stated that these privileges include the rights guaranteed by the Fourteenth Amendment, which include the equal protection of the laws.

Because Bruce Ackerman would overrule the *Slaughterhouse Cases*, he believes that *Bolling* is an easy case. In his view, the Constitution creates rights of national citizenship that bind state and national governments alike. The Fourteenth Amendment recognized and confirmed these rights and established the primacy of national citizenship. Thus, one need answer only two questions: First, is an adequate education one of the privileges or immunities of national citizenship? Second, if it is, does segregation of public schools treat blacks as second-class citizens? "If the answer to both questions is yes," Ackerman argues, "it makes no difference whether it is the national government or the states that have deprived Negroes of their birthright."

I. What Remedy?

The question of remedy was perhaps the most difficult question facing the Justices in the original *Brown* opinion, and it was the most difficult for the participants in this exercise. Warren's 1955 opinion in *Brown II* made three crucial decisions: First, the Court would not treat the cases as class actions and offer class-wide relief. This meant that only the named plaintiffs were entitled to a remedy and that each individual school district would have to be sued separately. Second, the Court would not insist on immediate desegregation. Instead it required only that desegregation proceed "with all deliberate speed," a term suggested by Frankfurter. Third, the Court would leave open most of the important questions about how to ensure that school districts complied with the principles of its *Brown I* decision. The Court allowed these questions to simmer in the lower courts for over a decade. It did not intervene significantly in remedial issues until its 1968 decision in *Green v. New Kent County School Board*.[39] The Court's subsequent decisions on school segregation were phrased almost entirely in terms of the forms of remedy available to courts rather than in terms of the rights of black schoolchildren. Obviously right and remedy are intimately related; a very narrow remedy tells us much about the nature of the right at stake.

For example, many opponents of integrated schools clung to a dictum by Judge Parker that appeared in the lower court opinion in *Briggs v. Elliott*. The Constitution, Parker argued, at most forbids segregation but does not require integration.[40] If the states simply stopped assigning pupils directly by race, it did not matter if private individuals chose to remain in segregated schools. Many southern school districts responded to *Brown II* with "pupil placement" and "freedom of choice" plans, which were neutral on their face but produced almost no integration. White parents refused to send their children to all-black schools, which had decidedly inferior facilities. Black parents were simply afraid to send their children to the white schools for fear of violent reprisal. Thus if *Brown* granted only a right to be free from racially based pupil assignments, it did not grant much to black children. Indeed, because the schools were technically "desegregated" once overt assignments by race ended, one could argue that there was no continuing obligation to equalize facilities between schools. The situation might then be even worse than it was before *Plessy*.

By contrast, if courts offered an expansive remedy, this implied a much more robust substantive right. In 1968, after years of silence on the issue, the Supreme Court decided *Green v. New Kent County School Board*, which is perhaps its most important school desegregation decision after *Brown*. Justice Brennan's opinion argued that racially identifiable schools were a vestige of segregation and must be eliminated.[41] Everyone knew which schools were the "white" schools and which were the "black" schools. As long as those social meanings were in place, there would never be real equality of opportunity. More money, more attention, better teachers, and better facilities would inevitably flow to the "white" schools, and white parents would shun the "black" schools. Thus, the goal of desegregation was achieving a "unitary" school district that would create no incentives for a white-controlled political process to deny blacks equal educational opportunity. In a delicious pun, Brennan argued that the point of *Brown I* and *Brown II* was "to convert promptly to a system without a 'white' school and a 'Negro' school, but just schools."[42] *Green* was the basis for the Court's later endorsement of busing as a remedy to achieve racial balance in *Swann v. Charlotte-Mecklenburg Board of Education.*[43] Obviously some whites would send their children to private schools, but these were expensive. If most whites had to go to the same schools as blacks, they would not leave their own children without a quality education.

Of course, what *Green* did not contemplate, or contemplate sufficiently, was that whites did have a way to avoid racial mixing and paying for equal educational opportunity for blacks—they could move to new political subdivisions and all-white suburban school districts. The crucial next step in the debate over remedies was whether *Brown I* and *Brown II* allowed courts to view metropolitan areas as a whole, rather than as collections of separate school districts that were increasingly defined by race. It was at this point the Court stopped its remedial expansion. In its 5-4 decision in *Milliken v. Bradley,*[44] the Court held that inter-district remedies were generally not permitted unless "racially discriminatory acts of the state or local school districts, or of a single school district have been a substantial cause of inter-district segregation." Without proof of a conspiracy to segregate, courts had to respect existing school district boundaries and could not combine school districts in a single plan. In effect, *Milliken* undermined *Green* because it allowed the recreation of "white" and "black" (or "Latino") schools in separate school districts rather than in the same school district.

This would not have been so bad, perhaps, if there had been a continuing obligation to equalize facilities between the white suburban and minority inner-city school districts. The previous year, however, in *San Antonio Independent School District v. Rodriguez*[45] the Court had held, also in a 5-4 decision, that education was not a fundamental right and reaffirmed that discrimination against the poor did not offend the Constitution. The combination of *Milliken* and *Rodriguez* meant that majority black and Latino school districts in inner cities had no remaining leverage under the federal Constitution to push for equal educational opportunity. (Nevertheless, many state constitutions did recognize a right to education, and this spawned considerable litigation in those states.)

The history of school desegregation litigation can be understood as a dialectic between the *Briggs* dictum—"desegregation not integration"—and *Green*'s focus on racially identifiable schools. Each is nominally a statement about remedies, but in effect each offers a different interpretation of the substantive right in *Brown I*. From one perspective, *Green* is an inevitable consequence of *Brown*. *Brown* was about racial subordination through practices that not only deny equal material benefits but also perpetuate the social meanings of white superiority and black inferiority. Racially identifiable schools perpetuate the subordination of racial minorities. As long as there are identifiable "minority" schools, whites will find ways to ignore them, and minorities will never achieve equal educational opportunity. From another perspective, *Green* is an unwarranted extension of *Brown*. The *Briggs* dictum is correct: *Brown* simply forbids pupil assignment on the basis of race. If schools become racially identified as "white" or "black" or "Latino" through a combination of demographic shifts, economic changes, and other "private choices," there is no Constitutional violation.

Along with these contrasting views about the relation between the remedy and the right, there are also contrasting views about whether it was wise to separate right from remedy. By structuring its post-1954 school desegregation decisions in terms of a debate about remedies rather than about the substantive rights of minority children, the Court may have underplayed the moral authority of *Brown I*. Viewing the controversy only in terms of remedies made it easier for people to proclaim their support for the ideal of racial equality while opposing the practical consequences of a commitment to that ideal.

On the other hand, it may have been wise to separate right from remedy. If *Brown I* meant that segregation was unlawful, state and local governments throughout the South might have been subject to enormous and potentially crippling money judgments, destroying the public school system. Although such lawsuits were rare in the 1950s for a number of reasons, it was only a matter of time before those practices changed. Leaving the terms of the remedy undecided allowed the Court to make a stronger statement of principle. As we have seen, Warren was able to get his unanimous opinion because he compromised on the issue of remedy with Frankfurter, Jackson, Clark, and Reed. If the right in *Brown I* had meant an immediate end to segregation and an ultimate right to racial balance in the public schools, the Court might have hesitated to overrule *Plessy* in the first place. Moreover, if Rosenberg and Klarman are correct in their assessments of how courts interact with the political branches in producing social change, it was wise to declare the right first and temporize on the remedy. Nothing would have been gained by pushing hard on remedial relief in 1954. The Court should have waited, as it did, for the formation of a powerful national political coalition that was committed to ending segregation.[46]

The revised versions of *Brown* in this book reflect these conflicting considerations. My opinion tries to solve the problem of remedy through a two-pronged attack. Because it finds that school districts violated the Constitution in two different ways—through segregation and through denial of a fundamental interest in education—it offers two separate remedial goals. One goal is the elimination of "racially identifiable schools," an idea taken from *Green*. *Green* held that freedom of choice plans did not comport with equal protection if their practical effect was to leave "black" and "white" schools in place. Simply refraining from classifying and assigning students by race would not cure the effects of years of segregation. Thus, facially neutral school assignment policies do not necessarily comply with equal protection. Rather, courts must take affirmative steps to remove the effects of previous segregation.

The second remedial goal is achieving the constitutional guarantee of equal educational opportunity. Racial segregation clearly hindered equal educational opportunity, and eliminating segregation and its effects is crucial to this second remedial goal. But the constitutional obligation to provide equality of educational opportunity applies even after racial segregation has been eliminated. The second remedial goal remains in force even if schools resegregate as a result of changing residential patterns and demographic shifts; moreover, the constitutional requirement of equal educational opportunity protects white children in poor districts as well as black children. Finally, the goal of equalizing educational opportunity is not limited by existing school district boundaries. Indeed, in order to make their case plaintiffs would have to compare inner-city school districts with neighboring suburban schools; in order to provide a remedy courts would probably have to reform traditional district-based systems of school finance.

The point of this two-pronged remedial scheme is to confront the realities that minority children—including Latino as well as black children—faced in the fifty years since *Brown*: Busing proved wildly unpopular, and the courts eventually gave up trying to desegregate the public schools. As a result, many minority children were increasingly isolated in public schools with dismal facilities and no chance at a decent education. A continuing obligation of equal educational opportunity might have served them better.

Michael McConnell's concurrence looks at the matter quite differently. Because he does not join in the holding that education is a fundamental interest, he does not think that courts have any independent constitutional obligation to remedy educational inequalities. Like Justice Thomas, he reasons that all the Constitution requires is that states employ racially neutral assignment policies. To be sure, states may not deliberately pursue racial segregation through ostensibly neutral policies like gerrymandering school district boundaries. But if there is no intent to segregate, school districts with overwhelmingly minority populations do not offend the Constitution. Racial mixing, or actual integration of the schools, is not required.

John Hart Ely reaches a similar conclusion: "[T]he Constitution does not dictate (nor does it forbid) that all schools be demographically identical, but rather that they not be intentionally segregated on the basis of race." Thus Ely finds no constitutional impediment to a policy that every child be assigned to the school nearest his or her home, as long as this policy is not a cover for intentional segregation by race.

Bruce Ackerman, by contrast, adopts a position closer to *Green*. He emphasizes that states may not allow blacks to become racially isolated in public schools. It is not enough to "erase all mention of racial categorization of students from . . . statute books and regulations." Rather, school districts must "take affirmative steps to integrate the races sufficiently to make it clear to the average student that historical patterns of subordination are no longer enshrined in the state's educational philosophy." Yet Ackerman emphasizes another, equally important theme: The Constitution requires school districts to provide students "with the practical skills required to function effectively as a free and equal American citizen." Racial isolation prevents students from learning to cooperate "across the lines of race and class on matters of common importance." Thus, integration is required not only to prevent stigmatization but to teach students of different races, cultures, and backgrounds "the practical arts of democratic cooperation."

The opinions were divided on how fast to proceed with desegregation. Catharine MacKinnon takes the most forceful position. She argues that the schools should have a maximum of one year to eliminate segregation on the basis of race. John Hart Ely agrees that there is little reason for delay: "[A]s of the fall of 1955" the constitutional requirement that schools may not assign pupils on the basis of race should "become fully applicable." Although Drew Days does not impose a specific time limit, he holds that "the process of desegregating the affected school systems must begin immediately."

By contrast, Frank Michelman argues that the desegregation must proceed in an "orderly fashion." Courts cannot achieve this alone but will have to rely on "the lively involvement . . . of state and local citizenries and officials," as well as on the leadership of Congress. Cass Sunstein maintains that issues of implementation must be left "to legislatures and district courts," but that courts should require that "in the beginning of the next school year, the defendants will make an immediate start toward full compliance with our ruling," including "[d]etailed schedules, with clear deadlines." Extensions of time are possible, but "[i]n no event should defendants be permitted an extension of more than one year."

By far the most interesting set of remedial proposals comes from Derrick Bell, who is technically a dissenter in the case because he does not argue for overruling *Plessy*. His ultimate goal, like that of my opinion and Ackerman's concurrence, is guaranteeing equal educational opportunity for minority schoolchildren. However, Bell goes about this task differently.

Bell argues that if the separate-but-equal doctrine of *Plessy* is to be retained, it should be "fully enforce[d] for all children," and this means more than merely equalizing facilities or admitting black children to white schools. Instead, Bell suggests a three-part remedy. First, the academic standards of each school district must be ascertained and made public. Once this is done, "[a]ll schools within the district must be fully equalized in physical facilities, teacher training, experience, and salary with the goal that each district, as a whole, will measure up to national norms within three years." Second, Bell argues that equality requires that parents and local communities have control of school boards. Hence, by the start of the 1955–56 school year courts should restructure school boards and other educational organizations so that they reflect the composition of the children who attend the local schools. Third, to monitor the first two goals, Bell would have federal district judges "set up three-person monitoring committees" to work with school officials, with "the Negro and white communities each selecting a monitor and those two agreeing on a third." Bell's idea is that through a combination of equalization of facilities, representation on school boards, and joint monitoring efforts by the white and black communities in each locality, blacks will be much better off than if they relied on the outcome of a struggle between judges and existing school officials.

After reading the nine opinions in *Brown*, and noting how they struggle with the deep and difficult issues of these cases, it is instructive to go back and look at Earl Warren's opinions in *Brown I, Brown II,* and *Bolling* again. Those opinions have often been criticized for sounding too matter-of-fact, for ducking some important issues, and for obscuring still others. Yet with the hindsight of fifty years' time, they seem to display a remarkable economy. Warren may have stumbled a bit in his use of social science and in his unfortunate adoption of Frankfurter's language of "all deliberate speed." On the whole, however, his three opinions stand up rather well. They do not try to do too much, but they get the basic job done with a minimum of exertion. In many respects Warren did less harm with his words than others, less gifted and less able, might have done. It became fashionable, especially among academic elites, to criticize Warren's opinion for either its lack of legal analysis or its lack of political passion. But from the perspective of fifty years, Earl Warren's work deserves no small degree of admiration.

The contributors to this volume tried to improve on Warren's work, with the benefit of half a century of hindsight. Nevertheless, I am sure that I speak for all of the participants in this book when I say that we learned enormously from the experience of working through the problems that Warren and his brethren faced. It is humbling indeed to compare our tentative efforts with a decision that, for all of its faults, seems far wiser and more well crafted than many gave it credit for when it was first written. Because no one knows the future, one can never be sure of the verdict of the generations that come after. Thus one must always do the best one can given the limited knowledge that one's time and circumstances afford. That was Warren's burden, and it is ours today. The difference is that his opinion would be tested by political events, whereas ours is an academic exercise.

Why then rewrite *Brown*? The answer is simple: Whether we realize it or not, each of us is always rewriting the central texts of our political heritage. In each generation we add new meanings and glosses to those texts based on our own experiences and understandings. In this fashion a tradition of readings and rereadings emerges that enriches our political life. *Brown* is such a central text, and our exercise in this volume merely makes explicit the processes of rereading and reinterpretation it has undergone in the last half century.

What is true of *Brown* is true even more of the Constitution itself. If we Americans truly love our Constitution, we will continually rewrite it, marking it up like a beloved but well-used volume—the more beloved because its margins are so full of scribblings and its pages so bent from constant recourse and reference. The Constitution that stays pristine on the page is the Constitution that shrivels and dies. Only the Constitution that is constantly reread and constantly rewritten lives.

NOTES

1. See *Simkins v. City of Greensboro*, 149 F. Supp. 562, 564 (M.D. N.C. 1957), aff'd *Greensboro v. Simkins*, 246 F.2d 425 (4th Cir. 1957). See also *Christian v. Jemison*, 303 F.2d 52, 55 (5th Cir. 1962).

2. 400 U.S. 112, 133 (1970)(Opinion of Black, J.).

3. 505 U.S. 833, 864 (1992) (Joint Opinion of O'Connor, Kennedy, and Souter, JJ.).

4. Kluger, *Simple Justice*, at 697.

5. 100 U.S. 303 (1880).

6. 339 U.S. 637 (1950).

7. 347 U.S. at 494.

8. Id.

9. 347 U.S. at 494

10. Kluger, *Simple Justice*, at 317–18.

11. Lucas A. Powe Jr., *The Warren Court and American Politics* (2000), at 43; John W. Davis used these points in his argument before the Court in *Briggs v. Elliott. Argument: The Oral Argument before the Supreme Court in* Brown v. Board of Education of Topeka, *1952–55* (Leon Friedman, ed. 1969), at 59.

12. Kluger, *Simple Justice*, at 321.

13. Id. at 321.

14. Powe, *Warren Court and American Politics*, at 42.

15. Id.

16. 320 U.S. 81, 100 (1943).

17. Alexander M. Bickel, "The Original Understanding and the Segregation Decision," 69 *Harv. L. Rev.* 1, 58 (1955).

18. Michael McConnell, "Originalism and the Desegregation Decisions," 81 *Va. L. Rev.* 947 (1995).

19. 388 U.S. 1 (1967).

20. *The Civil Rights Cases*, 109 U.S. 3 (1883).

21. See Kenneth L. Karst, *Belonging to America: Equal Citizenship and the Constitution* (1989); Kenneth L. Karst, "The Supreme Court 1976 Term—Foreword: Equal Citizenship under the Fourteenth Amendment," 91 *Harv. L. Rev.* 1 (1977). Two other major sources of the antisubordination model in the legal academy are Charles L. Black Jr., "The Lawfulness of the Segregation Decisions," 69 *Yale L.J.* 421 (1960), and Owen M. Fiss, "Groups and the Equal Protection Clause," 5 *Phil. & Pub. Aff.* 107 (1976).

22. 411 U.S. 1 (1973).

23. In his initial draft in *Bolling v. Sharpe*, Warren argued that "[j]ust as a government may not impose arbitrary restrictions on the parent's right to educate his child, the government must not impose arbitrary restraints on access to the education which government itself provides." Bernard Schwartz, *Super Chief* 99 (1983). In theory, this could have provided the basis for a fundamental right to education to be developed in later cases. The problem was that to justify this language Warren cited a number of Lochner era decisions, including *Meyer v. Nebraska*, 262 U.S. 390 (1923), and *Pierce v. Society of Sisters*, 268 U.S. 510 (1925). Both had been written by Justice James C. McReynolds, one of the Justices who defended the *Lochner*-era theory of substantive due process that had been used to strike down progressive social legislation both before and during the New Deal. Roosevelt appointees like Black, Douglas, and Frankfurter had been appointed precisely to oppose this sort of substantive due process reasoning about the meaning of "liberty." Bernard Schwartz reports that Hugo Black prevailed upon Warren to eliminate this language, because "Black was always sensitive about reliance upon, or even citation of, the pre–New Deal judicial philosophy." Schwartz, *Super Chief*, at 99.

24. *Brown I*, 347 U.S. at 493.

25. 83 U.S. (16 Wallace) 36 (1873).

26. 319 U.S. 624 (1943).

27. Id. at 499.

28. Id. at 500.

29. Id. at 500.

30. See *Washington v. Davis*, 426 U.S. 229, 239 (1976); *Frontiero v. Richardson*, 411 U.S. 677, 680 n. 5 (1973); *Shapiro v. Thompson*, 394 U.S. 618, 641–642 (1969); *Schneider v. Rusk*, 377 U.S. 163, 168 (1964). The phrase "equal protection component" appeared for the first time in a Supreme Court opinion in *USDA v. Moreno* 413 U.S. 528, 532 (1973).

31. Nomination of Robert H. Bork to be Associate Justice of the Supreme Court of the United States, Hearings Before the Committee on the Judiciary, United States Senate, Part I, 286–287 (1987).

32. Robert H. Bork, *The Tempting of America: The Political Seduction of the Law*, 83–84 (1990).

33. 381 U.S. 479 (1965).

34. 410 U.S. 113 (1973).

35. 323 U.S. 214 (1944).

36. Id. at 216.

37. 60 U.S. (19 How.) 393 (1857).

38. 83 U.S. (16 Wall.) 36 (1873).

39. 391 U.S. 430 (1968).

40. *Briggs v. Elliott*, 132 F. Supp. 776, 777 (E.D.S.C. 1955).

41. 391 U.S. 430, 442 (1968); see also *United States v. Montgomery County Board of Education*, 395 U.S. 225, 236 (1969).

42. 391 U.S. at 442.

43. 402 U.S. 1 (1971).

44. 418 U.S. 717 (1974).

45. 411 U.S. 1 (1973).

46. See Michael Klarman, "The Puzzling Resistance to Political Process Theory," 77 *Va. L. Rev.* 747, 813 (1991).

Part II

Revised Opinions in
Brown v. Board of Education

BROWN ET AL. v. BOARD OF EDUCATION OF TOPEKA ET AL.
No. 1
SUPREME COURT OF THE UNITED STATES
347 U.S. 483
May 17, 1954, Decided
Reargued December 8, 1953.

PRIOR HISTORY: APPEAL FROM THE UNITED STATES DISTRICT
COURT FOR THE DISTRICT OF KANSAS.[1]

CHIEF JUSTICE BALKIN announced the judgment of
the Court:

I.

These are school cases. They come from different parts of our country:
from Kansas and South Carolina, from Delaware and Virginia. They involve a national question, and, indeed, one case comes from the District
of Columbia, our nation's capital. Each case presents different facts and
different local conditions, but each presents a single common question,
which justifies our consolidated treatment.

In each of these cases, black schoolchildren, through their legal representatives, seek admission to public schools on a nonsegregated basis.
They argue that they have been denied admission to schools attended
by white children due to laws that either require or permit racial segregation, and that these laws deny them equal protection of the laws
under the Fourteenth Amendment. In the Kansas, South Carolina, Virginia, and District of Columbia cases, a three-judge federal district court
denied relief to the plaintiffs because of the so-called "separate but
equal" doctrine announced by this Court in *Plessy v. Ferguson*, 163
U.S. 537 (1896). Under that doctrine, equal protection of the laws is satisfied when the state provides persons of different races separate but

substantially equal facilities. In the Delaware case, the Supreme Court of Delaware held that under the separate-but-equal doctrine, the plaintiffs should be admitted to white schools because the schools that the state administered for blacks were markedly inferior.

The plaintiffs in these cases argue that segregated public schools are not equal and cannot be made so. They argue that by itself the segregation of public schools by race deprives them of rights guaranteed under the Fourteenth Amendment. Because of the obvious importance of this question, we took jurisdiction. We heard argument in the 1952 Term, and heard argument again in this Term based on questions asked by this Court.

II.

In our request for rehearing we asked counsel for both sides to brief and argue the question of the original understanding of the framers and ratifiers of the Fourteenth Amendment concerning the constitutionality of segregated schools. This discussion and our own investigations convince us that, although these sources cast some light on the matter, they are inconclusive. The most avid proponents of the postwar amendments undoubtedly intended them to abolish all legal distinctions among "all persons born or naturalized in the United States" and to guarantee full equality between whites and blacks. Other supporters believed in granting some forms of equality for blacks but not others. And the opponents of the amendments were antagonistic to both their letter and spirit, and wished them to have the most limited effect.

Perhaps the most often expressed view among the framers and ratifiers of the Fourteenth Amendment is that it granted blacks "civil" equality but not "political" or "social" equality. These terms were contested in their own day but had certain core meanings. Civil equality generally meant equal rights to sue and be sued, to testify and make wills, to make contracts, own and convey property, and to speak and follow one's own religious beliefs. Political equality generally meant the equal right to hold public office, to vote, and to serve on juries. Social equality was the most amorphous idea, and meant association with others as social equals. Many of the framers and ratifiers of the Fourteenth Amendment expected that amendment to grant only civil but not political or social equality to blacks. That is why it was thought necessary to pass the Fifteenth Amendment extending the franchise in 1870. Many framers and ratifiers had no desire to acknowledge as social and political equals people who had just emerged from slavery, and we must also admit that many of the framers and ratifiers wished to ensure that blacks remained inferior for all time. Yet even given the prejudices of their time, they were farsighted enough to use words that conveyed full and unalloyed equality for all persons at a moment in history when many of them were uncomfortable with recognizing the Negro as a full equal in every respect.[2]

If the distinction between civil, political, and social equality was contested and uncertain even when the Fourteenth Amendment was ratified, the distinction became even more unstable as years passed. Decisions of this Court increasingly recognized that these elements of equality could not be separated in practice. By 1880, this Court held in *Strauder v. West Virginia*, 100 U.S. 303 (1880), that states could not bar blacks from juries under the Fourteenth Amendment; yet for many in 1868 jury service was a core example of political equality. By the time of our decision in *Plessy* we acknowledged that the amendment granted political equality as part of its guarantee of "absolute equality of the races before the law." 163 U.S. at 544.

The distinction between civil and social equality also became increasingly unclear and unwieldy. Some persons in the generation that framed the Fourteenth Amendment probably imagined that although blacks and whites would be equal "before the law," the social inferiority of blacks would be maintained by the decisions of private parties in which the state played (and should play) no role. They presupposed a private sphere beyond law, in which social superiors and inferiors could choose whom to associate with and under what conditions. The state and its laws were not responsible for such private decisions, nor could they properly intervene in them.

However, as time passed, this belief in a racial private sphere untouched by the state's hand became increasingly untenable. In *Plessy v. Ferguson* itself, this Court upheld separate but equal facilities for blacks and whites as "reasonable" under the circumstances, but the rule separating the races was a regulation of the state. Indeed, the Court argued, striking down segregation laws would result in "enforced commingling" of the races. 163 U.S. at 551. In effect it held that state segregation laws were necessary to construct and preserve the so-called private sphere of social equality and inequality.

Nor was this an isolated example. During the period before and after *Plessy*, many states passed segregation laws that extended to churches, schools, housing, jobs, eating and drinking, public transportation, public facilities, places of public accommodation, drinking fountains, restrooms, sports and recreation facilities, hospitals, orphanages, prisons, asylums, and even funeral homes, morgues, and cemeteries. Enormous legislative and executive effort has been required to preserve this so-called private sphere of personal choice. Given this effort, the view that black and white were everywhere equal before "the law" but not in "private society" was increasingly shown to be a fiction. We recognized this fact in *Shelley v. Kraemer*, 334 U.S. 1 (1948), where we struck down the use of the state courts to enforce racially restrictive covenants that preserved housing segregation.

Perhaps even more telling, the state was implicated even in the decision as to who was white and who was black. The plaintiff in *Plessy*, Homer Plessy, was an "octoroon," one-eighth black. Although he appeared to be white, Louisiana held that he was black "by law," even though if he had crossed into Mississippi or Virginia he might be white "by law." In *Plessy*, although we insisted on "physical differences" between the races, we nevertheless held that the question of racial identity was one of *state law*. 163 U.S. at 552. And many states with segregation laws felt it necessary to determine who was white and who was black in order to enforce these laws.

In short, the power of the state, through its laws and practices, has been enlisted continuously in the century since the Civil War to keep blacks separate from whites and maintain the social superiority of whites to blacks. Thus the social inequality of the Negro has not been the result, as the framers imagined, of purely private decisions by individuals but has been produced through generations of state action that has enhanced and reinforced the social subordination of blacks. The social relations between the races have been and are produced in part by our system of laws, not despite them.

For these reasons, we cannot preserve the distinctions between civil, political, and social equality that motivated many of the framers and ratifiers of the Fourteenth Amendment. We must understand their desire to preserve elements of social inequality and white supremacy not as the great ideal underlying the Fourteenth Amendment, but as compromise with necessity, in a country that had just emerged from a system of chattel slavery and in which many whites were deeply afraid of surrendering all the social, economic, political, and dignitary privileges that came with their color. What is worthy of note and wonder is not that the generation that ratified the Fourteenth Amendment preserved to some extent the existing system of racial hierarchy, but that these people were willing to speak in language that undermined that system and recognized no special privileges for one group of citizens over another.

When the Constitution speaks in grand general phrases like "equal protection," or "due process," it speaks to generations long after those who drafted it. It asks those future generations to look beyond the compromises and hesitancies that are inevitable in any age and to do justice in their own time. We must regard the grand phrases of due process and equal protection as promises that we have made to ourselves as a people. They are promises, made in times of injustice, that respond to injustice, albeit haltingly and imperfectly. They are promises that cannot always be carried out fully in their own era; but they are promises that we nevertheless pledge ourselves to as a people so that someday they may redeemed by future generations. In this way our Constitution becomes more than a collection of rules and doctrines: it becomes a document of redemption.

Just as we may see the concrete practices of justice of those who framed and ratified the Constitution as compromised and imperfect, so we must recognize that others will someday see our own attempts at justice as equally flawed and deficient. That is why we owe it to previous generations to understand and apply their constitutional aspirations in their best light. We must carry on the work that they could only begin. If we read this document as fulfilling their best aspirations rather than chaining us to their worst fears, we do them greater honor than any slavish adherence to their concrete practices could; and perhaps, if we are fortunate, we may merit an equal charity from the generations that come after us.

III.

As we have seen, the belief that blacks and whites could be equal before the law and yet that the state could still enforce legal rules that promoted and preserved the social inferiority of blacks can no longer be maintained. Although many of the framers and ratifiers of the

Fourteenth Amendment gave only grudging acceptance to black equality, and many wished to preserve the legal and social supremacy of whites over blacks indefinitely, they nevertheless spoke in the general language of "equal protection of the laws" and not the more limited language of civil equality. They did so because their words pointed at a more general, just, and long-lasting principle than the mere preservation of social advantages for one race over another.

The framers and ratifiers of the Fourteenth Amendment, influenced by Jacksonianism, sought to prohibit "class legislation." Today this phrase may seem puzzling because all legislation makes classifications. Cf. *Railway Express Agency, Inc., v. New York*, 336 U.S. 106 (1949). However, the term had a special meaning in the early nineteenth century: it referred to legislation or state action that was designed to grant special privileges—usually to the wealthy—and that tended to create an aristocracy or favored class of citizens. In the beginning of the nineteenth century ordinary working people demanded and gained the franchise previously restricted in many states to men of wealth and property. They rejected any assertion that they should defer to "the best men," and they argued that rich and poor alike should have equal opportunities to work and to make a life for themselves.

The Jacksonian objection to "class legislation" has deep roots in the ideas behind the American Revolution. Americans revolted against monarchy and the hierarchical organization of society that monarchy implied. Monarchy was not merely a form of political organization; it was also a form of social organization, complete with elaborate elements of social distinction, rank, and duties of deference to social superiors. In the years after the Revolution, the new American nation tried to abolish social distinctions associated with monarchy and aristocratic rank and to substitute a new vision of equal republican citizens.

In the debates over the Fourteenth Amendment this principle of equal citizenship was given its logical extension: Just as the state should not create or preserve any kind of aristocracy, it should not be permitted to create an underclass or a disfavored class of citizens. In his proposed joint resolution for drafting the Fourteenth Amendment, for example, Charles Sumner claimed that the proposed Fourteenth Amendment should abolish "oligarchy, aristocracy, caste, or monopoly with particular privileges and powers."[3] Likewise Senator Howard, the floor manager of the Fourteenth Amendment, argued that the amendment should "abolis[h] all class legislation . . . and [do] away with the injustice of subjecting one caste of persons to a code not applicable to another."[4]

The deepest commitment of the Fourteenth Amendment, then, is a guarantee of equal citizenship. Our Constitution forbids the creation or perpetuation of a socially subordinate group through law. And any law or practice that creates or maintains such subordination is contrary to the spirit of our Constitution.

We come then to the question presented: Does segregation of children in public schools on the basis of their race deprive children of equal rights under our Constitution? We believe that it does. Separating children by race and maintaining schools that are understood to be "white" and "black" schools is a statement by the state that black children are not equal to white children and should not associate or mingle with them as equals. Laws of this kind help sustain and perpetuate the view that one class of our citizens is inferior and subordinate to the other. This our Constitution does not permit.

The *Plessy* Court well understood that social inequalities could be maintained by law and that maintaining them would violate the Constitution. It assumed that if separation of the races enforced a badge of inferiority upon blacks, it would be unreasonable and contrary to the Fourteenth Amendment. 163 U.S. at 550. It simply denied that separation of the races implied anything about the inferiority of blacks. It argued that "if this be so, it is not by reason of anything contained in the act, but simply because the colored race chooses to put that construction upon it." 163 U.S. at 551. Placed in the context of the many different forms of racial separation practiced by state governments in all parts of our country, it is hard to credit this argument today. Separation of blacks and whites is and has been a central device through which blacks have been subordinated in American society. We do not say that the subordination of a group might not occur through other means. We merely note that in our history the subordination of blacks has been accomplished by separating them from whites and by preventing them from acquiring the same opportunities as whites enjoy.

The "separate but equal" doctrine announced in *Plessy* and elaborated in later cases also assumed that separate facilities could be constitutionally permissible as long as they were substantially equal. *Missouri ex rel. Gaines v. Canada*, 305 U.S. 337, 344 (1938). This assumption has been eroded by subsequent experience. If the state separates a group as a statement of its inferiority in society, it is doubtful that this group will receive benefits equal to those received by more favored citizens. It comes as no great surprise when school districts preserve better buildings, better educational facilities, and better instruction for white children, given that the meaning of separation is to preserve the superior social meaning of being white as opposed to being black. It is unlikely that the state will give second-class citizens a first-class education.

Perhaps in recognition of this fact, cases following *Plessy* noted that separate facilities need be only "substantially" equal. But governments practicing segregation have often been unable to meet even this watered-down test. See, e.g., *Sweatt v. Painter*, 339 U.S. 629 (1950); *Missouri ex rel. Gaines v. Canada*, 305 U.S. 337, 344 (1938). Nor is this surprising, for higher status and greater material benefits usually go hand in hand. Moreover, as we pointed out in *Sweatt*, one's very inability to attend institutions reserved to whites affects one's connections to others in society and one's chance for success in later life. See 339 U.S. at 634; *McLaurin v. Oklahoma State Regents for Higher Education*, 339 U.S. 637, 641–42 (1950). When the state sends the message to a class of its citizens that they do not deserve the same concern and respect as others enjoy, it harms them in immeasurable ways.

Conversely, the isolation of white children from other races tends to teach them that they are entitled to look down on others, and it reinforces the notion that they should regard other races as deservedly inferior. It prevents white children from knowing people with different experiences from theirs, people from whom they equally could learn and by whom they equally could be influenced. It prevents white as well as black from learning to live together in a country that belongs to each equally. In short, segregation of facilities is harmful to both races, for "[t]he destinies of the two races, in this country, are indissolubly linked together, and the interests of both require that the common government of all shall not permit the seeds of race hate to be planted under the sanction of law." *Plessy*, 163 U.S. at 560 (Harlan, J., dissenting).

In *Sweatt* we found it unnecessary to consider the continued vitality of the constitutional doctrine of "separate but equal" and specifically reserved the question whether it might be wholly inapplicable to public education. See 339 U.S. at 631. Today the question is squarely before us, and we hold that *Plessy v. Ferguson* and its doctrine of "separate but equal" facilities are hereby overruled.

IV.

There is special reason to be concerned about the inequality of separate facilities in the area of education. Education is one of the most valuable assets that the state bestows on its citizens, and providing education is one of the most important functions of state and local governments. Today education is essential to make one's way in the world. Without education children are severely disadvantaged in their life chances. They are disadvantaged both in their ability to dream about the future and their ability to make those dreams into reality.

One of the central ideas behind the Thirteenth and Fourteenth Amendments was that all should be able to participate in civil society, choose their profession, and earn a livelihood on equal terms. The right to labor and to own one's labor was perhaps the most basic meaning of civil equality. Today this idea of civil equality is meaningless without genuine educational opportunity. When so many forms of work require literacy and education, to deny Americans an equal chance at education is to deny them a basic birthright of equal citizenship.

Equally important, education is essential to the basic functions of citizenship in a democratic society. Education gives children the skills they need to make choices and the means to act on their choices effectively, not only as workers, entrepreneurs, and consumers but as political actors who exercise their rights of conscience, free expression, assembly, and the franchise. Education is essential to service in the armed forces defending our country. Education awakens values in our children, socializes them to be good neighbors and good citizens, instills respect for the values of our society and our Constitution, and prepares children for life as citizens in a free and democratic republic.

At the time the Fourteenth Amendment was adopted, few states required education, especially in the South. The movement toward free common schools, supported by general taxation, had not yet taken hold. In the North, the movement toward public education was rudimentary. That is perhaps one reason why the legislative history on the question of segregated education is so sparse and inconclusive. Yet the importance of education to one's position in society was well understood even then. Very few blacks were able to receive an education, and in many states their education was forbidden by law. In these days, it is doubtful that any child may reasonably be expected to succeed in life if he is denied the opportunity of an education. Educational opportunity is an interest of the most fundamental nature in our society. Such an opportunity, where the state has undertaken to provide public schooling, is a right that must be made available to all on equal terms. Because separation of the races inevitably produces inferior educational opportunities for black children, it is inconsistent with the equal protection of the laws.

V.

We have also been asked to rule on the constitutionality of segregated schools in the District of Columbia, and on whether the principles of equal protection that apply to the states also apply to the federal government. We must decide, in other words, whether the promise of racial equality and of equal educational opportunity is a national commitment or merely a commitment that the federal government has imposed on the states, while reserving to itself the right to preserve racial inequalities. The answer to this question is clear. The United States has committed itself as a nation to the elimination of racial inequality, both in the passage of the Reconstruction Amendments and in its subsequent actions. Since Reconstruction the federal government has understood itself to have a special role in the promotion of civil equality for blacks. Under section 5 of the Fourteenth Amendment and section 2 of the Thirteenth and Fifteenth Amendments, the Congress of the United States was specifically given the power to promote the equality of blacks and other subordinated groups through remedial legislation. Indeed, in the very same year that *Plessy v. Ferguson* was decided, this Court declared that "the Constitution of the United States, in its present form, forbids, so far as civil and political rights are concerned, discrimination by the general government, or by the states, against any citizen because of his race."[5]

If equality is truly a basic commitment of our Constitution rather than a specialized obligation of the states, it must apply to the national and state governments alike. The goal of civil equality for blacks would mean little if it were secured against state interference but then could be taken away by arbitrary decisions of the national government. We have applied an analogous structural principle to the constitutional protections of speech, press, and religious liberty. By its terms, the First

Amendment binds only Congress, but it has long been understood to apply to the executive and the judicial branches, because executive action or judicial restraint could successfully destroy freedom of speech or religion even if Congress could not.[6]

Although the Equal Protection Clause of the Fourteenth Amendment applies to the states, the text of the same amendment recognizes and confirms the existence of privileges and immunities of national citizenship. If the states may not abridge these privileges or immunities, a fortiori neither may the federal government. In the *Slaughterhouse Cases*, 16 Wall. 36 (1873), we held that the privileges and immunities of national citizenship include the rights guaranteed by the Reconstruction Amendments, and, in particular the rights in section 1 of the Fourteenth Amendment. 83 U.S. (16 Wall.) at 81. These include the right to the equal protection of the laws.

Perhaps more important, the first sentence of the Fourteenth Amendment declares that "[a]ll persons born or naturalized in the United States, and subject to the jurisdiction thereof, are citizens of the United States." These words imply only one form of citizenship, and that is equal citizenship. They do not permit the national government to create first- and second-class citizens, whether on grounds of race or any other criteria.

Finally, principles of equality apply not only to all citizens but to all persons. The Due Process Clause of the Fifth Amendment states that the federal government may not deny any person due process of law. The concept of equal protection of the laws is implicit in the concept of due process, and it was so viewed by the framers of the Fourteenth Amendment. The inclusion of both phrases in section 1 of the Fourteenth Amendment reflects a desire to make what was already implicit in the concept of due process explicit to state governments that might have had strong motivations to deny equality to recently freed slaves. Our cases reflect the close connection between the concepts of due process and equal protection: In *Buchanan v. Warley*, 245 U.S. 60 (1917), we held that a statute that limited the right of a property owner to convey his property to a person of another race was a denial of due process because it constituted an unreasonable form of discrimination. And in a challenge to federal military policy under both the War Power and the Due Process Clause, we held that "all legal restrictions" by the federal government "which curtail the civil rights of a single racial group are immediately suspect" and "that courts must subject them to the most rigid scrutiny." *Korematsu v. United States*, 323 U.S. 214, 216 (1944). Whether that test was properly applied in that case is not before us today. But the applicability of equality principles to the federal government is before us, and we reaffirm our previously stated view.

VI.

We remand these cases for further proceedings. Each case presents a different factual situation and is best dealt with in the first instance by courts below. However, we offer a few remarks concerning the appropriate forms of relief.

First, the responsibility for moving toward integrated school systems rests with school authorities, who have an independent legal obligation to uphold constitutional principles. Courts should attempt to work with school authorities to find acceptable timetables for moving toward integrated schools. Nevertheless, courts must consider whether school authorities are acting in good faith in implementing constitutional principles, and should be prepared to take all necessary steps to enforce compliance. Although respect for local authority and expertise in education will be important in fashioning remedies that will work, courts must not allow deference to local authorities to hinder or prevent enforcement of constitutional obligations.

Second, in fashioning remedies, the equitable powers of federal courts are broad and flexible. Courts should be free to experiment with different ways of achieving constitutional equality. The most direct or most traditional approach may not always be the best approach. Courts should focus first and foremost on what works.

Third, in fashioning remedial relief, courts must keep in mind that the nature of the violation and the constitutional values at stake determine the nature and scope of the remedy. In the case of segregated schools, the remedial goal is equality of educational opportunity for all students, of whatever color or race. This is the central value toward which remedial efforts should strive.

Because this opportunity has been denied through the creation and maintenance of racially identified schools (i.e., "white" schools and "black" schools), racially identifiable schools must be eliminated. This is so whether the racial identification is due to deliberate assignment based on race, or is achieved through the use of facially neutral policies that have the foreseeable effect of perpetuating racially identifiable schools.

However, it is not enough for school authorities and the courts to end racially identifiable schools. Although such schools by themselves constitute a violation of equal protection, the deeper issue is equal educational opportunity. We hold today that both separate but equal facilities and denial of equal educational opportunity violate the Constitution. The constitutional obligation to provide such equality of opportunity continues even if all systems of racially identifiable schools were dismantled overnight. No matter which students sit next to each other in our public schools, all deserve an equal chance at life.

There will be inevitable demographic shifts in response to federal equitable remedies, as some parents attempt to avoid sending their children to formerly black schools and formerly white schools that become integrated. Courts should not ignore these changes. They must not allow school boards to facilitate the creation of new school districts and school district boundaries that effectively shut out most racial minorities. Nevertheless, courts cannot control the long-term growth of our towns and cities. Thus, as times change, courts must ensure that their remedies always work to the benefit of equal educational opportunity for the least advantaged—in this case minority students.

If the past is any prediction of the future, unless courts intervene to enforce constitutional obligations of equal protection, schools with large proportions of minority children are likely to receive the least qualified teachers, the poorest facilities, and the smallest amount of educational resources. Such relative deprivation is the legacy of a social and legal system that reserved the best for its most favored citizens and thought nothing of the injustices that resulted. Therefore, in fashioning remedies for school desegregation, federal courts are specifically authorized to require that states and school districts alike devote additional resources to such schools in the interests of achieving equal educational opportunity, even if such remedies do not affect the proportion of black and white students who attend these schools. Once a constitutional violation has been found, a state's schools should not be considered fully in compliance with the Constitution until equal educational opportunity is achieved.

In determining whether a state is providing equal educational opportunity in different schools, courts should look not only at the inputs to the system but also at its outputs. They should ask whether, on average, the state is producing students of comparable educational achievement among its various schools. If minority students are left to fend for themselves in inferior schools with inferior educational opportunities, the Constitution is violated even if this state of affairs does not result from a conscious state policy of minority isolation.

Accordingly, the judgments below, with the exception of the Delaware case, are reversed. The cases are remanded to the district courts for further proceedings in light of this opinion, with instructions to achieve, in an expeditious fashion, the goal of equal educational opportunity. The judgment of the Delaware case, which ordered the immediate admission of plaintiffs to formerly all-white schools, is affirmed, and the case is remanded to the Supreme Court of Delaware for further proceedings consistent with this opinion.

It is so ordered.

NOTES

1. Together with No. 2, *Briggs et al. v. Elliott et al.*, on appeal from the United States District Court for the Eastern District of South Carolina, argued December 9–10, 1952, reargued December 7–8, 1953; No. 4, *Davis et al. v. County School Board of Prince Edward County, Virginia, et al.*, on appeal from the United States District Court for the Eastern District of Virginia, argued December 10, 1952, reargued December 7–8, 1953; and No. 10, *Gebhart et al. v. Belton et al.*, on certiorari to the Supreme Court of Delaware, argued December 11, 1952, reargued December 9, 1953.

2. See the *Slaughterhouse Cases*, 16 Wall. 36, 67–72 (1873); *Strauder v. West Virginia*, 100 U.S. 303, 307–8 (1880).

3. *Cong. Globe*, 39th Cong. (1st Sess.) 674 (1866). Although the joint resolution failed, Sumner's argument shaped the final language of the amendment and influenced the general understandings of its meaning. See *Adamson v. California*, 332 U.S. 46, 51 n.8 (1947).

4. *Cong. Globe*, 39th Cong. (1st Sess.) 2766 (1866). This understanding of the principles behind the amendment is reflected in one of our earliest decisions construing it, *Strauder v. West Virginia*. In describing the "spirit and meaning" of the Fourteenth Amendment, Justice Strong held that it

declar[es] that the law in the States shall be the same for the black as for the white; that all persons, whether colored or white, shall stand equal before the laws of the States, and, in regard to the colored race, for whose protection the amendment was primarily designed, that no discrimination shall be made against them by law because of their color[.] The words of the amendment . . . contain . . . a positive immunity, or right, most valuable to the colored race,—the right to exemption from unfriendly legislation against them distinctively as colored,—exemption from legal discriminations, implying inferiority in civil society, lessening the security of their enjoyment of the rights which others enjoy, and discriminations which are steps towards reducing them to the condition of a subject race. 100 U.S. at 307–8

5. See *Gibson v. Mississippi*, 162 U.S. 565, 591 (1896).

6. This point was recognized as early as 1833 by Justice Baldwin. See *Magill v. Brown*, 16 F. Cases 408, 427 (C.C.E.D. Pa. 1833) (holding that the First Amendment "wholly prohibits the action of the legislative or judicial power of the Union on the subject matter of a religious establishment, or any restraint on the free exercise of religion"). Following our recognition that the guarantees of the First Amendment apply equally to the states, see *Gitlow v. New York*, 268 U.S. 652 (1925), it has been repeatedly reaffirmed that the legislative, executive, and judicial departments of state governments are equally bound by the constitutional guarantees of freedom of speech, press, and religious exercise. See, e.g., *Near v. Minnesota*, 283 U.S. 697 (1931)(freedom of speech and press), *Kedroff v. St. Nicholas Cathedral of the Russian Orthodox Church in North America*, 344 U.S. 94 (1952)(free exercise of religion); see also *West Virginia State Bd. of Educ. v. Barnette*, 319 U.S. 624, 642 (1943)("If there is any fixed star in our constitutional constellation, it is that no official, high or petty, can prescribe what shall be orthodox in politics, nationalism, religion, or other matters of opinion or force citizens to confess by word or act their faith therein").

DAYS, J., concurring.

For almost three generations, this Court has defaulted in its duty to enforce the Equal Protection Clause of the Fourteenth Amendment with the full force and vigor that it justly deserves. In declaring racial segregation in public education unconstitutional, we take a major stride on the road toward rectifying that default. As the Court's opinion today reminds us, the central purpose of the Civil War Amendments was "the freedom of the slave race, the security and firm establishment of that freedom and the protection of the newly made freeman and citizen from the oppressions of those who had formerly exercised unlimited dominion over them." *Slaughterhouse Cases*, 83 U.S. (16 Wall.) 36, 71 (1873). The words of the Fourteenth Amendment in particular, we have held, contain "a necessary implication of a positive immunity, or right, most valuable to the colored race,—the right to exemption from unfriendly legislation against them distinctively as colored,—exemption from legal discriminations, implying inferiority in civil society, lessening the security of their enjoyment of the rights which others enjoy, and discriminations which are steps towards reducing them to the condition of a subject race." *Strauder v. West Virginia*, 100 U.S. 303, 307–08 (1880).

Yet, this Court, in the case of *Plessy v. Ferguson*, 163 U.S. 537 (1896), created out of whole cloth the separate-but-equal doctrine, contending that it was consonant with the core purpose of the Fourteenth Amendment Equal Protection Clause. Pursuant to that doctrine, the Court in *Plessy* upheld state laws requiring racial segregation in the provision of railroad transportation, the question specifically at issue there. The *Plessy* Court relied heavily, however, upon the existence of state-imposed racial segregation in public schools in the North as evidence that such arrangements did "not necessarily imply the inferiority of either race to the other." 163 U.S. at 544. The flaws in *Plessy* were many, as the opinions of several of my fellow Justices make clear. Within relatively little time, however, jurisdictions throughout the South and border states embraced the separate-but-equal doctrine to mandate racial segregation, not only in public transportation and schooling, but in the provision of a broad range of governmental and governmentally regulated activities.

The damage done by the *Plessy* decision to the Negroes' quest for first-class citizenship to which they are entitled under the Fourteenth Amendment was grievous enough. But the Court must also accept responsibility for the reflexive and superficial way in which this institution continued to give life and legitimacy to the separate-but-equal doctrine for the three decades after *Plessy*. In *Cumming v. Richmond County Board of Education*, 175 U.S. 528 (1899), decided only three years after *Plessy*, we upheld a decision by authorities to close a colored high school in order to have sufficient funds to operate a high school for whites. In that case, "equal" clearly meant everything for white high school students and nothing for Negro students in the same grades.

In *Berea College v. Kentucky*, 211 U.S. 45 (1908), the outcome turned technically on questions of state corporations law. The Court in effect held, however, that Kentucky possessed the power to preclude a private college from educating white and Negro students together. *Plessy* had upheld a state's right to require separate but equal facilities to prevent the *involuntary* interaction between members of the two races. Berea College, however, provided instruction to students *voluntarily* enrolled in its institution.

Gong Lum v. Rice, 275 U.S. 78 (1927), presented the question of "whether a Chinese citizen is denied equal protection of the laws when he is classed among the colored races and furnished facilities equal to that offered to all whether white, brown, yellow or black." *Plessy* itself was largely obiter dictum on the question of whether separate but equal educational facilities satisfied the requirements of the Fourteenth Amendment, and neither *Cumming* nor *Berea College* addressed itself to that question. Nonetheless, this is how the Court responded in *Gong Lum*:

> Were this a new question, it would call for very full argument and consideration; but we think that it is the same question which has been many times decided to be within the constitutional power of the state Legislature to settle, without intervention of the federal courts under the federal Constitution.

275 U.S. at 85–86.

The list of authorities cited by the Court in support of this proposition was headed by *Roberts v. City of Boston*, 59 Mass. (5 Cush.) 198 (1849), a Massachusetts case, the centerpiece of *Plessy's* argument for the constitutionality of the separate-but-equal doctrine. *Roberts* was decided almost twenty years before the Fourteenth Amendment was ratified.

How does one even begin to explain this pitiful record in defense of rights to equal citizenship secured by the Fourteenth Amendment? Of course, this Court has noted that

> it is bound by two rules, to which it has rigidly adhered, one, never to anticipate a question of constitutional law in advance of the necessity of deciding it; the other never to formulate a rule of constitutional law broader than is required by the precise facts to which it is to be applied. These rules are safe guides to sound judgement. It is the dictate of wisdom to follow them closely and carefully.

Liverpool Steamship Company v. Emigration Commissioners, 113 U.S. 33, 39 (1885) (quoted in *Ashwander v. Tenn. Valley Authority*, 297 U.S. 288, 346–47 (1936) (Brandeis, J., concurring)).

I would be the first to agree that the foregoing rules have served the Court and the country well, for the most part. But there are circumstances—and I view the obvious, pervasive, long-lived, and pernicious effect of the separate-but-equal doctrine on racial equality as one such—when it is incumbent upon the Court to act to remedy injustice. "[T]here comes a point where this Court should not be ignorant as judges of what we know as men." *Watts v. Indiana*, 338 U.S. 49, 52 (1949) (Frankfurter, J.). For more than a quarter century, this Court failed to discharge that judicial responsibility faithfully.

More recently, in the *Graduate School Cases, Missouri ex rel. Gaines v. Canada*, 305 U.S. 337 (1938), *Sipuel v. Oklahoma State Board of Regents*, 332 U.S. 631 (1948), *Sweatt v. Painter*, 339 U.S. 629 (1950), and *McLaurin v. Oklahoma State Regents for Higher Education*, 339 U.S. 637 (1950), the Court, although resisting all invitations to reconsider the constitutionality of the separate-but-equal doctrine, demanded of state authorities *actual* equality in tangible resources between facilities for white and Negro students. This result was in sharp contrast to what it did in *Cumming*. Moreover, in *Sweatt* and *McLaurin*, the Court held that equality with respect to *intangible* resources is required in order to comport with constitutional requirements. This new sense of the Court's responsibilities under the Fourteenth Amendment is captured, I believe, by the following quotation from its opinion in *Sweatt*: "It may be argued that excluding petitioner from that school [the University of Texas Law School] is no different from excluding white students from the new law school. *This contention overlooks realities.*" 339 U.S. at 634 (emphasis added). It is this unwillingness to "overlook reality" in the Court's recent decisions that distinguishes them from *Cumming, Berea College,* and *Gong Lum.* It is an approach that has brought us to this momentous day in American history when racial segregation in public education may no longer look to this Court for constitutional approval or ratification. For once again, after generations of students have endured the burdens imposed by *Plessy,* we are declaring that "all persons, whether colored or white, shall stand equal before the laws of the States."

I have recited the foregoing history of this Court's school segregation decisions, one well known to its current members, and with their kind indulgence, as a cautionary tale. For, despite my general agreement with the Court's decision, I am left with concern about whether, as we address issues related to school desegregation or other challenges to vestiges of *Plessy*'s separate-but-equal doctrine, we will move in the cautious, self-conscious fashion dictated by the *Liverpool* case or in the spirit of acknowledging realities as judges that we know as men and women. I feel this concern most keenly in the apparent unwillingness on the part of several of my fellow Justices to overrule *Plessy v. Ferguson* outright and generally, not only with respect to public schools but also as to transportation—the context in which it was originally announced—and to other sectors of American life where the separate-but-equal doctrine has dropped deep roots. An authoritative study on race relations reports as follows in this regard:

> Most other public facilities—such as libraries, parks, playgrounds—are available to Negroes with about the same amount of discrimination in the various regions of the country, as in schools. Negroes are not permitted to use these in the South unless they are acting in a servant capacity. Many Southern cities have separate parks, playgrounds, and libraries for the Negroes, but in all cases they are poor substitutes for those available to whites.

Gunnar Myrdal, *An American Dilemma* 634 (1944).[1]

There is, in my estimation, no justification for judicial timidity in this regard. For we know as men and women that until the *Plessy* doctrine is eliminated "root and branch," true progress in achieving racial equality will be significantly frustrated and retarded. We have also learned through our own decision-making process that racial segregation practices reinforce, and are in turn reinforced by, numerous official acts of outright denials of constitutionally protected rights on a racially discriminatory basis. This pattern has repeated itself during the 20th century, to cite just a few examples, in the field of housing, *Barrows v. Jackson*, 346 U.S. 249 (1953) (holding that award by state court of damages against co-covenantor for breach of racially restrictive housing covenant constitutes state action depriving non-Caucasians of equal protection of the laws), *Shelley v. Kraemer*, 334 U.S. 1, 19, 22 (1948) (holding that enforcing racially restrictive housing covenants in equity would constitute state action "in the full and complete sense of the phrase" because "but for the active intervention of the state courts, supported by the full panoply of state power, petitioners would have been free to occupy the properties in question without restraint. . . . Equal protection of the laws is not achieved through indiscriminate imposition of inequalities"), *Hurd v. Hodge*, 334 U.S. 24, 36 (1948) (Frankfurter, J., concurring) ("[I]t cannot be 'the exercise of a sound judicial discretion' by a federal court to grant the relief here asked for when the authorization of such an injunction by the State of the Union violates the Constitution— and violates it, not for any narrow technical reason, but for considerations that touch rights so basic to our society . . ."), *Buchanan v. Warley*, 245 U.S. 60, 82 (1917) (holding that a municipal ordinance preventing "the alienation of . . . property . . . to a person of color [i]s not a legitimate exercise of the police power of the state, and is in direct violation of the fundamental law enacted in the Fourteenth Amendment of the Constitution preventing state interference with property rights except by due process of law"); in the field of employment, *Brotherhood of Railroad Trainmen v. Howard*, 343 U.S. 768 (1952) (holding that a discriminatory employment agreement signed between exclusively white union and railroad violates the constitutional rights of Negro employees) and *Steele v. Louisville & N.R. Co.*, 323 U.S. 192 (1944) ("Congress, in . . . authorizing the union . . . did not intend to confer plenary power upon the union to sacrifice, for the benefit of its members, rights of the minority of the craft, without imposing on it any duty to protect the minority"); in the field of voting, *Smith v. Allwright*, 321 U.S. 649, 664–65 (1944) (holding that restricting the privilege of party membership based on race is unconstitutional because "when, as here, that privilege is also the essential qualification for voting in a primary to select nominees for a general election, the state makes the action of the party the action of the state"), *Lane v. Wilson,* 307 U.S. 268 (1939) (holding that the Fifteenth Amendment "nullifies sophisticated as well as simple-minded modes of discrimination. It hits onerous procedural requirements which effectively handicap exercise of the franchise by the colored race although the abstract right to vote may remain unrestricted as to race"), *Nixon v. Herndon,* 273 U.S. 536 (1927) (holding that Texas statute denying Negroes the right to vote in primaries was in violation of the Equal Protection Clause of the Fourteenth Amendment), *Guinn v. United States,* 238 U.S. 347, 361 (1915) (holding state suffrage standards unconstitutional because the standards "involve[] an unmistakable, although . . . somewhat disguised, refusal to give effect to the prohibitions of the 15th Amendment . . . creating a standard which . . . calls to life the very conditions which the Amendment was adopted to destroy and which it had destroyed"); in the field of transportation, *Henderson v. United States,* 339 U.S. 816 (1950) (holding that capping the admission of Negroes to a train dining car at a fixed number violates the Interstate Commerce Act), *Mitchell v. United States,* 313 U.S. 80 (1941) (holding that a railroad's refusal to allow a Negro to ride in a first-class car solely on the basis of his race and despite his having purchased a first-class ticket constitutes "an invasion of a fundamental individual right which is guaranteed against state action by the Fourteenth Amendment") (citations omitted); and in the field of public accommodations, *District of Columbia v. John R. Thompson,* 346 U.S. 100 (1953) (holding that congressional acts banning discrimination by restaurateurs were valid despite nonenforcement by licensing authority). Moreover, we have developed criteria for evaluating the constitutionality of racial classifications that do not depend upon findings of psychic harm or social science evidence. They are based rather on the principle that "distinctions between citizens solely because of their ancestry are by their very nature odious to a free people whose institutions are founded upon the doctrine of equality," *Hirabayashi v. United States,* 320 U.S. 81 (1943), and must bear a very heavy burden of justification. With these tools, I am confident that we will be able to provide protections against racial discrimination that the Constitution forbids.

I have two final points to make. First, I concur in the view that the first sentence of section 1 of the Fourteenth Amendment, "All persons born or naturalized in the United States and subject to the jurisdiction

thereof, *are citizens of the United States* and of the State wherein they reside" (emphasis added), establishes a national standard of citizenship
and all the rights pertaining thereto. Although the Due Process Clause
of the Fifth Amendment and the Equal Protection Clause of the Fourteenth Amendment are not congruent, the first sentence of the latter
amendment provides more than sufficient constitutional and "think-
able" justification for subjecting the District of Columbia in *Bolling v.
Sharpe* to the same injunction against racial segregation in its public
schools that the Court has imposed on those defendant states involved
in *Brown*. A distinguished, biracial, nation-wide citizens' group properly noted:

> In many ways, the color bar in the public schools is basic to discrimina-
> tion elsewhere. Education has always been central to Americans. The
> public school system has been the great instrument by which we hoped
> to overcome inequalities of birth and station, and give each American an
> equal chance to make good. It has been the great unifying principle of the
> Republic. When the public schools of the capital are used instead to di-
> vide citizens on racial lines, to perpetuate inequalities, to increase them,
> and worse, to justify them, then the time has come to consider what kind
> of an America we want to build for the future.

Kenesaw M. Landis, *Segregation in Washington: A Report of The National
Committee on Segregation in The Nation's Capital* 80 (1948).

Second, as to the question of remedy, I am mindful of the fact that
these are class actions that will require remedial adjustments affecting
literally hundreds of school districts and thousands of people. But I join
the Court in believing that the process of desegregating the affected
school systems must begin immediately and that any requested delays
in implementation must be weighed against the critical consideration
that the right of Negro students to secure public education without
racial discrimination is "personal and present." *Sweatt*, 339 U.S. at 851.

We have come a long way as a nation, and as a Court, from *Plessy* to
today's decision. The road ahead will be neither easy nor straight in
America's journey to realize its highest constitutional ideals. But we
have no choice but to go forward. As the President's Committee on
Civil Rights observed not too many years ago:

> Our American heritage further teaches that to be secure in the rights he
> wishes for himself, each man must be willing to respect the rights of other
> men. This is the conscious recognition of a basic moral principle: All men

are created equal as well as free. Stemming from this principle is the obligation to build social institutions that will guarantee equality of opportunity to all men. Without this equality, freedom becomes an illusion. Thus the only aristocracy that is consistent with the free way of life is an aristocracy of talent and achievement. The grounds on which our society accords respect, influence or reward to each of its citizens must be limited to the quality of his personal character and his social contribution.

President's Committee on Civil Rights, *To Secure These Rights* 4 (1947).

I concur.

NOTE

1. The Carnegie Corporation commissioned this study and selected Myrdal, a Swedish social economist, to be its leader. The researchers, who conducted extensive fieldwork, aimed to collect, analyze, and interpret existing knowledge on race relations in America and the social, political, and economic status of the Negro.

ACKERMAN, J., concurring.

Four score and six years ago, our fathers struggled to find meaning in a bloody war that took 600,000 lives, tearing apart families, friends, and the nation itself. With the solemn ratification of the Fourteenth Amendment, America chose the revolutionary path of free and equal national citizenship. We consider today how far we have come, and where we must go, if we are to remain faithful to this great commitment.

Before the Civil War, this Court systematically read the Constitution in favor of slavery. It showed no patience with free states that refused to cooperate with the return of fugitive slaves to their condition of bondage.[1] Going further, our *Dred Scott* decision declared that free blacks could never become citizens of the United States.[2] This was a white man's country, forever.

As schoolchildren, we are all taught President Lincoln's Gettysburg Address. But at the end of the Civil War, the nation hesitated before broadening its commitment to government of the people, by the people, and for the people. The Thirteenth Amendment, enacted in 1865, abolished slavery, but it did not overrule *Dred Scott*. Blacks were no longer slaves, but they remained aliens amongst us.

And aliens they should remain, argued President Andrew Johnson, who took Lincoln's place after an assassin's bullet put him in the White House in 1865. Vetoing Congress's proposed civil rights act and freedman's bureau bill, Johnson rejected the Republicans' vision of a strong national government dedicated to the affirmative protection of free and equal citizens. The Republican Congress responded with the Fourteenth Amendment, which served as the party's platform for the crucial elections of 1866.

Rarely has a fundamental issue been the subject of such profound popular debate. In an unprecedented act, President Johnson left the

White House for a barnstorming campaign through the country—appealing to the People to throw the Republicans out of office, urging his fellow citizens to reaffirm the proposition that this was a "white man's country," and that a national government dedicated to equal citizenship would inexorably degenerate into a centralized despotism.[3]

But the American people refused to believe him. They gave their support to the competing vision advanced by the Republican Congress and sustained its demand for a reconstruction of the very foundations of our Union. This country would no longer be a place where citizenship was defined by race. The Fourteenth Amendment explicitly instructed this Court to repudiate the path taken in *Dred Scott*, declaring native-born and naturalized Americans to be "citizens of the United States, and the State wherein they reside."

National citizenship was made primary; state citizenship, derivative. We are Americans first, and when we move from Maine to Mississippi or back, the second sentence of the amendment protects us in sweeping terms: "No state shall make or enforce any law which shall abridge the privileges or immunities of citizens of the United States." Only then does the amendment extend its concern to all "persons," whether or not they are citizens, and forbid the states from depriving them of "life, liberty, or property without due process of law" or denying them the "equal protection of the laws."

And yet, until today, this Court has ignored the opening lines of our greatest constitutional amendment. We have sought, to the best of our understanding and ability, to assure every person due process and equal protection of the laws. But we have utterly failed to reflect on the meaning of national citizenship or systematically guarantee all Americans their rightful privileges against state infringement. While this Court went out of its way before the Civil War to declare that black men and women could never enjoy the privileges of national citizenship, it fell silent when the time came to change course and redeem the promise of citizenship for all Americans. We cannot repeal the past, but we will not remain silent in the future.

We hold today that a public school education is a privilege of American citizenship and that the defendant states, as well as the District of Columbia, have abridged its full and equal exercise by the black petitioners in these cases.

I.

The founders began the long process of putting the nation first. At their meeting in Philadelphia, they launched a revolutionary assault on the premises of America's first constitution, the Articles of Confederation, which had made the national government into a mere creature of the states. According to the Articles, "Each state retains its sovereignty, freedom, and independence, and every power, jurisdiction, and right, which is not by this Confederation expressly delegated to the United States, in Congress assembled."[4] And the Articles gave the Congress very few express powers.

In contrast, the founders planted the seeds of a new nationality. They spoke self-confidently in the name of We the People of the United States, and denied that any single state could veto their constitutional initiative for "a more perfect Union." What is more, they gained popular support for the creation of an independent national government with large, if limited, powers.

But the founders were not full-fledged nationalists. Whatever their personal beliefs, they knew that their fellow countrymen were not yet prepared explicitly to affirm the unconditional priority of the nation over the states. As a consequence, their Constitution failed to define a concept of national citizenship, let alone explicitly affirm its primacy. The text simply guaranteed that "citizens of each state shall be entitled to all privileges and immunities of citizens in the several states," without explicitly defining any of the contestable terms in this formulation. The text was also silent on the right of any state, and its citizens, to secede from the Union—leaving it open for both sides to debate the matter endlessly throughout the antebellum period.

But this period of debate came to a decisive close during Reconstruction. Despite the efforts of President Johnson and constitutional conservatives throughout the land, the American people self-consciously resolved to put American citizenship first and to extend it broadly to all who are lucky enough to be born in this land of liberty and equality.

When read as a whole, the Reconstruction Amendments create four tiers of national protection. The first tier is established by the Thirteenth Amendment, abolishing "slavery" and "involuntary servitude." This by itself creates a vast grant of freedom to every American. We should not view "slavery" and "involuntary servitude" as the names of ancient practices long since abolished. The Thirteenth Amendment requires an ongoing test of existing status relationships to determine whether they mask these forbidden conditions under another name. A man or woman is in a position of involuntary servitude whenever he or she lacks the freedom to exercise a wide range of legal rights of self-determination. See, e.g., *Pollock v. Williams*, 322 U.S. 4 (1944); *United States v. Gaskin*, 320 U.S. 527 (1944); and *Taylor v. Georgia*, 315 U.S. 25 (1942).

The second tier is established by the Fourteenth Amendment's requirement of due process of law in protecting every person's "life, liberty or property." This represents an explicit authorization to the courts to sustain the great tradition of Anglo-American law in assuring fundamental fairness for all. See *Palko v. Connecticut*, 302 U.S. 319, 325 (1937).

The third tier was less familiar at the time. In contrast to the other formulas we are examining, the "equal protection of the laws" had no echoes in the previous language of the Constitution. In supporting this new demand, everybody was perfectly aware that black freedmen did not enjoy many of the most basic legal rights that white men took for granted. Even many "free" states barred Negroes from many common occupations and often refused to allow them to testify in court.[5] With the enactment of the Equal Protection Clause, all these stigmatizing discriminations would henceforth be blatantly unconstitutional. In short, any thoughtful American reading the Equal Protection Clause in 1866 could not help but recognize that it was inaugurating a fundamental revolution in race relations in this country.

Given the radical character of the textual demand, it is not surprising that this Court has sometimes stumbled in translating the principles of equality into legal doctrine. These failures, however, should not obscure the repeated occasions on which we have sought to recognize and redeem the exigent character of this new commitment. See, e.g., *Strauder v. West Virginia*, 100 U.S. 303 (1879), *Yick Wo v. Hopkins*, 118 U.S. 356 (1886), *Buchanan v. Warley*, 245 U.S. 60 (1917), *Shelley v. Kraemer*, 334 U.S. 1 (1948), *Sweatt v. Painter*, 339 U.S. 629 (1950).

But we are today concerned primarily with the fourth tier of national protections created by our Reconstruction Constitution. To gain a sense of its majestic promise, put yourself in the position of an ordinary American reading the text of the Fourteenth Amendment during the great electoral struggle between President Andrew Johnson and the Reconstruction Congress in 1866. In moving beyond the promise of due process and equal protection, the citizenship clauses were granting

Negro Americans something different from the kind of respectful legal treatment provided to any white Englishman or Frenchman who permanently resided in this country. In extending citizenship, the opening lines of the Fourteenth Amendment were offering Negro Americans nothing less than a revolution in the human spirit. These lines proposed to rebuild the American community on a new foundation. By supporting this amendment, whites were pledging to recognize black Americans as full citizens in the ongoing American project of democratic self-government—a government that was truly of the people, by the people, and for the people.

This decision to reconstruct the very foundations of citizenship was not made lightly, as if it were a gift from the dominant race to the previously subordinate one. Negroes had *earned* their claim to citizenship by sacrificing for the Union during the darkest hours of the Civil War; dying by the thousands so our great experiment would endure. And for the first time in history, they entered American politics as active voters in the debate over the Fourteenth and Fifteenth Amendments, providing crucial political support during the struggle for ratification in the southern states. The citizenship clauses, in short, were a legal token of a more profound act of mutual recognition occurring among the American people themselves. This pledge was further enhanced by the Fifteenth Amendment's explicit bar on any effort to restrict the suffrage on the basis of race.

Undoubtedly, there were many who bitterly opposed these great acts of communal redefinition. But few could doubt their profound significance. As the text makes plain, the Reconstruction Constitution goes far beyond the guarantee of basic human rights. Indeed, the citizenship clauses do not speak of rights at all, but make the national government the guarantor of the *privileges* of citizenship. To an ordinary person reading these lines in 1866, the sweeping character of this grant would have been apparent. Only yesterday, freed blacks had been subordinated everywhere by ignoble limitations on their freedom; and now they were being proclaimed full equals, not only in the rights but in the privileges of American citizenship.

Given the speed of this transformation, no well-worked-out understanding of these privileges had emerged in the short time after the Civil War. Since no formal definition of American citizenship had been attempted at the time of the founding, the problem of interpretation could not be solved by granting Negroes the precise set of federal privileges already guaranteed whites. Rather than dealing with a well-articulated idea, both blacks and whites were coming to a new understanding of themselves as citizens of the nation. Moreover, the scraps of legal materials generated in the antebellum period were neither sufficiently considered, nor sufficiently diffused among the general public, to warrant giving them authoritative status.[6] The paucity of legal materials should not blind us to the main point: the supporters of the Fourteenth and Fifteenth Amendments fully understood that the color of one's skin was no test of loyalty to the Union, and that the effective recognition of Negroes as citizens of the nation was a practical necessity if the Reconstruction vision of the Union was to endure.

If anything was clear during this creative period of flux, it was that the precise legal meaning of this great grant of citizenship privilege was not to be settled in a single day, or by a single generation. It was hard enough to mobilize the American people to write new words into their constitutional covenant; but it would be harder still to change old habits. It was one thing to recognize the principled claim of Negroes to recognition as equal members of the national community; quite another to work out the implications of this claim by a critical appraisal of many fundamental practices. This would inevitably be the work of generations, each reflecting on the strengths and weakness of its predecessors' efforts to redeem the great promises of the Reconstruction Constitution.

II.

We begin this process of reassessment with our fateful decision, in the *Slaughterhouse Cases* of 1873, to consign the citizenship clauses into constitutional oblivion. Looking back over the past eight decades, it is easy to see how profoundly this early opinion has distorted the shape of our law. But its fateful character is clearer in retrospect than in prospect. The facts raised by these cases gave our predecessors very misleading cues about the future problems they would encounter in enforcing the commands of the Fourteenth Amendment.

Three features of the *Slaughterhouse Cases* conspired to cloud the Court's understanding. The first involved the nature of the plaintiffs. They were a group of white butchers protesting against New Orleans' decision to require them to slaughter all livestock in central facilities operated by a specially chartered monopoly. This monopoly grant, they argued, deprived them of one of the central privileges of their new-found national citizenship—the right to engage on competitive terms in their lawful occupation.

The Court was understandably surprised to encounter these ingenious plaintiffs on its first encounter with a then-unfamiliar text. As it explained, all three of the Reconstruction Amendments had "one pervading purpose . . . lying at the foundation of each, and without which none of them would have been even suggested; we mean the freedom of the slave race, the security and firm establishment of that freedom, and the protection of the newly-made freeman and citizen from the oppressions of those who had formerly exercised unlimited dominion over him."[7] And yet here were a group of white men who were asking this Court to extend the newly minted privileges of national citizenship on their behalf.

Strictly speaking, there was nothing wrong with this request. The amendment does not restrict its express concerns to the underdogs in society, but extends its protections to all citizens. Nevertheless, the Court was right to be cautious. After all, white men were already skilled in the political art of protecting their interests in the rough-and-ready democracy of nineteenth-century America. But there was no assurance that the new American citizens created by the Fourteenth Amendment would be equally successful. Far better, then, for the courts to focus their energies on the paradigm cases for protection, leaving less central problems for later consideration if a compelling need should arise.

The second peculiarity of *Slaughterhouse* involved the nature of the defendant. The case was handed down during the first flush of Reconstruction, when the free Negroes of New Orleans were full participants in city politics and government. The Court was not confronting the tragic situation that would eventually become the standard case—in which many state governments effectively denied Negro Americans all participatory rights and yet subjected them to harshly subordinating legislation. Nor could the Court guess that, despite the explicit command of section 2 of the Fourteenth Amendment, all-white state governments would one day maintain their full representation in the federal House of Representatives and the Electoral College without a deduction in their voting strength as a penalty for unconstitutional acts that had disenfranchised their Negro fellow citizens.[8]

The third peculiarity involved the substance of the lawsuit. *Slaughterhouse* was an invitation to open-ended judicial supervision of each state's efforts to regulate its economy. The facts sufficed to warn against the dangers of too ready an acceptance of this extraordinary mission. On its face, New Orleans' decision did not seem arbitrary or capricious. Animal slaughter, if left unregulated, is a noxious business, harmful to the health of neighbors. It was reasonable for the city to require that it be conducted in a small number of locales (see *Euclid v. Ambler Realty Co.*, 272 U.S. 365 (1926)), and that it proceed under the generalized control of a carefully selected corporate body (see *Tennessee Electric Power Co. v. T.V.A.*, 306 U.S. 118 (1939)). Since New Orleans had expressly required the Slaughterhouse Company to open its facilities to all at reasonable rates,[9] the Court was on firm ground in rejecting the butchers' complaint. Surely our recent judicial experience confirms the *Slaughterhouse* Court's wisdom in allowing broad scope for democratic control over the economy. See *Federal Power Commission v. Hope Natural Gas*, 320 U.S. 591 (1944).

In short, the Court's refusal to grant federal relief in *Slaughterhouse* was entirely appropriate, and we reaffirm its holding today. But unfortunately, the Court used some very blunt conceptual instruments to come a to sensible conclusion. It did not content itself with an opinion emphasizing the democratic authority of the states to control the predictable abuses of a free market economy. Instead, it trivialized the majestic idea of national citizenship, rendering it unusable in later cases by Negro Americans and other subordinate groups, who were originally understood as its primary beneficiaries.

The narrowing interpretation was offered up by Mr. Justice Miller for a majority of five Justices. He began by noting that the amendment denies a State (call it Missouri, for illustrative purposes) only the power to "abridge the privileges or immunities of citizens of the *United States.*" It does not forbid Missouri from depriving Missourians of the privileges or immunities they possess by virtue of their *Missouri citizenship.* This is a distinction, he correctly insisted, that was well worth pondering. To apply it to the claims of petitioner Linda Brown, we must begin by asking whether her interest in obtaining an education is a privilege of her national citizenship or whether it is merely a privilege available to her as a citizen of Missouri.

But it is at this point where Mr. Justice Miller went wrong. He suggested that such questions might be resolved at wholesale, not retail. Rather than considering the distinctive character of each claim of privilege, Justice Miller proposed to solve his problem in one fell swoop and once and for all. Pointing vaguely to a vast, and poorly defined, class of "civil rights," he proclaimed all of them to be exclusively privileges of state citizenship. In contrast, he placed an odd assortment of privileges on the federal side of the ledger, generating his list without much rhyme or reason.

We reject this categorical mode of proceeding. We have recently had occasion to witness the bankruptcy of an analogous approach to another fundamental issue: the meaning of the Commerce Clause. Not too long ago, this Court sought to allocate federal and state regulatory responsibilities through the similar use of talismanic labels: if a firm were engaged in a large and ill-defined activity we called "manufacturing," we insisted that only the individual states could constitutionally regulate it; only when a firm had ceased "manufacturing" and offered its products into interstate "commerce" did we allow the federal government to enter the scene. We have found, however, that this categorical style of reasoning is utterly inadequate to the realities of modern life in our federal system. See *NLRB v. Jones & Laughlin Steel Corp.*, 301 U.S. 1 (1937).

We have substituted in its place a much more functional, fact-specific, and discriminating analysis. For example, the nationalization of our economic life has made it constitutionally appropriate for the federal government to regulate intensively activities like family farming, which would have been deemed "intrinsically local" under our older conceptual jurisprudence of federalism. See *Wickard v. Filburn*, 317 U.S. 111 (1942).

The present case requires an identical jurisprudential turn. The allocation of privileges of citizenship between the state and the nation demands the same kind of contextual sophistication that we now bring to the allocation of state and federal responsibilities in other areas. Compare *Erie Railroad Co. v. Tompkins*, 304 U.S. 64 (1938) (Brandeis, J.).

From this perspective, the central mistake of the *Slaughterhouse Cases* is simple enough to see. For reasons never explained, the majority opinion analyzes the privileges of citizenship in sharply dichotomous terms: a particular interest can qualify as a privilege either of state citizenship or of national citizenship, but not both. Why?

To be sure, there are some privileges that fit into only one conceptual box. The privilege of obtaining an American passport is obviously one of national citizenship, since states have no independent power to conduct foreign relations. See *United States v. Curtiss-Wright Export Corp.*, 299 U.S. 304 (1936). Similarly, the states may sometimes claim ownership of certain natural resources on behalf of their own citizens, though this power is subject to stringent limitation. See *Toomer v. Witsell*, 334 U.S. 385 (1948).

But there is no reason to suppose that all privileges of citizenship can be so easily dichotomized in our complex federal system. Ours is largely a collaborative federalism of interdependent functions, with states and nation joining together to discharge the responsibilities of government. This basic point is incompatible with a view of the privileges of citizenship as sortable into two hermetically sealed boxes. Given the multiple interdependencies of our two governments, it is only natural that some of the same privileges will be fundamental to *both* state and national citizenship.

This point was already implicit in the leading case of *Crandall v. Nevada*,[10] decided by this Court in 1868, the very year the Fourteenth Amendment was ratified. Though the amendment was not yet on the books, the Court began to elaborate a concept of national citizenship in language that suggests the tenor of the debate in the country at the time. Nevada had imposed a tax of one dollar on "every person leaving the State by any [vehicle engaged] in the business of transporting passengers for hire." This Court struck the statute down, but refused to ground its decision on any of the potentially applicable constitutional texts, basing it instead on the unwritten but robust notion of national citizenship then in the ascendancy:

> The people of these United States constitute one nation. They have a government in which all of them are deeply interested. This government has necessarily a capital established by law, where its principal operations are conducted. . . . That government has a right to call to this point any or all of its citizens to aid in its service, as members of the Congress, of the courts, of the executive departments, and to fill all its other offices; and this right cannot be made to depend upon the pleasure of a State over whose territory they must pass to reach the point where these services must be rendered. The government, also, has its offices of secondary importance in all other parts of the country. . . . In all these it demands the services of its citizens, and is entitled to bring them to those points from all quarters of the nation, and no power can exist in a State to obstruct this right that would not enable it to defeat the purposes for which the government was established. . . .
>
> But if the government has these rights on her own account, the citizen also has correlative rights. He has the right to come to the seat of govern-

ment to assert any claim he may have upon that government, or to trans-
act any business he may have with it. *To seek its protection, to share its of-
fices, to engage in administering its functions.*[11]

These paragraphs express the vibrant national spirit that gave life to the
Fourteenth Amendment and its expansive vision of national citizenship. It also provides a basis for transcending the simplistic either/or
approach to citizenship taken by *Slaughterhouse* five years later. Suppose that Nevada had not merely placed a dollar tax on exit, but had
trenched on the privileges of Americans in more fundamental ways—
for example, by imposing a severe regime of censorship on the state's
newspapers, making it impossible for them to discuss issues of national
political importance. Such an action might well have offended the privileges of state citizenship guaranteed by Nevada's constitution. However this might be, it would also deprive Nevada residents of their privileges and immunities as *American* citizens. Without a vigorous press,
Nevadans could hardly participate in the process of national self-government envisioned by *Crandall.* Our recent cases have recognized this
point, imposing the basic principles of the First Amendment on the
states no less than on the federal government. *Bridges v. California*, 314
U.S. 252 (1941), *Cantwell v. Connecticut*, 310 U.S. 296 (1940). These decisions are best understood as an elaboration of privileges of American
citizenship.

No less important is *Crandall*'s understanding of the reciprocal relationship between a citizen's rights and responsibilities. We are in an especially good position to appreciate this logic today in the aftermath of
another great war for American freedom. As in the late 1860s, we have
recently witnessed black Americans laying down their lives by the
thousands in a struggle to sustain our great experiment in liberal
democracy. In recognition of their sacrifices, President Truman has
ended the practice of consigning Negroes to segregated regiments and
barracks. Having once again established their claims to citizenship with
their blood, Negroes have finally been granted "equality of treatment
and opportunity . . . in the armed services without regard to race, color,
religion or national origin."[12]

Shall America greet its Negro servicemen, and increasingly women,
with open arms when it comes to the great responsibilities of national
citizenship, and yet turn a cold shoulder when they demand their
rightful privileges? Shall blacks and whites fight and die together in

defense of American democracy, but send their children to schools that split them apart?

III.

At the time of the Fourteenth Amendment, public education was in its infancy. We remained a nation of vast frontiers and weak school systems, where many learned to read and write from parents or ministers or private tutors. As President Johnson himself proved, it was still possible for an American to become president without any formal education whatsoever.

This world has vanished with the closing of the frontier and the rise of a society based on knowledge obtained through years of formal education. Homeschooling has become the rare exception and no longer serves as a standard path to economic independence and political participation. Public education has become a fundamental part of the process by which we pass on our democratic values to the next generation. If we do not provide the young with a solid education in democratic citizenship, our larger project in self-government will not endure.

This is the reason why state constitutions throughout the land declare public education to be a fundamental element of the American system.[13] But as we have seen, this broad recognition by the states does not preclude a similar recognition on the national level. To the contrary, public schooling is equally fundamental to the functioning of national democracy. If children of all races, religions, and creeds are not invited to understand themselves as equal citizens of the nation in the public schools, precisely where is this precious sense of national identity to be acquired?

Just as a state cannot disable the local press from reporting on national matters, so too it cannot disable local public schools from training the next generation of Americans to associate with one another as equal citizens of the United States.

The great precedent in this field involves not race but religion. In *West Virginia State Board of Education v. Barnette*, 319 U.S. 624 (1943), the state required the children of Jehovah's Witnesses to violate their religious convictions by saluting the flag at the beginning of each school day. If they refused, they would be expelled from public school and left to receive an education in the private sector or at home. In the America of the mid-nineteenth century, a required ritual like the flag salute might not have seemed such a large price for the state to impose in exchange for a grant of free primary education.[14] But by 1943, this Court was already treating public education as fundamental to the framework of national life. While parents might choose a private education so long as it complied with statutory requirements, their children could not be denied a public education in disregard of the constitutional values established by the nation.

The particular constitutional values at stake in *Barnette* are easily mischaracterized. While First Amendment principles were involved, the case did not involve a classic right to freedom of expression. Students in public schools are not free to remain silent when their teachers ask them questions. To the contrary, teachers regularly require student participation in educational exercises. If a student fails to come up with the "correct" answers on an examination, he will fail the course and suffer the consequences. It is far too simple, then, to say that *Barnette* grants schoolchildren a general First Amendment right to express themselves in any way they like.

Similarly, *Barnette* was not a straightforward case involving the free exercise of religion. As a general rule, no child has the constitutional right to insulate himself from those parts of the public school curriculum that he or his parents consider offensive. There are simply too many competing and conflicting creeds in America to allow for such free-floating vetoes. With every religious and philosophical sect shielding its children from different parts of the curriculum, the very idea of the public school as a training ground in *common* democratic values would dissolve. The general shape of the public curriculum must remain a matter for democratic deliberation and control.

Given these points, our decision in *Barnette* may seem paradoxical. If, as we have insisted, the public schools play an essential part in our national democracy, why not begin each school day with a brief ritual saluting the flag? Isn't this a perfectly appropriate tool for civic education? By what authority do distant judges sitting in Washington, D.C., have the right to intervene in such delicate questions of pedagogy?

Our answer was based on an understanding of the privileges of American citizenship. We focused on the situation of the young Jehovah's Witnesses who would be excluded from public education by the school board's decision: Are not these children also Americans? To be sure, they hold beliefs that set them apart from the majority. But should this difference in belief suffice to exclude them from our common training ground for citizenship?

As Mr. Justice Jackson explained, "If there is any fixed star in our constitutional constellation, it is that no official, high or petty, can prescribe what shall be orthodox in politics, nationalism, religion, or other matters of opinion or force citizens to confess by word or act their faith therein."[15]

Nobody could suppose that the State of West Virginia might evade these constitutional principles by establishing a specially segregated school for Jehovah's Witnesses and other members of dissenting creeds who refused to salute the flag. Even if the segregated school for dissenters were equal in every other respect, the resulting system would still disparage their equal standing as citizens. Isolated from the rest of their peers, they would be a natural object of disdain to students in the other public schools, who would have little opportunity to test their prejudices by real-world contact. Deprived of the opportunity to engage with their fellow Americans on a day-to-day basis, the dissenting students would themselves begin to wonder whether their segregated treatment suggested a second-class status.

This dynamic of mutual estrangement would occur even if the schoolbooks in both mainstream and minority institutions proclaimed the equality of all citizens. Actions speak louder than words. If all are equal citizens, why are some cordoned off from the wider world, as if they were the carriers of some social disease?

The same question applies here. The defendant states, and the District of Columbia, concede that they have fallen far short of providing Negroes with the same educational resources—measured in terms of buildings and books and the like—that white students receive as a matter of course. In response to this lawsuit, they profess a willingness at last to remedy these inequalities—so long as they can retain their segregated systems intact.

But this remedy mistakes the nature of the petititoners' claim. They do not merely demand equal textbooks or gymnasiums. They demand an education worthy of an American citizen—an education that enables each and every one of them, to the extent of their abilities, to collaborate with their fellow Americans on a free and equal basis. Such an education is a priceless constitutional privilege of American citizenship and cannot take place when minority children are cordoned off in schools isolated from the mainstream of social life. Just as it would be unconstitutional to segregate children of dissenting creeds, it is equally unconstitutional to isolate children of minority races.

IV.

Our brother McConnell suggests that *Bolling v. Sharpe*, coming to us from the District of Columbia, raises very different issues from the cases arising out of the states. In particular, he denies that "the Privileges or Immunities Clause avail[s] petitioners. Even assuming that there are certain rights that pertain to Americans as citizens, the plain language of the Clause begins: 'No State shall make or enforce any law. . . .'"[16]

By beginning his quotation with the second sentence of the Fourteenth Amendment, Mr. Justice McConnell invites us to ignore the relationship between the rights enumerated in that sentence and the more fundamental rights created by the amendment's opening line: "All persons born or naturalized in the United States, and subject to the jurisdiction thereof, are citizens of the United States and of the State wherein they reside." This great grant would be meaningless if American citizens had no privileges that Congress was constitutionally obliged to protect.

Consider, for example, the status of one of the very few national privileges explicitly recognized by the *Slaughterhouse* majority: the right of Americans "to demand the care and protection of the Federal government . . . when on the high seas or within the jurisdiction of a foreign government."[17] Despite the long-established recognition of this privilege, Mr. Justice McConnell's interpretation would require this Court to uphold a congressional statute stripping Negro citizens of *any* such protection, leaving them at the mercy of foreign governments. To repeat his words, the "plain language of the clause begins: 'No State shall make or enforce any law'"; and if, as he asserts, this clause serves as a *limitation* on the amendment's opening grant of national citizenship, the fate of Negroes overseas would be entirely dependent upon their political power to induce Congress to repeal its hypothesized endorsement of second-class citizenship.

But even the *Slaughterhouse* Court refused to read the amendment's initial sentences in this restrictive way. The majority's opinion was based on a much more straightforward understanding of the relationship between the amendment's opening lines. As Justice Miller made clear, the second sentence of the amendment does *not* implicitly authorize the national government to deny Americans the privileges granted them by the first sentence.[18] To the contrary, the second sentence *expands* the protection that American citizens would otherwise have the right to expect.

To appreciate this fundamental point, suppose the Fourteenth Amendment had included only the first sentence but not the second. Under this scenario, this Court would have predictably encountered a threshold objection whenever it sought to prevent a state from denying Americans their privileges of national citizenship. By definition, these national privileges did not have their source in the state's own constitution; moreover, absent the second sentence, the federal Constitution would have contained no provision that expressly required the states to refrain from abridging the privileges of national citizenship. Why, then, could not a state proudly declare that, so far as it was concerned, the privileges of American citizenship were no more sacrosanct than those created by some foreign nation like France or Germany?

Such extreme claims of state "sovereignty" were entirely familiar to Americans as they were hammering out the terms of their Reconstruction Constitution. It was precisely such constitutional rhetoric that the South had used to legitimate the Civil War. By including the second sentence in the Fourteenth Amendment, Americans were indeed trying to make their meaning plain—but not in the way that Mr. Justice McConnell suggests. Rather than implicitly granting the federal government the power to play fast and loose with the privileges of national citizenship, Americans were explicitly repudiating familiar notions of state sovereignty that might otherwise authorize the local abuse of national citizens.[19]

Mr. Justice McConnell is quite wrong to read the Reconstruction Constitution as if it contained a single citizenship clause relevant to this litigation. To the contrary, the Fourteenth Amendment contains two basic provisions. The first—call it the Grant of Citizenship Provision—extends national citizenship to both native-born and naturalized Americans, and thereby forbids the national government from creating second-class citizens. The second—call it the Privileges or Immunities Provision—elaborates upon the primacy of national citizenship by explicitly preventing the states from abridging its privileges and immunities. Under both provisions, the dispositive questions are the same: Is an adequate education part of the birthright of every American citizen? If so, does the education provided to Negro children in one or another part of the nation treat them as second-class citizens?

If the answer to both questions is yes, it makes no difference whether it is the national government or the states that have deprived Negroes of their birthright. The opening lines of the Fourteenth Amendment bar both the national and state governments from stripping away any of the constitutional privileges of citizens of the United States.

V.

We are now in a position to summarize and elaborate our central holding: The democratic republic contemplated by our Reconstruction Constitution cannot survive under modern conditions without *all* Americans receiving an education worthy of free and equal citizens. When states discharge their educational responsibilities under their own constitutions, they must organize their school systems in ways that do not abridge this fundamental privilege of national citizenship. This command of the Citizenship Clauses of the Fourteenth Amendment imposes both negative and affirmative obligations on each of the states and the District of Columbia.

We begin with a fundamental "thou shalt not": the states and the District are barred from any educational practice that foreseeably disparages the status of Negro Americans as equal citizens.

The question of foreseeability should be approached from the point of view of the children themselves. When a youngster is only five or ten years of age, he cannot be expected to make nice legal distinctions between those all-Negro schools that are created by law and those that are the consequence of city boundaries or residential patterns. If he finds himself in a school that is racially isolated from the broader community in his metropolitan area, it is only natural for him to wonder why; and it is only natural for the children in the majority schools to think they know the answer: the racial isolation of Negroes betokens their pariah status as second-class citizens.

As we have seen, similar problems can arise in the case of religious minorities, but thankfully, no state has ever sought to emulate the Nazis by requiring citizens to attend segregated schools on the basis of their religion. In contrast, the states in these cases have been categorizing students on the basis of race for generations. Against this historical background, it will be a very long time indeed before racial isolation will be commonly interpreted as a product of happenstance rather than governmental design, by either the children or their parents.

Petitioners would have us ignore this point by reaffirming a famous dictum by Mr. Justice Brown in *Plessy v. Ferguson*, which upheld state-enforced segregation on railroad cars:

> We consider the underlying fallacy of the plaintiff's argument to consist in the assumption that the enforced separation of the two races stamps the colored race with a badge of inferiority. If this be so, it is not by reason of anything found in the act, but solely because the colored race choses [*sic*] to put that construction upon it.[20]

We refuse to reaffirm this dictum, but defer its full-blown reconsideration to another time. Whatever its relevance to other areas of the law, this dictum proceeds on obviously defective premises where public education is concerned. Schoolchildren are simply too immature to "choose" among rival interpretations of social reality in the way Mr. Justice Brown supposes. Indeed, it is precisely because children are unprepared to make intelligent choices that the state is constitutionally obliged to provide them with an educational environment that will prepare them for life as responsible adults.

In its capacity as educator, the state simply cannot be indifferent to the "construction" that its children place upon their educational experience. To the contrary, it is pervasively concerned with the impact of the school environment on the hearts and minds of the young. Every time a teacher disciplines one of his students, every time he passes out an examination, he is seeking to shape the child's "construction" of social reality so as to prepare him for the responsibilities of citizenship that lie ahead. Given the state's pervasive concern with the impact of the educational environment, it cannot profess indifference when it comes to the predictable stigmatizing consequences on Negro children of their continued racial isolation from the larger community. Instead, the Citizenship Clauses of the Fourteenth Amendment require the states to organize their educational systems to avoid stigmatizing Negro children as second-class citizens in their own eyes and in the eyes of the majority.

This negative command—"thou shalt not disparage the status of Negro Americans as equal citizens"—suffices for us to conclude that, as a practical matter, it will not be enough for the District of Columbia or the states to erase all mention of racial categorization of students from their statute books and regulations. They must instead take affirmative steps to integrate the races sufficiently to make it clear to the average student that historical patterns of subordination are no longer enshrined in the state's educational philosophy.

This conclusion is reinforced when we consider that the Fourteenth Amendment does not simply demand that the states avoid stigmatizing Negro children. It requires them affirmatively to provide each child an education with the practical skills required to function effectively as a free and equal American citizen. This practical training cannot occur if school systems effectively restrict Negro children to ongoing engagement with members of their own discrete and insular minority. If this vast nation is to function effectively as a democracy, its children must be taught to cooperate across the lines of race and class on matters of common importance. This basic point will continue to apply even on that distant day when a policy of racial integration will have managed to overcome the weight of our historical experience and the number of Negro children in a school will have no greater social meaning than the number of children with brown eyes or red hair. Even then, it will remain constitutionally important for the public schools to continue teaching all their children that despite their obvious differences in race and culture and class, they can indeed develop the practical arts of democratic cooperation that make them all Americans.

It follows that when any public school isolates Negro children from the broader community, this simple fact suffices to place a heavy burden of justification on the state. First, the state must show that further integration is not reasonably practical. It is, of course, important to keep transportation costs within reasonable bounds—in terms of both public funds and lost student time. But the minimization of such costs was never an absolute priority in the era of segregated education, when children were routinely bussed past neighborhood schools of the "wrong" race. It should not suddenly be transformed into an absolute priority in the new era. Second, even where racial isolation must continue to some extent, the state must demonstrate that it is taking special steps to provide young Negro Americans with the skills and associations they will require to engage constructively with the wider world as adults.

There are, then, two remedial priorities—to end formal racial segregation and to achieve racial integration. Both will call upon the judges of the district courts and courts of appeals to exercise a great deal of equitable discretion. It will be only reasonable for them to put first things first and focus initially on the end of formal segregation. But even during this early period, they should keep the ultimate objective of the Citizenship Clauses firmly in mind.

VI.

It is past time to put the Civil War behind us and to fulfill the solemn commitments of the Reconstruction Constitution. We are all Americans, and we should give all our children an education worthy of their common citizenship. This is the only way to realize the constitutional promise of democratic life made after so much bloody sacrifice.

Education is not enough. The Constitution confers other privileges of national citizenship and extends its exigent demands for equal protection and due process into many other spheres of life.

But education is special. The curse of slavery has afflicted America from its very beginning, and it would be naive to suppose that any single generation can magically resolve its tragic aftermath. Whatever else we do, or fail to do, to meet our constitutional obligations, we must prepare our successors to move beyond us.

Reversed and remanded for proceedings not inconsistent with this opinion.

NOTES

1. See *Prigg v. Pennsylvania*, 41 U.S. (16 Pet.) 539 (1842).

2. See *Dred Scott v. Sandford*, 60 U.S. (19 How.) 393 (1857).

3. See the president's vetoes of the Freedman's Bureau Bill, 6 *Messages and Papers of the Presidents* 398, 398–402 (Feb. 16, 1866), and Civil Rights Bill, id. at 405 (March 26, 1866).

4. Art. 2, 1 Stat. 4 (July 9, 1778).

5. See George W. Williams, *History of the Negro Race in America: 1800 to 1880*, chaps. 10 and 11 (1882).

6. Probably the most familiar legal text was an opinion in *Corfield v. Coryell* delivered by Justice Bushrod Washington while riding circuit in Pennsylvania in 1823. By necessity, the case did not involve the then-nonexistent textual guarantee of national citizenship, but it did involve the clause of the

1787 Constitution that dealt with the "privileges and immunities" of state citizenship: "the citizens of each state shall be entitled to all privileges and immunities of citizens in the several states."

The facts of the case were entirely unprepossessing. John Keene, a citizen of Pennsylvania, had been caught oystering in New Jersey waters, contrary to a New Jersey statute reserving the oysters to New Jersey citizens. He attacked the statute on the ground that the Constitution had given citizens of Pennsylvania "all the privileges and immunities" of citizenship in New Jersey. In response, Justice Washington rejected the idea that oystering rose to the dignity of a constitutionally protected interest: "We feel no hesitation in confining these expressions to those privileges and immunities which are, in their nature, fundamental; which belong, of right, to the citizens of all free governments." To reassure himself that this formula embraced a significant bundle of rights, Justice Washington enumerated a host of privileges and immunities he believed constitutionally protected, and when he exhausted himself, he cautioned his reader that "many others . . . might be mentioned."

Judge Washington's definition was quoted at length by Senator Howard when he presented the Fourteenth Amendment to the Senate on behalf of the Joint Committee on Reconstruction. Howard expressly included Washington's open-ended reference to "many others which might be mentioned," as he invited his fellow senators to "gather some intimation of what probably will be the opinion of the judiciary" as to the scope of the amendment's protection of "privileges" and "immunities." Cong. Globe, 39th Cong. 1st Sess., 2765 (May 23, 1866). After quoting *Corfield* at length, he explained that "these privileges and immunities . . . *are not and cannot be fully defined in their entire extent and precise nature*" (emphasis added). Id.

Other debates on related matters before the Thirty-ninth Congress, particularly the Civil Rights Act, reveal that leading Republicans were familiar with Judge Washington's opinion and understood it as an open-ended text. See Statement of Rep. Lawrence, Cong. Globe, *Corfield*, as well as note in Brightly's 39th Cong., 1st Sess. 1835–36 (April 7, 1866) (quoting *Digest*, which described the rights enumerated in *Corfield* and other opinions as "*some* of the particular privileges and immunities of citizens which are clearly embraced by the general description of principles deemed to be fundamental" (emphasis added)); Statement of Rep. Shellabarger, Cong. Globe, 39th Cong., 1st Sess., app. 293 (asserting that the privileges and immunities of "general or national citizenship" include "*at least*" those rights enumerated by Judge Washington (emphasis added)).

After all is said and done, however, *Corfield*'s formulation represents a few remarks rendered by a single judge in the course of resolving an oystering dispute. While the legislative history plainly indicates that leading Republicans, in citing and quoting *Corfield*, recognized that their invocation of "privileges" and "immunities" opened up a broad judicial inquiry into the fundamental principles of national citizenship, every detail of Washington's particular formulation does not deserve canonical status.

7. *Slaughterhouse Cases*, 83 U.S. (16 Wallace) 36, 71 (1873).

8. The relevant section reads:

Representatives shall be apportioned among the several States according to their respective numbers. . . . But when the right to vote at any election for the choice of electors for President and Vice President of the United States, Representatives in Congress, the Executive and Judicial officers of a State, or the members of the Legislature thereof, is denied to any of the male inhabitants of such State, being twenty-one years of age, and citizens of the United States, or in any way abridged, except for participation in rebellion, or other crime, the basis of representation therein shall be reduced in the proportion which the number of such male citizens shall bear to the whole number of male citizens twenty-one years of age in such State.

Article II, Section 1 regulates the selection of the president and provides that "Each State shall appoint . . . a Number of Electors, equal to the whole Number of Senators and representatives to which the State may be entitled in the Congress."

9. *Slaughterhouse Cases*, at 61.

10. 73 U.S. (6 Wall.) 35 (1867).

11. Id. at 43–44 (emphasis supplied).

12. Executive Order No. 9981, 3 CFR 722 (June 26, 1948) (1943–48 Compilation).

13. The constitutions of all forty-eight states ensure the provision of free public education in some manner. Most contain separate articles requiring the legislature to establish and maintain free public schools and creating a perpetual school fund of some sort. See Ala. Const. art. XIV, § 256 ("The legislature shall establish, organize, and maintain a liberal system of public schools"); Ariz. Const. art. XI, § 1 ("The legislature shall . . . provide for the establishment of a general and uniform public school system"); Ark. Const. art. XIV, § 1 ("[T]he state shall ever maintain a general, suitable and efficient system of free schools"); Cal. Const. art. IX, §§ 1, 5; Colo. Const. art. IX, § 2; Conn. Const. art. VIII, § 2; Del. Const. art. X, § 1; Fla. Const. art. XII, § 1; Ga. Const. art. VIII, § 2-6401 ("The provision of adequate education shall be a primary obligation of the state of Georgia"); Idaho Const. art. IX, § 1; Ill. Const. art. VIII, § 1; Ind. Const. art. VIII, § 1; Iowa Const. art. IX, Pt. 2, § 3; Kan. Const. art. VI, § 2; Ky. Const. § 184; La. Const. art. XII, § 1; Me. Const. art. VIII; Md. Const. art. VIII, § 1; Mass. Const. Pt. 2, Ch. 5, § 2; Mich. Const. art. XI, § 1; Minn. Const. art. VIII, § 1; Miss. Const. art. VIII, § 201; Mo. Const. art. IX, § 1(a); Mont. Const. art. XI, § 1; Neb. Const. art. VII, § 6; Nev. Const. art. XI, § 2; N.H. Const. art. 83; N.J. Const. art.

XII, § 4; N.M.. Const. art. XII, § 1; N.Y. Const. art. XI, § 1; N.D. Const. art. VIII, § 147; N.D. Const. art. VI, § 2; Okla. Const. art. XIII, § 1; Or. Const. art. VIII, § 3; Pa. Const. art. X, § 1; R.I. Const. art. XII, § 1; S.C. Const. art. XI, § 5; S.D. Const. art. VIII, § 1; Tenn. Const. art. XI, § 12; Tex. Const. art. VII, § 1; Utah Const. art. X, § 1; Vt. Const. Ch. 2, § 64; Va. Const. art. IX, § 129; Wash. Const. art. IX, § 2; W. Va. Const. art. XII, § 1; Wis. Const. art. X, § 1; Wyo. Const. art. VII, § 1. A few states include education in their constitutions' declaration of rights. See Md. Const., Declaration of Rights, art. 43 ("That the legislature ought to encourage the diffusion of knowledge and virtue, the extension of a judicious system of general education . . ."); N.C. Const. art. I, § 27 ("The people have a right to the privilege of education, and it is the duty of the state to guard and maintain that right."); Wyo. Const. art. I, § 23 ("The right of the citizens to opportunities for education should have practical recognition").

Many other constitutions contain language emphasizing the relationship between education and stable republican government, the importance of education to the exercise and protection of the people's rights, and the relationship between education and welfare generally. See Ark. Const. art. XIV, § 1 ("Intelligence and virtue being the safeguard of liberty and the bulwark of a free and good government . . ."); Cal. Const. art. IX, § 1 ("A general diffusion of knowledge and intelligence being essential to the preservation of the rights and liberties of the people . . ."); Idaho Const. art. IX, § 1 ("The stability of a republican form of government depending mainly on the intelligence of the people . . ."); Ind. Const. art. VIII, § 1 ("Knowledge and learning, generally diffused throughout a community, being essential to the preservation of free government . . ."); Me. Const. art. VIII ("A general diffusion of the advantages of education being essential to the preservation of the rights and liberties of the people . . ."); Mass. Const. Pt. 2, Ch. 5, § 2 ("Wisdom, and knowledge, as well as virtue, diffused generally among the body of the people, being necessary for the preservation of their rights and liberties; and as these depend on spreading the opportunities and advantages of education among the different orders of the people . . ."); Mich. Const. art. XI, § 1 ("Religion, morality and knowledge being necessary to good government and the happiness of mankind . . ."); Minn. Const. art. VIII, § 1 ("The stability of a republican form of government depending mainly upon the intelligence of the people . . ."); Mo. Const. art. IX, § 1(a) ("A general diffusion of knowledge and intelligence being essential to the preservation of the rights and liberties of the people . . ."); N.H. Const. art. LXXXIII ("Knowledge and learning, generally diffused through a community, being essential to the preservation of a free government; and the spreading of the opportunities and advantages of education through the various parts of the country, being highly conducive to promote this end . . ."); N.D. Const. art. VIII, § 147 ("A high degree of intelligence, patriotism, integrity and morality on the part of every voter in a government by the people being necessary in order to insure the continuance of that government and happiness of the people . . ."); R.I. Const. art. XII, § 1 ("The diffusion of knowledge, as well as virtue, among the people, being essential to the preservation of their rights and liberties . . ."); S.D. Const. art. VII, § 1 ("The stability of a republican form of government depending on the morality and intelligence of the people . . ."); Tenn. Const. art. XI, § 12 ("Knowledge, learning, and virtue, being essential to the preservation of republican institutions . . ."); Tex. Const. art. VII, § 1 ("A general diffusion of knowledge being essential to the rights and liberties of the people . . .").

14. In fact, the "pledge of allegiance" was a creation of the late nineteenth century and did not exist at the time of the enactment of the Fourteenth Amendment. Our thought experiment should not be understood as an exercise in divining the "original understanding" on such matters.

15. West Virginia State Board of Education v. Barnette, 319 U.S. 624, 642 (1943).

16. See McConnell, p. 166.

17. *Slaughterhouse Cases*, at 79.

18. Id. at 72–73.

19. While my interpretation is solidly rooted in both *Slaughterhouse* and the original understanding, Mr. Justice McConnell provides absolutely no evidence that *anybody* explicitly advanced his restrictive interpretation of the amendment's second sentence during Reconstruction.

20. 163 U.S. 537, 551 (1896).

MICHELMAN, J., concurring in part and concurring in
the judgment.

I.

The Chief Justice and Justice Days show compellingly that no state-
mandated system of race-based segregation, whether in public places
generally or specifically in the public schools, can stand against a constitutional principle of civil equality. I join the Court's conclusion that
such a principle is brought to bear on the states by the Equal Protection
Clause of the Fourteenth Amendment, and that *Plessy v. Ferguson* must
accordingly be overruled.

As I understand it, the legal principle that decides these cases
is one of equality of membership in the civil community. It is an
antimonarchical, anti-aristocratical principle of one-size-fits-all civil
membership, opposed to the legal imposition of caste or any graded
public status.[1] It was first made applicable to the states, as a matter of
national constitutional law, by the Fourteenth Amendment. I wish to
make clear, however, my view that the principle in question is not
one that entered our Constitution for the first time with the enactment of the amendment. Rather, it has been from the beginning a
basic premise of the American constitutional venture, not the less so
for having been honored in the breach for the greater part of our history. Only by so understanding it can we explain robustly our legal
conclusions in all of the cases before us.

II.

One of these cases, no. 8, *Bolling v. Sharpe*, involves a constitutional
challenge to segregation in the public schools of the District of Columbia, while four of them are from the states. My colleagues all give

the main weight of their attentions to the state cases. That they should do so is understandable. It is nevertheless regrettable for this reason: It suggests that the right approach to the work of constitutional exegesis we are called on to perform today is first to decide the relevant legal implications of the restrictions on state government conduct imposed by the Fourteenth Amendment's second, prohibitory sentence and only then to consider, as a subordinate and relatively minor matter, where that leaves the question of the federal government's obligations under provisions of the Constitution applicable to it. With respect, I find that mode of proceeding in these cases to be putting the cart before the horse.

I agree with the majority of my colleagues who find that a constitutional question is before us in the *Bolling* case and disagree, in this respect, with Justice McConnell.[2] The prohibitions of the Fourteenth Amendment's second sentence do not apply to the conduct of the federal government. They do not do so in terms, and Justice McConnell demonstrates convincingly why we may not set aside that plain textual fact as an oversight or drafting error.[3] I nevertheless conclude that the operation of segregated schools by the governmental authorities of the District is prohibited by the same principle of single civic membership that prohibits this practice to the states. The question is not without some relevance, in my mind, to our consideration of the state cases themselves, for I cannot share Justice McConnell's equanimity about a Constitution that, taken as a whole, would leave Congress legally free to pursue a course of conduct that this same Constitution treats, when practiced by the states, as a violation of a legal right as basic as that of equal membership.

To my mind, such a posture would defy reason. Justice McConnell explains cogently why the authors of the Fourteenth Amendment, meaning to make Congress and not this Court the amendment's chief arbiter and enforcer, declined to subordinate Congress, in that regard, to the direction of this Court by bringing Congress itself within the amendment's own prohibitions. It is nevertheless hard to fathom how the authors could have acted thus, lacking a firm belief that Congress was itself *already* legally bound by the core, at least, of a parallel principle with regard to its own conduct of the affairs of the federal government. Lacking such a belief, the authors would have been acting in the most unprincipled way. That is so whether we think of the authors as being the Reconstruction Congress that framed and promulgated the amendment, the representatives who ratified it in the states, or the voters in the states who chose those representatives. It may indeed be true that the members of that Congress, proposing to make certain great principles of justice legally enforceable against the states, trusted themselves (so far as they could know themselves) to follow those principles spontaneously. Such a belief would hardly have given them either cause or excuse for long-term exemption of the United States from the legal force of the Constitution's most basic standards of justice. So much the less would such a temporal difference in trust have given the country's people reason thus to act. We little honor the amendment's authors, whether in Congress or in the states, by imagining them blind to the fact that it was a Constitution they were amending.

I thus agree with those who have suggested to us that it borders on the unthinkable that the Constitution should dictate a conclusion in the District of Columbia case opposite from the one it dictates in the state cases. Of course "unthinkability" of that kind can never in itself supply a warrant for finding in the Constitution what is not there or for refusing to see in it what is there. We need not look abroad to learn that it is possible for highly dedicated and capable authors to write into a Constitution that which goes against all reason and divides the Constitution against itself. Equally surely, however, this Court ought not lightly to conclude thus of the Constitution we have been specially entrusted to expound. We are, I believe, obliged in our entrusted work to seek avoidance of any unprincipled disparity in the Constitution's treatment of the states and the United States.

That obligation, as a wholly abstract matter, no more necessitates a decision in favor of the *Bolling* plaintiffs than it potentially embarrasses a decision in favor of the plaintiffs in the state cases based strictly on the second, prohibitory sentence of the Fourteenth Amendment. No doubt one can say that if the prohibitory sentence does not allow Kansas to follow the practice of separate-but-equal schooling in the Topeka schools then the Constitution outside the prohibitory sentence ought not, at least not without strict textual compulsion, be read to allow Congress to follow it in the District schools. With exactly equal force, one can say that if the Constitution outside of the prohibitory sentence does not prohibit that practice in the District then the prohibitory sentence ought not, at least not without strict textual compulsion, be read to prohibit it in Topeka. This is why I find that our identification of a constitutional ground of objection to segregated schooling outside of the prohibitory sentence bears inescapably on our consideration not only of *Bolling* but of the state cases, too. It is for this reason that I say that the most robust legal conclusion against the constitutional permissibility of segregation, whether imposed by the states or by the United States, will be one that draws its normative premise, at least in part, from sources beyond a constitutional sentence that leaves the federal government untouched.

III.

Two proposals for such a common source of the state and federal obligations appear in the opinions of my colleagues.

A.

Justice Sunstein would find the common source in the "substantive" aspect of the duty not to deprive anyone of liberty without due process of law, imposed on the United States by the Fifth Amendment and on the states by the Fourteenth. It is true, as Justice Sunstein says, that a chastened doctrine of substantive due process—revised and narrowed as the doctrine is by our decisions in cases such as *West Coast Hotel Co. v. Parrish* and *United States v. Carolene Products Co.*—remains to condemn any legislation burdensome to liberty for which there cannot be shown any plausible connection to a legitimate pursuit or interest of the state. With respect, however, I cannot agree that rational-basis substantive due process can supply a robustly principled ground for our decisions in these cases.

A first difficulty is that, by relying on rational-basis due process for our decision in the *Bolling* case while basing the state decisions on the Equal Protection Clause (not the Due Process Clause) of the Fourteenth Amendment's second sentence, we rather establish than avoid a troubling disparity between the most fundamental constitutional obligations of the states and of the United States. For why would we not be content today to base the state decisions on rational-basis due process as well, were we not anticipating the possibility of future cases in which a more robustly substantive principle of anticaste or antisubordination—applicable to the states but not to the United States—would cut ice where a bare, rational-basis requirement of due process would not?

On the other hand, sole or central reliance on rational-basis due process as our ground for decision in all the cases, state and federal, would inevitably commit us to extended uncertainty and conflict over the application of our rulings today both to the specific matter of segregated schooling and, all the more so, to state-imposed segregation in other public places and facilities. Such a reliance seemingly would dictate remands of these cases for further proceedings, in which the defendants—not to mention future defendants in other localities not yet involved in litigation—predictably will propose innumerable allegedly rational bases for segregated schooling, some of them doubtless locally specific and many of them doubtless purportedly supported by expert testimony and social-scientific evidence. Undeniably, educational effectiveness and efficiency are permissible pursuits of the state. How may we, in all reason, preclude the attempts of state and local governments to show that those pursuits are served by the practice of segregation, whether locally or generally, "temporarily" or permanently? When will the process end? Of course we could cut it short by announcing today that no pragmatic reason could ever be *sufficiently weighty* to provide a "rational" justification for the moral enormity of state-enforced segregation in public schools, but to do so would obviously be to rely on some constitutional principle beyond that of a rational-basis due process requirement.

B.

Neither the Chief Justice nor Justice Ely would have us rely on rational-basis substantive due process. Rather, both assert that the Fourteenth Amendment's Equal Protection Clause is designed to pick up a principle of equality before the law that had always been understood to be imposed on the federal government by the original Bill of Rights, in order to make that principle for the first time applicable to the states as a matter of national constitutional law. Theirs is an astute and helpful proposition, but not yet sufficient to the conclusion we reach in these cases. It may well be true that the original American constitutional conception of due process of law reflected a natural right tradition—a "higher law background," as it has been called—containing a requirement of formal generality in law and formal equality before the law.[4] That natural right tradition is not, however, in itself an anticaste tradition, and it is anything but clear that antebellum American constitutional understandings, cut from its cloth, would have precluded a material legal policy of separation of the races in various public settings. No support for such a preclusion in legal history, text, or precedent has been brought to our notice.

IV.

Is there something, then, in the Reconstruction Amendments that pours the wine of anticaste into the more ancient American due process bottle?

A.

As an original matter, we might have found the answer in section 1 of the Thirteenth Amendment. We cannot do so now, however, without calling into the most serious question our long-standing, well-entrenched doctrine, reared on our decision in the *Civil Rights Cases*, that section 1 does not reach discrimination by nongovernmental agents in which no state official or "state function" is directly involved, no matter how public the setting, the meaning, or the ramifications of the discrimination in question.[5]

The English language contains different terms for caste and slavery, and the two terms are usually understood to refer to different things. That the two things they refer to have much that is morally atrocious in common does not mean that lawmakers writing a law to ban "slavery" should be read to have included a prohibition of caste, whether intentionally or willy-nilly. Our view in the *Civil Rights Cases* was that so to conclude would be "running the slavery argument into the ground."[6] We cannot now upend that view without reopening afresh the question of the constitutional-legal status, under section 1 of the Thirteenth Amendment, of race-based discrimination in arguably public places and activities where no state action is found. Whatever may be the merits of doing so, I do not see a majority of the Court prepared to do it today.

B.

Like the first sentence of the Thirteenth Amendment, the first sentence of the Fourteenth is not specifically directed to the states. In fact, that sentence does doubtless affect the application of legal rights and protections guaranteed against the federal government by the original Bill of Rights. Declared as they are in universal terms, those rights and protections must surely appertain to everyone who is constitutionally declared a "citizen of the United States." The Fourteenth Amendment's first sentence thus does have the plain legal effect of extending the enjoyment of those rights and protections to a previously excluded group of persons, namely, the ex-slaves and their descendants.

But to say so does not answer the question of what these rights and protections were, and are. Admission of African Americans to enjoyment of rights against the federal government that whites had previously enjoyed would not ipso facto have the effect of expanding the content of those rights to include what it did not previously include. If that content did not previously include a right against government-imposed public separation of the races, it is not clear how admission of African Americans to the enjoyment of these rights would alter any such limitation of their content.

V.

It thus appears to me that, after we have taken the constitutional text and its legislative history as far as defensible legal argumentation can take them, decision in the *Bolling* case, at least, finally comes to rest on an attribution of national purpose and commitment for which no internal legal-textual or textual-historical demonstration can be found. Decision becomes a matter of attributing or not attributing to the Constitution, from its very beginnings, an overriding purpose and premise of excluding caste institutions from these shores, a premise that most Americans today doubtless would trace to the Declaration of Independence.[7] Decision thus also becomes a matter of explaining American affairs of race during the Constitution's first seventy-five years as a visionary eclipse or occlusion. It was an occlusion consisting, while it lasted, in a refusal to envision inhabitants of African lineage as belonging at all to the civic company of one-size-fits-all civil membership—an accompaniment to the legal condonation and normalization of African slavery during those years, wrought by laws and judges of this country and of many of its states. It was lifted, if not fully cleared away, as those laws were destroyed, by the momentous events of the Civil War and its aftermath.

VI.

That is a plausible construction of the United States and our history in the respects pertinent to our decisions today, perhaps on the whole the historically most persuasive one. It is nevertheless a contestable construction, and one that can hardly claim entire independence of the moral outlook of whoever presumes to make it.

On this occasion, if ever, our duty is to speak plainly to our fellow citizens about the task they have entrusted to this Court by acceding, as they have since near the beginning of the republic, to our role of judging independently the constitutional legality of statutes, state and federal, when the question of constitutionality is raised by a case coming properly before us. What is it that we do when we judge a statute to be against the law of the Constitution? Of course it is and can only be the Constitution to which we look in passing such a judgment. That is why we place upon the text and its legislative history as much of the weight of decision as they can bear. There are, however, cases in which that text and that history cannot bear the full weight of decision, without receiving a construction in the light of a controlling but unwritten national orientation or purpose that those charged with the duty of decision must take some responsibility to identify and supply.

In a government of laws, there is no shirking such a responsibility when it arises, as surely it will. By the force of practice that we must now regard as settled, the responsibility sometimes falls on this Court. It does so not because of any special moral or intellectual virtue, or any special relevant wisdom, that any of us possesses, but only because, in a government of laws, the responsibility must rest somewhere and Americans have made or acquiesced in the choice to place it in this Court. It will not do, in a government of laws, to turn away the plaintiffs in these cases upon the plea that no body of mere judges can be permitted to find elected officials in violation of the law upon such a ground as I have mentioned. A plaintiff who files a claim of a deprivation of rights secured by existing principles of law is entitled to a decision on that claim and on the law that claim invokes. That entitlement does not lapse if it happens that we find the law not finally decidable, either in favor of the plaintiff's claim *or against it*, by analysis of legal text and legislative history without some supplementary illumination from unwritten premises and purposes.[8]

VII.

Today we thus decide that a constitutional-legal principle of equality of civil membership controls the operation of public schools by any and all governments in the United States, and that it prohibits the operation of a "dual" school system in which schools are reserved exclusively for "white" or colored attendance. We must accordingly direct the lower courts in these cases to see to the termination of such operations as speedily as it may be accomplished in orderly fashion.

The formal termination of dual schooling may not be all that is required by the applicable constitutional principle. We can easily imagine untoward, even self-defeating, consequences from the enforcement of formal desegregation. We can imagine evasive tactics, more or less plausible pleas of impossibility, compliance in form but not in spirit, and even compliance both in form and in spirit that will nevertheless leave materially uncorrected constitutionally intolerable deprivations of equality of citizenship in the field of education. We ought, however, to leave to the future any speculation about what further recognition of constitutional obligations, or further remedies against failure to perform the obligation to desegregate we recognize today, may be constitutionally in order.

Having identified the applicable legal principle of equality of civil membership and its central meaning as applied to dual school systems, it behooves us to leave further elaboration of what that principle requires in the operation of public schools to be arrived at in as broadly democratic a manner as is consonant with the rule of law. That is especially so insomuch as the task of legal decision in these cases has required the Court to summon to its aid an attribution of a national moral vision that it cannot be the exclusive business of this Court to fashion for the country in detail at a given moment of its history. Our course now is to await not only the lively involvement in this work of state and local citizenries and officials, but also the assumption by Congress of its constitutionally assigned responsibility of leadership in the substantiation and effectuation of the principles of law imposed on the states, as we decide today, by the Fourteenth Amendment.

NOTES

1. I speak of public status and membership, rather than of citizenship, for a reason explained in footnote 7, below.

2. It is not clear to me that Justice McConnell has entirely avoided, or could possibly avoid, the constitutional question in the *Bolling* case. He would hold that in the absence of specific authorization from Congress to run their public schools on a segregated basis, District officials act beyond their lawful powers in doing so. The precept on which he would rely is that a court should not presume that Congress has authorized any subordinate federal agency to depart from general principles of law protecting the basic rights of citizens elsewhere in the country. Thus stated, the precept is surely right. It is, however, insufficient to the task of deciding the case before us. A court need not, after all, "presume" anything in order to find or conclude that the time-honored practice of segregating the District schools by race has indeed been authorized by a long-acquiescent Congress that can hardly be suspected of either ignorance of the practice or obliviousness to the great issues of policy and justice it raises.

What my colleague McConnell must precisely mean, therefore, is something rather stronger than that courts of law ought not to presume in favor of such a delegation. Fully unfolded, his view is that courts of law ought to presume *against* such a delegation—that is, by erecting or recognizing special, institutional safeguards against its occurrence. But if that is the judicial duty, it must be so by reason of some legal policy derived from some legal source. It is not clear to me what the legal source in this case would be, if not the Constitution. In the last analysis, it appears to me that my colleague McConnell's position is not far from a proposition that constitutional law obliges us to construe the congressional enactments regarding schooling in the District of Columbia to include an unstated prohibition against segregating the schools by race (in order, as it might be said, to avoid constitutional doubts).

3. Nor, in my view, may we regard it as a lapse now cured by stare decisis. *Buchanan v. Warley*, 245 U.S. 60 (1917), is very much in point, but I do not agree with the suggestion of the Chief Justice that our decision in that case reflects the presence of a civil equality motif or component in our conception of due process. If anything, the fact that we found it necessary to rest our decision there on constitutional protection of property rights points in the opposite direction. The dicta in *Korematsu v. United States*, 323 U.S. 214 (1944), also fall short of the mark. The Court there was confronted with a set of laws that utterly and peremptorily stripped a single racial group of the most basic entitlements of

property and freedom. Such a set of laws might well be held covered by the Fifth Amendment Due Process Clause without implying the contrariety to due process of laws mandating public separation of the races.

4. *Calder v. Bull*, 3 U.S. (3 Dall.) 386 (1798); Edward Corwin, "The 'Higher Law' Background of American Constitutional Law," 42 *Harv. L. Rev.* 149, 365 (1928–29); cf. *Loan Ass'n v. Topeka*, 87 U.S. (20 Wall.) 655 (1874).

5. See, e.g., *Terry v. Adams*, 345 U.S. 461 (1953); *Shelley v. Kraemer*, 334 U.S. 1 (1948); *Smith v. Allwright*, 321 U.S. 649 (1944).

6. See the *Civil Rights Cases*, 109 U.S. 3, 24 (1883).

7. There is no immediately obvious reason why such a constructive American constitutional-legal principle of unitary civil membership should be understood to be confined in its application to persons who are "citizens" in the technical legal sense specified by the first sentence of the Fourteenth Amendment, and we need not today decide whether and how that principle might apply to short- or long-term, temporary or permanent, residents of this country who were not born here and have not (yet) been naturalized here. It is with a view to possible future consideration of such questions, whenever they may come properly before us, that I frame the applicable principle in terms of civil membership rather than of citizenship.

8. Perhaps some would say that the pertinent, constructive constitutional premise is not unwritten, having in mind that the Constitution prohibits the United States from "grant[ing any] Title of Nobility." U.S. Const. Art I, § 9, cl. 8. We may well regard the Title of Nobility Clause as an outcropping or manifestation of a constructive constitutional premise of equal civil membership, but we ought not to treat it as the premise itself declared. We should be careful about running any constitutional clause into the ground.

ELY, J., concurring in the judgment (except as to remedy).

I.

A.

Defendant school boards are probably right in asserting that most of the framers and ratifiers of the Fourteenth Amendment did not expect that ratification would result in the immediate desegregation of the public schools. This is, however, of scant if any relevance to the cases before us. The "public school system" in 1868 bore essentially no resemblance to its contemporary counterpart.[1] More fundamentally, the Equal Protection Clause—like the other clauses of section 1 of the Fourteenth Amendment—is among the Constitution's clearest examples of a provision whose exact content was understood not to be frozen in time. This does not make the Equal Protection Clause, any more than any other provision of the Constitution, infinitely malleable, capable of bearing any meaning that strikes this Court (or anyone else) as a good idea at the time. It is limited in application to situations of officially imposed inequality, specifically inequality that negatively affects the former slave race or other groups that can on principled grounds be regarded as relevantly analogous thereto, in that they are the victims of mindless prejudice and lack the political power to protect themselves.[2]

This is not the occasion to ruminate about what other groups should be protected with unusual force by the Equal Protection Clause, but this much is clear: its core concern was the protection of racial minorities, most specifically Negroes, from unequal treatment at the hands of the law, and (as its language alone would be sufficient to demonstrate) it was not intended to be tethered by any 1954 or other future attempt to guess what particular instances of inequality our 1868 forebears had at the forefront of their minds. They were accustomed to interpreting the 1789 and 1791 documents in terms of the principles they set forth rather than trying to read the minds of the founding generation for further specificity, and there is no convincing indication that they intended their own unratified thoughts to be given any greater deference. It was a *constitution* they were writing.

B.

The school boards' principal argument seems to be that the "mere" segregation, or separation, of the races into different schools does not harm anybody—specifically it does not harm children thus relegated to a "Negro school"—and thus there can be no claim of a denial of equality.[3] This view can find support in the 1896 case of *Plessy v. Ferguson*, upholding state-enforced racial segregation on trains:

> We consider the underlying fallacy of plaintiff's argument to consist in the assumption that the enforced segregation of the two races stamps the colored race with a badge of inferiority. If this be so, it is not by reason of anything found in the act, but solely because the colored race chooses to put that construction upon it.[4]

However, time has set its face against *Plessy v. Ferguson*. Petitioners have directed us to various studies suggesting that enforced racial segregation necessarily—and not because the members of certain ethnic groups are unusually sensitive—inflicts psychological harm upon the minorities on whom it is imposed. We need not pause to consider the details of these studies, however, for as of the mid-twentieth century it is apparent that their conclusion is correct. An all-white legislature tells a Negro child that because of her color she is not fit to go to school with their own children, and if she is hurt it is because she "chooses" to be? The claim is self-evidently absurd. Absent an inner self-confidence that borders on the superhuman—surely none of us would claim it—separating a Negro child from white children of similar age and qualifications solely because of her race is bound to generate feelings of insecurity, even inferiority, that will not only impede her ability to learn, but affect her heart and mind in a way unlikely ever to be undone.[5] *Plessy v. Ferguson* is overruled.

C.

The school boards argue secondarily (and with understandably lessened vehemence) that even if we assume that racially segregated

schools injure children of the Negro race, they can nonetheless be justified. They point out that laws often treat some people better than others, but that does not render them unconstitutional unless they are irra-
tional. That is true so far as it goes. However, this is a case of racial discrimination, understood from the beginning to be the core concern of
the Equal Protection Clause.

> The existence of laws in the States where the newly emancipated negroes
> resided, which discriminated with gross injustice and hardship against
> them as a class, was the evil to be remedied by this clause, and by it such
> laws are forbidden.

Slaughterhouse Cases, 16 Wall. 36, 81 (1873). See also *Strauder v. West Virginia*, 100 U.S. 303 (1879) (invalidating a statute limiting jury service to
white males). The scrutiny applied to business regulations and most
other classifications is notoriously, albeit correctly, lenient. See, e.g.,
Railway Express Agency v. New York, 336 U.S. 106 (1949). Unless the scrutiny applied to racial classifications is considerably stricter than this,
however, most of them would stand, if only on the flimsy but "rational"
ground that they are calculated to reduce the opportunities for racial
strife,[6] thereby defeating the central point of the Fourteenth Amendment. See generally *United States v. Carolene Products Co.*, 304 U.S. 144,
152 & n.4 (1938). This Court has therefore stated that "all legal restrictions which curtail the civil rights of a single racial group are immediately suspect" and "courts must submit them to the most rigid scrutiny." *Korematsu v. United States*, 323 U.S. 214, 216 (1944).[7]

Thus in these cases the argument that desegregating the schools will
increase the possibility of violence, thereby rendering students of all
races less secure and decreasing their capacity for learning, is not fanciful. It does not, however, rise to the level required in a case involving
racial discrimination. It is circular, in that the possibility of strife stems
in no small measure precisely from the fact that the schools have long
been segregated. It is consequently time-bound as well, in that over
time desegregation will increase interracial understanding and thereby
decrease the likelihood of racial strife. It also violates the salutary principle that we cannot allow vigilante threats of resistance to thwart the
commands of the Constitution. E.g., *Terminiello v. Chicago*, 337 U.S. 1, 5
(1949). Certainly the beginnings of desegregation will carry some risk,
as doing the right and constitutional thing often does. It is the duty of
the state to deploy its police to ensure, as they plainly have the capacity

to, that that risk does not degenerate into violence during the unavoidable period of adjustment.

The argument that, overall, white children score higher on aptitude and achievement tests than Negro children, and that segregating the schools can therefore be defended as a form of "tracking" on the basis of capacity to learn, suffers from the same defects and another as well. Negro children who test comparatively low undoubtedly do so, at least in part, *because* they have been forced to attend inferior schools and essentially told they are not good enough to study with white children. The test score argument too is thus both circular and time-bound. Moreover, it is openly based on a statistical generalization, one that itself is probably tainted by prejudice and in any event is entirely unnecessary. Many Negro children test at or near the top despite the adverse conditions under which they are being educated. Many white children test at or near the bottom. If the state genuinely wanted to "track" on the basis of capacity to learn, it could do so (and undoubtedly would, were its rationalization actually its intention) by individual measurements that are far from prohibitively expensive, and vastly more accurate than crude and ill-fitting racial stereotypes.[8] School segregation is thus not justifiable in terms of any argument that can remotely satisfy the Constitution.

II.

One of these cases concerns the school system of the District of Columbia, to which the Equal Protection Clause does not in terms apply. It is suggested that it would be "unthinkable" were the Constitution read to impose a more stringent command of equality on the states than on the federal government. On the other hand we are assured that if we were today to invalidate school segregation in the states but not in the nation's capital, Congress would complete the job by desegregating the District's schools. We certainly hope that is the case, but must also take into account the likelihood that such a congressional transformation might take years, and in the process involve an ugly and counterproductive struggle, both of which factors would give aid and comfort to those who would resist today's decision. The search for a responsible constitutional basis for desegregating the District's schools must therefore continue.[9]

We are urged to hold that the Equal Protection Clause is somehow "incorporated" into the Fifth Amendment's Due Process Clause. Passing the question whether the term "due process" can responsibly be read to contain such a command of equality, it would be turning somersaults with history to hold that an amendment ratified in 1791 incorporated part or all of an amendment ratified in 1868. Such somersaults are not required, however, to conclude that it was the office of the Equal Protection Clause unequivocally to apply to the states a command of equality of the sort that the original framers, and this Court among others, had already acknowledged in various contexts to be constitutionally applicable to the federal government.[10] Indeed, the issue can be regarded as already settled: *Korematsu*, involving a federal law, correctly assumed without argument that the demands of the Equal Protection Clause were fully applicable.

III.

We therefore hold that neither the states nor the federal government can constitutionally maintain schools segregated on the basis of race. Noting that today is May 17, 1954—almost the end of the school year—we do not require this holding to be fully implemented at once. Although we do not require it, however, those school districts in a position to do so would be well advised to desegregate their schools, at least certain grades thereof,[11] as of this fall. As of the fall of 1955 our order should—though apparently I do not speak for a majority of my colleagues on this issue—become fully applicable. Neither any state nor the federal government can constitutionally maintain separate schools reserved for white, Negro, or any other group of children defined by ethnicity. Neither may they assign children on the basis of attendance zones (or for that matter school districts) that were delineated with an eye toward segregating the races, or permit children to choose which public school to attend, as one can be virtually certain that most children would "choose" (out of fear or simple familiarity) to remain in the school they currently attend, thereby thwarting the constitutional requirement that the schools be desegregated.[12]

More than this the Constitution does not require. It does not, for example, demand that all schools within a district or other area contain the same percentages of white and Negro children. Aside from the inconvenience and risk to which any such command would necessarily subject children of all races, especially minorities, the Constitution does not dictate (nor does it forbid) that all schools be demographically identical, but rather that they not be intentionally segregated on the basis of race.[13] We realize that even with a year's grace period, the transition we require today will be challenging to all concerned.[14] However, the Constitution requires nothing less. It is long past time it was enforced.

NOTES

1. Public schools basically did not exist in the South, and in the North, school—where there was one—generally was in session no more than three months a year, and was not compulsory.

2. Unlike the Thirteenth Amendment, ratified a scant two and a half years before the Fourteenth, and the Fifteenth, ratified two years after, the Fourteenth Amendment is not limited in terms to the protection of groups defined by race.

3. In fact "Negro schools" are notoriously inferior to "white schools" in facilities and faculty educational background. Plaintiffs understandably decline to rely on that disparity here, however, so as to obviate the need to prove such tangible inferiority school by school, nationwide. The facts that in virtually (perhaps literally) every case such proof would be probably available (if burdensome to produce), and that the situation is likely to remain as it is in that regard for the foreseeable future, would likely provide strong alternative support for our holding today. However, we do not rely on it, as it is clear that "mere" segregation would harm Negro children even if the facilities were in fact tangibly equal. Proof of any difference between the facilities provided whites and Negroes is not required today and is not to be required in the future. This aspect of the situation is also deplorable, but unnecessary to a successful segregation challenge.

4. 163 U.S. 537, 551.

5. In fact this Court has already recognized this, rendering reliance on *Plessy v. Ferguson* at this late date doubly courageous. In two cases decided in 1950, desegregating state law schools and universities despite the states' contention that equal facilities were provided for Negro students, the Court relied in substantial part on the consideration that interaction with students of races other than one's own enhanced the education one received. *McLaurin v. Board of Regents*, 339 U.S. 637, 641 (1950); *Sweatt v. Painter*, 339 U.S. 629, 634 (1950). (Any contention that the opportunity to interact with students of different races is less important earlier in life could not be taken seriously. Racial prejudice, and for that matter insecurity, are most effectively inculcated early on.) See also *Bu-*

chanan v. Warley, 245 U.S. 60 (1917), invalidating the "mere segregation" of Negroes and whites in terms of where they could live.

6. In the long run that is probably backwards, but a legislature could rationally believe it.

7. Whether *Korematsu* correctly applied its own test is not a question that needs answering today. God forbid that it ever will again.

8. Or, as Mr. Marshall of the NAACP Legal Defense Fund more bluntly put it during oral argument, "Put the dumb colored children in with the dumb white children and put the smart colored children in with the smart white children."

9. If "unthinkability" were a constitutional test, *Plessy* and other unconstitutional decisions would be justifiable on the ground that racial integration was widely deemed unthinkable throughout the nineteenth century.

10. Most conspicuous, perhaps, was the Declaration of Independence's first "self-evident truth," that "all Men are created equal." To the same effect, see 2 Del. Laws, ch. 53 (S. and J. Adams 1797); 1 N.C. Public Acts, ch. 22 (J. Iredell ed., F.X. Martin rev. 1804). See also *The Federalist* n. 57 (Madison):

> I will add, as a fifth circumstance in the situation of the House of Representatives, restraining them from oppressive measures, that they can make no law which will not have its full operation on themselves and their friends, as well as on the great mass of society.

To the same effect, see *Ervine's Appeal*, 16 Pa. 256, 268 (1851); *De Chastellux v. Fairchild*, 15 Pa. 18, 20 (1850). Sometimes this command of equal treatment was attributed to specific provisions, such as the Privileges and Immunities Clause of Article IV, summarized in *Toomer v. Witsell*, 334 U.S. 385, 395 (1948) ("It was designed to insure to a citizen of State A who ventures into State B the same privileges which the citizens of State B enjoy"); the Commerce Clause, see *Brown v. Maryland*, 12 Wheat. 419 (1827); and other clauses granting federal powers, see *McCulloch v. Maryland*, 4 Wheat. 316, 436 (1819), but the general command is probably most comfortably attributed to the Ninth Amendment, ratified in 1791 and designed to protect against federal infringement of rights analogous to those recognized elsewhere in the Constitution.

11. For example, elementary schools might be desegregated this fall, middle and high schools a year later. As noted above, children are born without racial prejudice and develop it only as their elders teach it to them.

12. Thus every child should be assigned to the public school nearest his home, subject only to genuine and neutrally applied considerations of existing building capacity. (It should go without saying that the fallback question, of which school a student is to attend in the event the one closest to his home is filled to capacity with children who live even closer to it than he, is one that cannot constitutionally be answered even in part on the basis of race but instead must also be determined by geography.) Moreover, whatever new schools are

built should be given a capacity sufficient to maximize the chances that over time every single child will be able to attend the school nearest his home.

13. Mr. Marshall made it clear in oral argument that the NAACP was not asking for anything beyond nonracially designated geographic schools zones, noting correctly that "in most Southern areas . . . there are very few areas that are predominantly one race or the other." In an area where most or all of the children are Negroes, however, a Negro child is unlikely to infer from the fact that most or all of his schoolmates are also Negroes that the state has placed them in a separate school because it believes them to be inferior.

Of course, the relative percentages (considered in the context of residential patterns) will often constitute the evidence most probative of segregatory intent. Moreover, if it can be proven that existing residential patterns are themselves the product of racially motivated government action, the state should be required to take whatever steps are necessary to approximate the situation that would have obtained in the schools in the absence of such unconstitutional action.

14. Should a majority of my colleagues persist in their present resolve to grant a grace period of indefinite length extending over a number of years, the transition is likely to become more difficult still.

MacKinnon, J., concurring in the judgment.

Beneath and beyond the victory for Black schoolchildren in these five cases—a step for all toward what Mr. Silas Hardrick Fleming, a plaintiff testifying in *Brown*, called "the light"[1]—lie hazards for the principle of equality under law and for the social equality it aims ultimately to promote.

The risk we run today is not of going too far too fast, as defendants fear, but of going too slowly and not far enough. Insuring a future consistent with the Fourteenth Amendment's purpose and promise, as my colleagues document and interpret it, calls not only for dismantling racially segregated public schools but for squarely facing why official separation on the basis of race ever was seen as consistent with a constitutional equality rule in the first place. This deeper history has roots and remains in legal concepts, as well as in the social dynamics and political events my colleagues report. Because this case requires us to define no less than what equality, as guaranteed in the Constitution, means, I write separately to draw out and repudiate this theoretical legacy, which began long before slavery on this continent.

Plaintiffs in these five cases argue that public school segregation on the basis of race, officially permitted or required, relegates Negro children to inferior status, denying them equal protection of the laws within the meaning of the Fourteenth Amendment by depriving them of equal educational opportunities. On reargument before this Court, plaintiffs[2] squarely challenge the rule of "separate but equal," as formulated in *Plessy v. Ferguson*, 163 U.S. 537 (1896), a transportation case under the aegis of which racially segregated public schools have been permitted so long as they were substantially equal in facilities. Plaintiffs argue, in this and in *Bolling v. Sharpe*, post, challenging racial segregation in schools in the nation's capital, that "separate but equal" is intrinsically inconsistent with the Fourteenth Amendment's guarantees of equality and due process of law.

Specifically, they contend that our rulings in *Sweatt v. Painter*, 339 U.S. 629 (1950), and *McLaurin v. Oklahoma State Regents*, 339 U.S. 637 (1950), effectively vitiate racial segregation in higher education even with equal facilities. Our principled opposition to drawing official race-based lines in *Shelley v. Kraemer*, 334 U.S. 1 (1948), and *Buchanan v. Warley*, 245 U.S. 60 (1917), a due process case; our repudiation in doctrine if not result of racial distinctions except in extremity of *Hirabayashi v. United States*, 320 U.S. 81 (1943), and *Korematsu v. United States*, 323 U.S. 214 (1944); and the larger backdrop of the emancipatory purpose of the Fourteenth Amendment as articulated in the *Slaughterhouse Cases*, 16 Wall. 36 (1872), properly understood, and *Strauder v. West Virginia*, 100 U.S. 303 (1879)—this context, they argue, compels a ruling in their favor. Given these precedents, they say the "separate but equal" rule of *Plessy* is incorrect on principle, out of step and out of line with our Fourteenth Amendment jurisprudence, and at the very least distinguishable from the cases before us. They also argue that its standards were unmet in the South Carolina and Virginia cases, in which educational facilities were concededly (one could add grotesquely) unequal.

The plaintiffs' principal argument is that *Plessy* was wrong the day it was decided: that to separate on the basis of race in the circumstances of these cases is intrinsically to treat equals unequally. Secondarily, even assuming the Fourteenth Amendment does not invalidate racial distinctions per se, they argue that the racial segregation of schools bears no reasonable relation to any valid legislative purpose or educational goal, given the predicate of the Equality Clause of the Fourteenth Amendment that intellectual capacity is equal by racial group.

The official defendants for their part do not explicitly argue that racial segregation in education is reasonable. Rather, they seek shelter under *Plessy*'s rule that racial segregation is permissible state behavior under the federal Constitution, supported by this Court's decisions in *Berea*, *Cumming*, and *Giles*. *Berea College v. Kentucky*, 211 U.S. 45 (1908) (finding school segregation statute does not violate due process when applied to a state-chartered corporation); *Giles v. Harris*, 189 U.S. 475 (1903) (refusing to remedy violation of Fifteenth Amendment right to vote by ordering Blacks put on voter registration lists); *Cumming v. Board of Education of Richmond County*, 175 U.S. 528 (1899) (holding denial of injunction against funding school for whites, where no equivalent school for Blacks existed, did not violate Equal Protection Clause). They claim, with emphasis varying among the cases at bar, that the

Fourteenth Amendment was never meant by its drafters or ratifiers to integrate public schools racially; that school segregation by race does not arise from or promote racial prejudice but was benevolently meant and "presented a way of life," Transcript of Oral Argument of Justin Moore, Dec. 10, 1952, at 25; that said segregation does no harm when educational facilities are materially equal; that there is no showing of individual harm to students in any of the cases; that state policy is powerless to affect whether individuals feel inferior; and that ending segregation would produce dislocation and chaos, interracial violence and social unrest. Finally, they assert that federalism mandates leaving to states and localities the policy choice of how to administer schools. In short, they do not defend segregated education as a reasonable classification, but rather contend that it is harmless and even constitutionally privileged.

We find for the plaintiffs in law and in fact in the state cases. No one on this Court supports the view that our doctrines of federalism permit states to do what the Equality Clause of the federal Constitution forbids them from doing.[3] In the District of Columbia case, we find no valid reason why federal authorities should be permitted to violate the constitutional equality principles to which states are held. In the process, my colleagues implicitly adopt a variety of positions on the legal meaning of equality. Convinced that emphasis is all, see *Bethlehem Co. v. State Board*, 330 U.S. 767, 780 (1947) ("In law also the emphasis makes the song") (Frankfurter, J.), I attempt to clarify my colleagues' common implicit substantive ground. I have also come to believe that it is difficult to err in speaking too plainly of who has done what to whom on this question.

I.

The question of the harm of school segregation by race where physical facilities are comparable (as in fact they seldom are) is the central question of this litigation. The Kansas court, where substantial equality of facilities was conceded, found as fact in *Brown* (finding no. 8):

> Segregation of white and colored children in public schools has a detrimental effect upon the colored children. The impact is greater when it has the sanction of the law; for the policy of separating the races is usually interpreted as denoting the inferiority of the negro group. A sense of inferiority affects the motivation of a child to learn. Segregation with the

sanction of law, therefore, has a tendency to [retard] the educational and mental development of negro children and to deprive them of some of the benefits they would receive in a racial[ly] integrated school.

Brown v. Board of Education of Topeka, 98 F. Supp. 797 (D. Kan. 1951) (No. T-316).

In a similar finding left undisturbed by the Supreme Court of Delaware, the chancellor in the Delaware case found as fact that "in our Delaware society," state segregation in education "itself results in the negro children, as a class, receiving educational opportunities which are substantially inferior to those available to white children otherwise similarly situated," *Belton v. Gebhart,* 87 A.2d 862, 865 (1952)—in essence finding that racially separate schools, ipso facto, provide inferior educational opportunities for Black children.

Expert witnesses also testified without contradiction in the South Carolina case, *Briggs v. Elliott,* that compulsory racial segregation injured Negro students by impairing their ability to learn, deterring their personality development, depriving them of equal status in the school community, destroying their self-respect, denying their full opportunity for democratic social development, subjecting them to the prejudices of others, and stamping them with a badge of inferiority. Brief for Appellants in nos. 1, 2, and 4 and for Respondents in no. 10 on Reargument at 29. The same view of racial segregation in higher education was reflected in the opinions of this Court in the *Sweatt* and *McLaurin* cases. Certainly, it is difficult to see how the educational deprivation done by separate education with equal facilities that intrinsically harms graduate and professional students does no injury to younger children. The reverse is more likely to be true.

This record documents injuries to public education by official action done through injury to the children's status as human beings in society. In my view, it is a misnomer to label these injuries "psychological," if by that is meant that the harm to equality is to be found in the children's inner response to the conditions imposed upon them, rather than in the imposition of the conditions themselves. The damage to which the experts testified in these cases[4] is one measure of the consequences of authoritative relegation of equals to a social status of inferiority. Being categorically ranked low among humanity on a hierarchical scale on a group basis by operation of law is a harm in itself: the quintessential harm of official inequality. It is always harmful, although some individuals deal with it better than others. We dare not fall into the trap of *Plessy*, in which whether or not "the colored race chooses to put that construction upon it," 163 U.S. at 551, is seen to constitute the harm or not. It is the construction put upon the colored children by the imposed arrangements that constitutes the harm of the segregation that forms the core of the injury to equality rights in these cases. Nothing the children thought or felt—their construction of it, as it were—created or could have changed that.

Indeed, what the children were found to have thought and felt was simply what that practice, in social reality, meant: they were assumed inferior, their presence contaminating, to white children. The children's response is also one measure of what that practice, in reality, did to them: it imposed inferior status and often inferior education on them in life. The tracks left on their hearts and minds is real damage; it is useful to have it documented. But the injury itself is done *to* them in the outward social world they inhabit, not in any sense *by* them or solely inside their heads.

The equality injury, hence the violation of law in these cases, thus lies not in the children's response to the state practice but in the practice itself. When a man is cut, he bleeds. Here, it is as if experts had to be called in to study the blood before the cut that produced it would be seen to be an injury. Simply put, the injury is one thing, the damages are another. Although injuries to equality typically do inflict, inter alia, psychic harm, inequality injuries are not subjective ones. Even if Black children do not think they are inferior, and many do not think so, they are still injured by the school segregation that makes that official assumption about them on a racial basis. That injury happens in the real world. The inequality takes place not when the children feel hurt by the unequal arrangements. That they often do is one real and intolerable measure of its damage. But they feel hurt because they are *being* hurt. The inequality takes place in material, not merely psychic, space. In these cases, the inequality inheres in the official imposition of unequal status on equal persons—that is, in the arrangement of racial segregation itself.

II.

Mr. Justice Harlan, early in his dissent in *Plessy* vindicated today, observed: "Every one knows that the statute in question had its origin in the purpose, not so much to exclude white persons from railroad cars occupied by blacks, as to exclude colored people from coaches occupied by or assigned to white persons. . . . The thing to accomplish was, under the guise of giving equal accommodations for whites and blacks, to compel the latter to keep to themselves while traveling in railroad passenger coaches. No one would be so wanting in candor as to assert the contrary." 163 U.S. at 557. The candor to which he referred could not be taken for granted, beginning with the *Plessy* majority. So, too, here. The statutes in question in these cases originated in, and accomplish, not a symmetrical exclusion of all children from all but their own racial group, but an exclusion of Black children from schools for whites. The thing for white people to accomplish, under the guise of equal educational facilities for all, was to keep white children, in particular white girls—in large part for reasons that implicate that distinguishability that makes the color line, hence white privilege, visually possible—from being educated with Black children, in particular young Black men.[5]

The segregation in the cases before us is no more equal a separation than the one in *Plessy*. The reason it is unequal is not that Black children felt bad about themselves as a result of it. One reason is, as plaintiffs put the point on reargument, "that the plain purpose and effect of segregated education is to perpetuate an inferior status for Negroes which is America's sorry heritage from slavery." Brief for Appellants in nos. 1, 2, and 4 and for Respondents in no. 10 on Reargument at 17. The point and premise of segregation laws, as they argue, was "to organize the community upon the basis of a superior white and an inferior Negro caste." Id. at 50. Segregation excludes Negro children from state public schools created for the children of dominant white groups. "Such a practice can only be continued on a theory that Negroes, *qua* Negroes, are inferior to all other Americans." Id. at 198. The United States recognized the same reality when it observed in these cases that the school systems litigated presented an instance of "[t]he subordinate position occupied by Negroes in this country as a result of governmental discriminations ('second-class citizenship,' as it is sometimes called)." Brief for the United States as Amicus Curiae at 31. The American Jewish Congress, in unvarnished terms, called the racial segregation of schools in these cases what it plainly is: "white supremacy."[6]

The point is that the evil of segregation we confront here is one not of mere differentiation but of hierarchy; not a categorization as such but an imposed inferiority; not an isolated event but an integral feature of a cumulative historical interlocking social and legal system; not a separation chosen by a subordinated group to seek their equality, but a segregation forced on them by a dominant group; not an abstract distinction made on the basis of race, but an officially imposed ordering of one race, white, over another, people of African descent. And note that "white," as pointed out by Thurgood Marshall in oral argument, is undefined by these school systems except by default; in South Carolina, he observed, the term in practice means everyone but Blacks. Transcript of Oral Argument of Thurgood Marshall, Dec. 9, 1952, at 12–13.[7] In these cases, Black students are treated one way, worse, and everyone else is treated another, better. The sting of the state-imposed segregation we invalidate in these cases is that it is imposed by white people on Black people and imposes and validates daily the discredited theory of superiority of the so-called white race over people of African descent—the same theory that long served to justify the institution of ownership of Black people by white people as their chattel property.

The cautionary note being sounded is that we avoid taking the ringing indictment of the Brief of the United States as Amicus Curiae at 13 of "separate and hence unequal" schools, or their equally correct observation that "'separate but equal' is a contradiction in terms," id. at 17, as stand-ins for the concrete conditions and groups and history and context and substantive social status—the reality of experience—that give these phrases their meaning. Those conditions, to repeat, have been the institutionalization by white Americans of inferior status for persons of African heritage, a rule of white supremacy. The policies invalidated today institutionalize white supremacy as public policy in education. Because supremacy of one race over another is inimical to an equality rule, we invalidate these policies. A premise of human equality and a premise of natural group-based hierarchy or valid racial social ranking cannot occupy the same space.

This is not to limit the Fourteenth Amendment's reach to these facts alone, but to establish that it is group dominance in historical space that is the enemy of equality. Our observation in *United States v. Carolene Products*, 304 U.S. 144, 153 n.4 (1938), that, for purposes of equal protection solicitude, the treatment of "discrete and insular minorities" deserves heightened scrutiny compared with other types of official distinctions, is animated by this same awareness. Group-based disadvantages other than to Negroes have been, *see, e.g. Yick Wo v. Hopkins*, 118

U.S. 356 (1886), and, when appropriate, will be prohibited. Expectably, which groups are "discrete and insular minorities," even whether it is only minorities who are unequally treated, has changed over time, *see e.g., Leser v. Garnett,* 258 U.S. 130 (1921) (holding the Nineteenth Amendment granting suffrage to women validly part of the federal constitution), and will properly continue to evolve.[8]

Conversely, however, not every official notice of the situation of Black people will be prohibited as discriminatory, although all, because of a history that is far from over, must be treated with "immediate suspicion," *Korematsu,* 323 U.S. at 216, and grave concern. But an embargo on official notice of race could, given widespread racial inequality, preclude official attention to the very substantive realities of racism that have made us rightly suspicious of race as a designation. In sum, our ruling today should be read to hold not that separate is inherently unequal in the abstract, but that forced segregation of Black from white, in a racially hierarchical society of white supremacy, is a practice of inequality and cannot stand.

Fortunately, the Fourteenth Amendment was passed to dismantle precisely the substantive reality of imposed systematic inferiority of Black to white. More words on the history of the Thirteenth, Fourteenth, and Fifteenth Amendments can scarcely make this clearer. As we noted in *Strauder*: "The very fact that colored people are singled out . . . is practically a brand upon them, affixed by the law, an assertion of their inferiority, and a stimulant to race prejudice," 100 U.S. at 308. *Strauder* speaks further of the Fourteenth Amendment's granting "the right to exemption from unfriendly legislation against them distinctively as colored, exemption from legal discriminations, implying inferiority in civil society," 100 U.S. at 307–08. In *Ex Parte Virginia,* 100 U.S. 339, 344–45 (1879), we stated that "[o]ne great purpose of these amendments was to raise the colored race from that condition of inferiority and servitude in which most of them had previously stood, into perfect equality of civil rights with all other persons within the jurisdiction of the States." And in *Virginia v. Rives,* speaking of the Reconstruction statutes, we noted that "[t]he plain object of these statutes, as of the Constitution which authorized them, was to place the colored race, in respect of civil rights, upon a level with whites." 100 U.S. 313, 318 (1879).

Many of our precedents in this area can be read as rejecting abstraction severed from and insisting on the substantive content of concrete inferiority socially imposed. In a salient recent example given surprisingly little attention in my colleagues' opinions today, this Court in *Shelley v. Kraemer* firmly grasped substance and repelled the argument from abstraction in rejecting the potential equality of application of restrictive covenants against any race. We said: "It is . . . no answer [to plaintiff's claim] . . . to say that the courts may also be induced to deny white persons rights of ownership and occupancy on grounds of race or color. Equal protection of the laws is not achieved through indiscriminate imposition of inequalities." 334 U.S. 1, 21–22 (1948). Put affirmatively, we have long rejected a presumption of hierarchy among humans on particular group grounds as the gravamen of the Fourteenth Amendment's Equality Clause. Put another way, we must not take the road of building a better Fourteenth Amendment law of "rational" discrimination on the ashes of *Plessy*, vitiating segregation today but leaving standing *Plessy*'s rule of "reasonable" differentiation—a rule of categorization by correspondence that makes equality law tautologous with social inequality rather than resistant to it.

III.

It is time to admit that the notion of equality that found race-based segregation by law congenial has ancient roots and a beachhead in our jurisprudence in the "similarly situated" requirement. Well before *Plessy*, this Court in *Barbier v. Connolly* stated that while "class legislation, discriminating against some and favoring others, is prohibited, . . . legislation which, in carrying out a public purpose, is limited in its application, if within the sphere of its operation it affects alike all persons similarly situated, is not within the amendment." 113 U.S. 27, 32 (1885). In 1920, we similarly distinguished the wide legislative discretion to classify from that which the Fourteenth Amendment prohibits in these terms: "[T]he classification must be reasonable, not arbitrary, and must rest upon some ground of difference having fair and substantial relation to the object of the legislation, so that all persons similarly circumstanced shall be treated alike." *F. S. Royster Guano Co. v. Virginia*, 253 U.S. 412, 415 (1920). See also *Hayes v. Missouri*, 120 U.S. 68, 71 (1887).

This "similarly situated" test will be recognized as a restatement of Aristotle's principle of formal equality, long thought axiomatic, even obvious, that "things that are alike should be treated alike, while things that are unalike should be treated unalike in proportion to their unalikeness," Aristotle, *The Nicomachean Ethics* V.3, 1131a–b (W. Ross, trans., 1925), a notion recently embraced and formulated by Joseph T. Tussman and Jacobus tenBroek, "The Equal Protection of the Laws," 37 *Calif. L. Rev.* 341 (1949), while *Plessy* was still good law.

The logic of Aristotle, who supported slavery, was followed precisely in *Plessy*: segregating those seen as likes from unlikes constitutes equality. In the racist mind, race is always a relevant unalikeness, and nothing in the notion of treating "likes alike, unlikes unalike" requires the assumption of equal humanity across racial or any other lines, or clarifies when (if ever) race is relevant to policy and when it is not. This inherited approach to equality from the Greeks through the Enlightenment, one that has been treated as common sense in our law until today, ratifies legal categories that are hand in glove with social inequalities. In the present cases, a rule of "likes alike" would support segregated schools, overlaying "unalikeness" of race from nineteenth-century theories of "scientific racism" drawing on Darwin and Spencer that purported to prove race-based intellectual inferiority and superiority with schools legally divided on the same lines. Just as consistently, Aristotle's equality reasoning justified the Nuremberg laws of the Third Reich. See Ulrich Scheuner, "Der Bleichheitsgedanke in der volkischen Verfassungsordnung," 99 *Zeitschrift für die gesamte Staatswissenschaft* 245, 260–67 (1939). Similar treatment—ultimately, extermination—was contemplated for all Jews, seen as "alike" by virtue of being Jewish and "unlike" Aryans. The American Veterans Committee aptly observes that the segregation at bar is cut of the same cloth as the racism over which we just prevailed in World War II. Brief of American Veterans Committee Inc., Amicus Curiae, at 2. See also *The Yellow Spot* (1936) (documenting official segregation and other inequalities imposed on Jews in Germany).

Nothing in *Plessy*'s equality rule requires an assumption that all racial groups possess equal humanity or equal capacities. Nothing precludes imposing by law a condition of inferiority upon a group that is deemed inferior in society—in fact the opposite is true. Nothing in its notion of "rationality" stops giving a group less on the grounds that, having been given less in the past, it might appear less deserving today. Nothing, in other words, precludes law from simply replicating the consequences of social inequality and calling that "equal protection of the laws." Rather, the *Plessy* rule encourages, and *Plessy* achieved, precisely that.

Examples of the circular relation between this equality rule and unequal social reality are numerous. The thin guise of equal facilities that has been formally necessary for confronting the "separate but equal" rule as such is one. The "separate but equal" doctrine placed litigants challenging segregation as such in the perverse position of having to show that segregated facilities were equal when, because of the racism that produced the segregation that they wished to confront, facilities virtually never were equal. To have to deny an inevitable component of the harm of segregation in order to be able to challenge its legality is a litigation posture engendered by the approach to equality that produced the legal fiction that, under existing conditions of inequality, imposed separation along the same unequal lines can be equal in the first instance. It plays out the "similarly situated" approach in requiring that litigants must first present themselves as being in an equal situation before they are heard to complain of unequal treatment—when, in fact, due to the very inequality they challenged, they could not be "similarly situated." To be required first to have material equality before one can complain of unequal treatment, and then be told that due to material equality there is no harm, is a classic vicious circle.[9]

Plessy's "reasonableness" test is another example. In *Plessy*, separation with equal facilities was justified as having a reasonable basis in the "established usages, customs and traditions," 163 U.S. at 550, of the surrounding society. On the sad record before us, experts were thus constrained to document, See Transcript of Oral Argument of Louis L. Redding, Dec. 11, 1952, at 25, what should go without saying: there are no racial differences in inborn intellectual capacity. There is, thus, no rational basis for educational differentiation on a racial basis. However, an ominous indication that the reasonableness approach of *Plessy* is not interred can be found in the amicus brief for the United States on reargument here. The government speculates that, had the issue of rationality of separate schools been raised shortly after the Civil War, "constitutional justification for such action might conceivably have been found in the illiteracy and retarded social and economic status of a race so recently liberated from the bonds of slavery." Supplemental Brief for the United States on Reargument at 142. In other words, social inequality could rationalize legal inequality.

Applying *Plessy*, the doll studies in this record, Testimony of Dr. Kenneth Clark, Record of Trial at 2:87096, *Briggs v. Elliott*, 103 F. Supp. 920 (E.D.S.C. Mar. 13, 1952) (No. Civ. T-316); Appendix to Appellants'

Briefs, The Effects of Segregation and the Consequences of Desegregation: A Social Science Statement at 3–7; Transcript of Oral Argument of John W. Davis, Dec. 10, 1952, at 6–7, could be read not as we do, to show the damage of segregation, but as finding a race-based inferiority or difference, to justify segregation. Permitting what might be called rational discrimination was what *Plessy* was all about. By implication, under *Plessy*, when enough social equality had been achieved over imposed inequality, official segregation would be rendered "unreasonable." Equality, on this approach to reasonableness, could be achieved by law only when it was no longer socially necessary to seek it.

We are not constrained to reproduce the inequality the Fourteenth Amendment aimed to end. To escape the hall of mirrors—the endless regress in which inequality in society makes "rational" inequality by law, which imposes inequality on society, which makes "rational" further inequality by law—we must take a substantive principled contextual approach. Guided by a record of harm, we need not pretend not to know as judges what we know as members of our society. Treating equals equally does not reduce to treating likes alike. The value of groups may lie in their variety, just as the value of individuals may lie in their singularity. But it is not for us to judge their value. An equality rule presumes it to be equal. Our equality question is not whether groups are alike or unalike in the abstract, but whether, assuming human equality on a group basis, a practice or statute promotes the social disadvantage of a historically disadvantaged or subordinated group. This contextualized determination mobilizes the clear purpose of the framers of the Fourteenth Amendment to *promote* equality, not merely to preside passively over a Constitution that reflects social inequality by sorting people by law in the same order into which an unequal society has ranked them. That *Plessy* would see that process as making a regulation reasonable, hence equal, is what we overrule when we overrule *Plessy* today.

On the view that "[t]hat which is unequal in fact cannot be equal in law," Brief on Behalf of ACLU et al. as Amicus Curiae at 5, emphasizing one part of our tradition and rejecting another, in an attempt to insure that the reality of social inequality never again becomes a constitutional reason that equality rights can be denied, this analysis of basic principles is offered so that, fifty years from now, we have no cause to wonder why nothing has changed.

IV.

Change is not slow; it is resistance to change that makes it take a long time. At oral argument, Kansas laudably conceded that eliminating segregation would not have serious administrative or other consequences for them. The Supreme Court of Delaware in *Gebhart v. Belton*, 91 A.2d 137, 149 (1952), having already ordered admission of Black children into formerly white schools, observed that "[t]o require the plaintiffs to wait another year under present conditions would be in effect partially to deny them that to which we have held they are entitled." In Delaware, they have been attending those schools without incident. For these same reasons, I would give the schools a maximum of one year from the date of this decree to eliminate race-based segregation from their school systems. On account of segregated schools, let there be not one more "dream deferred." See Langston Hughes, "Harlem [2]," *Montage of a Dream Deferred* (1951).[10]

N O T E S

1. Describing why he "got into the suit whole soul and body," Mr. Fleming, said: "[M]y point was that not only I and my children are craving light; the entire colored race is craving light. And the only way to reach the light is to start our children together in their infancy and they come up together." Record of Trial at 109–10, *Brown v. Board of Education of Topeka*, 98 F. Supp. 797 (D. Kan. 1951) (No. T-316).

2. "Plaintiffs" here refers to the original moving parties in these consolidated cases, Appellants in *Brown* (No. 1), *Briggs* (No. 2), and *Davis* (No. 4), and Respondents in *Belton* (No. 10).

3. Defendant Topeka School Board, having determined to integrate racially in the midst of the litigation, did not resist the claim of the *Brown* plaintiffs beyond trial, taking acquiescence in the plaintiffs' position far enough to have raised the question of mootness. See Transcript of Oral Argument of Robert L. Carter on Reargument, Dec. 8, 1953, at 1–4 (responding to questions by Justice Frankfurter on reargument). Topeka sought only gradualism in the relief ordered. Brief for the Board of Education, Topeka, Kansas, on Questions Propounded by the Court at 2. The State of Kansas, while not defending racial segregation as a policy and "grant[ing] that segregation may not be the ethical or political ideal," defended its statute permitting local choice of racial segregation before the Supreme Court on the ground that constitutional law "permits

determination of state and local policy to be made on state and local levels." Brief for the State of Kansas on Reargument at 14, 56. We reject this argument from federalism. Equality in public schools is not an ethical or political matter alone, but one that has been made a matter of constitutional right by the Fourteenth Amendment.

4. See Testimony of Dr. Kenneth Clark and Dr. David Krech in *Briggs*; Testimony of Louisa Holt and Hugh Speer in *Brown*; Testimony of M. Brewster Smith and Isidor Chein in *Davis*.

5. This widely known but little acknowledged motivation for and function of segregation was alluded to obliquely by the American Jewish Congress in discussing the role of segregation statutes by quoting a Kentucky court's reference to "the general feeling everywhere prevailing [that] the Negro, while respected and protected in his place, is not and cannot be a fit associate for white girls." Brief of American Jewish Congress as Amicus Curiae at 13 (quoting *Axton Fisher Tobacco Co. v. The Evening Post*, 169 Ky. 64 (1916)). The missing persons in the Kentucky court's analysis—Black women in "the Negro," at least the entire Black community in "everywhere"—serve to highlight the subliminal obsession.

6. Brief of American Jewish Congress as Amicus Curiae at 14 argues that the enforced separation of races affirms "white dominance," and further that racial segregation of schools incorporates the doctrine of "white supremacy" into the provision of facilities for citizens, id. at 20.

7. The racial particulars have varied arbitrarily, see *Gong Lum v. Rice*, 275 U.S. 78 (1927) (permitting state to define race so as to send student of Chinese descent to schools for Black children), but what does not vary, in segregated systems, is the exclusion of Black children from schools principally for whites.

8. The disenfranchisement and exclusion of women as a group from public life and their often lower status in private life suggest that it is not entirely due to lesser numbers that so-called minority groups are discriminated against or can be kept unequal.

9. Treating "unlikes unalike" in the Aristotelian language could even have gone beyond "separate but equal" and supported unequal facilities—justified, for example, by lower performance, even if that lower performance was shown to be due to poor facilities. In reality, if not in doctrine, the *Plessy* rule accomplished exactly this.

10.
> What happens to a dream deferred?
> Does it dry up
> Like a raisin in the sun?
> Or fester like a sore—
> And then run?
> Does it stink like rotten meat?

Or crust and sugar over—
like a syrupy sweet?
Maybe it just sags
like a heavy load.
Or does it explode?
Langston Hughes, "Harlem [2]," *Montage of a Dream Deferred* (1951).

McConnell, J., concurring in the judgment.

These cases force us to confront a moral, political, and legal issue that divides this nation more deeply than any other. Throughout the southern region of these United States, it is customary for children attending public schools to be assigned to classrooms segregated according to race. Similar laws require segregation in other public and private facilities, from swimming pools to municipal buses to courtrooms. In these states, racial segregation is a deeply entrenched social institution. By contrast, throughout the northern and western regions—and among many citizens even in the South—racial segregation has come to be recognized as a serious injustice. Segregation, it is believed, rests on the untenable idea that people of one group are inherently superior to those of another group, by virtue of nothing more than the accident of race. It falls to this Court to determine whether the system of segregated education that prevails in the schools operated by respondent Boards of Education is consistent with the Fourteenth Amendment.

This Court must approach such a question with profound humility. No one familiar with this Court's record in the field of human rights could believe that the members of this Court are especially blessed with moral foresight. It was this Court's decision in *Dred Scott v. Sandford*[1] that, on the basis of an almost fanciful reading of constitutional text, stripped Congress of its ability to confine the expansion of slavery. It was this Court's decision in *Plessy v. Ferguson*[2] that (as will be explained more fully below) turned its back on the original promise of the Fourteenth Amendment and inaugurated the era of Jim Crow. It was this Court that, in *Cumming v. Board of Education*,[3] effectively abandoned even the requirement that separate schools be equal, and that, in *Berea College v. Kentucky*,[4] forced even a private religious educational institution to segregate white students from black. It was this Court, in *Giles v. Harris*,[5] that eviscerated the Fifteenth Amendment and left black Americans without the republican means of obtaining redress of grievances through voting and representation.

I do not invoke these ghosts to point the finger at benighted predecessors. I have no doubt that the honorable members of this Court who decided *Dred Scott*, *Plessy*, *Cumming*, *Berea College*, and *Giles* took their oaths of office to support the Constitution no less seriously than we do. No doubt they thought they were "calling the contending sides of a national controversy to end their national division by accepting a common mandate rooted in the Constitution."[6] I invoke this history only as a warning against the hubris that can infect any institution. There is no reason to assume that members of this Court today have moral compasses superior to those of our honorable predecessors, or of the legislators, executive officials, and voters who also have had to grapple with the problem we face today.

Fortunately, the awesome authority of constitutional judgment was not placed in the members of this Court on account of our superior moral judgment. We are not philosopher kings, but only judges, and we have authority only to enforce rules imposed by others—by the framers and ratifiers of the Constitution and its amendments. It is our responsibility, in the context of cases of a judicial nature, to keep faith with the historic commitments Americans have made as a people through the instrument of the Constitution. We approach that task not as prophets or as moralizers, but as interpreters of a document written in understandable language with discernible purposes.

Some litigants ask us to take note of studies by social scientists suggesting that segregated education is harmful to black schoolchildren. That we cannot do. No one has elected us to make decisions about effective pedagogy. And some litigants ask us to take note of the extraordinary importance of education, and to craft special rules of constitutional law appropriate to so vital an institution. That is similarly beyond our authority. The limits on state power embodied in the Fourteenth Amendment are not confined to education, or to matters of grave importance. If segregation is unconstitutional with respect to matters of importance, it is no less unconstitutional with respect to other matters to which the Constitution applies. Others ask us to postpone judgment, to make prudential accommodations for entrenched practices and popular prejudices. That, also, we cannot do. In a case properly before us, it is our obligation to give force and effect to the supreme law of the land. It is not our job to engage in social engineering.

Let us turn, then, to the Fourteenth Amendment, and to the legal issues in this case.

I.

It is common ground that the Fourteenth Amendment requires the
states to treat all citizens (and in some contexts, all persons) equally
with respect to their civil rights. As an original matter, this requirement
was most obviously embodied in the clause of the Fourteenth Amendment forbidding states to "make or enforce any law which shall abridge
the privileges or immunities of citizens of the United States." After
this Court's dubious interpretation of that clause in the *Slaughterhouse
Cases*,[7] however, Congress and this Court have treated the Equal Protection Clause as the textual locus of this requirement of equality. There
is no need in these cases to dwell on which of those clauses is the proper
source. In these cases, the respondent school boards do not dispute that,
as public entities, they are required to treat all persons equally with respect to their civil rights. Nor do the respondents deny that the benefits
of public education are among the civil rights protected by the Fourteenth Amendment. Their position is simply that segregation on the
basis of race is not inherently unequal.

It is obvious why respondents do not question the status of public
education as a civil right. If public education were not a civil right, then
it would follow that public school districts would have no obligation to
provide schools to black children that are materially equal to those provided to white children, or indeed to provide schools to black children
at all. Such an extreme position, however, would find no support in the
precedents of this Court or in the established practices of the southern
states. While they have not lived up to the obligation of providing
"equal" facilities in the past, the leaders of the southern states have un-
hesitatingly accepted the responsibility of doing so, and have represented to this Court that they are expeditiously improving the material
facilities at schools for black children.[8] To claim that segregation is not
inherently unequal has some support in practice and precedent; to
claim a right to deprive black children of any semblance of equal educational opportunity would be universally condemned.

This point bears attention, however, because the history of desegregation efforts in Congress during Reconstruction, to which I will turn

momentarily, shows that educated legal minds of that era had not yet arrived at a clear and consistent understanding of the status of publicly funded benefits as "civil rights." Although most defenders of segregated public education during Reconstruction based their argument on the legitimacy of "separate but equal" schools,[9] a not insignificant minority was of the opinion that the equality norms of the Fourteenth Amendment did not apply to schooling, because schooling was a mere benefit and not a "right."[10] To them, the equality dictates of the amendment applied to natural rights (such as the right to contract or to freedom from bodily injury) and to common law rights (such as the right of access to common carriers, or the right to bequeath property), but not to governmental largesse.[11] In the years since Reconstruction, however, the distinction between natural rights, common law rights, and rights grounded in positive law has ceased to define the limits of constitutional protection, if it ever did. Indeed, much of the challenge of interpreting the Bill of Rights today lies in preserving limits on governmental power that were crafted in an age of small government,[12] in the new era of widespread regulation and provision of welfare. Any attempt to confine civil rights to protection against overt acts of governmental coercion would be untrue to the historic purposes of the Bill of Rights. I take it as settled, therefore, that states do not have the authority to grant or withhold generally available public benefits on the basis of constitutionally forbidden considerations, even though those benefits are creatures of positive law and could be repealed at legislative whim.

The dispositive question, then, is whether segregation by race is a form of inequality within the meaning of the Fourteenth Amendment.

As distinguished counsel for the respondents acknowledges, the debates in Congress and the ratifying legislatures over the Fourteenth Amendment cast little light on the issue. Indeed, the substance and meaning of section one of the amendment were barely discussed. During debate over the Civil Rights Act of 1866, opponents charged that language prohibiting "discrimination in civil rights or immunities" would bar segregated schools[13]—as well as guarantee voting rights,[14] a step that moderate members of Congress were not yet prepared to take. Accordingly, to prevent "latitudinarian construction not intended," the House voted to remove this broad language from the statute.[15] Significantly, however, the framers of the Fourteenth Amendment used similarly broad language ("privileges or immunities of citizenship"); and once moderate members of Congress were assured that this language would not encompass political rights, they joined in providing the necessary two-thirds majority. It is impossible to tell, from this evidence, whether the language of the Fourteenth Amendment should be interpreted to require desegregation.

Defenders of segregation therefore rely heavily on the practice of the day. Schools in many northern states—and even in the District of Columbia—were racially segregated at the time of adoption of the Fourteenth Amendment, as were the galleries in the halls of Congress. Defenders of segregation argue, therefore, that the amendment should be read so as not to disturb that practice. On the other hand, Congress throughout the 1860s voted to desegregate transportation facilities in the District of Columbia, using language indicating that it understood segregation to be a form of "discrimination." In 1873, this Court interpreted an 1863 law forbidding "discrimination" as applying to the practice of racial segregation—and dismissed the railroad's argument that a policy of separate but equal is nondiscriminatory as "an ingenious attempt to evade a compliance with the obvious meaning of the requirement."[16] We cannot assume that the amendment was intended to perpetuate the practice of segregation.

Fortunately, we have more to go on than the legislative history of the amendment (which is silent) or the social practice of the day (which is ambiguous). Under section five of the amendment, Congress had authority to pass legislation to enforce the dictates of the new amendment, and thus had occasion to deliberate over its meaning. During the years immediately following ratification of the amendment, the constitutionality of segregation was the most hotly debated issue in Congress. Senator Charles Sumner of Massachusetts and Representative Benjamin Butler, chairman of the House Judiciary Committee, championed legislation that would prohibit racial segregation of common carriers, places of public accommodation, and public schools.[17] The debate was conducted in expressly constitutional terms, with proponents maintaining that segregation of public facilities was unconstitutional and thus that the bill was an appropriate measure to enforce section one of the amendment,[18] and opponents maintaining the opposite.[19] These debates provide the most direct evidence of the meaning ascribed to the Fourteenth Amendment during Reconstruction.

Opponents of the legislation defended segregation in much the same terms used today. Senator Orris Ferry of Connecticut argued that if the "same facilities, the same advantages, the same opportunities of education are given to the white child and the black child," it is not necessary that they "receive those equal facilities and advantages in the same school-room."[20] Senator Joshua Hill of Georgia denounced the proposition that "if there be a hotel for the entertainment of travelers, and two classes stop at it, and there is one dining room for one class and one for another, served alike in all respects, with the same accommodations, the same attention to the guests, there is anything offensive or anything that denies the civil rights of one more than the other."[21] Senator Augustus Merrimon of North Carolina conceded in debate that it would be "a violation of the fourteenth amendment" to exclude black children from the schools, but argued that "it is competent for the State to make a distinction on account of race or color if it shall make the same provision for the black race that it makes for the white race."[22]

In response, supporters of the desegregation bill argued that official segregation is a form of inequality barred by the Fourteenth Amendment. Sumner declared that "any rule excluding a man on account of his color is an indignity, an insult, and a wrong."[23] Representative John Lynch of Mississippi called racial segregation "an unjust and odious proscription."[24] Many Republicans called segregation a form of "caste" legislation.[25] Senator Frederick Frelinghuysen of New Jersey, floor leader for the bill after Sumner's death, called segregation by law "an enactment of personal degradation" and a form of "legalized disability or inferiority," effectively a denial of citizenship and a return to slavery.[26] The chairman of the House Judiciary Committee stated that supporters of the bill "have all come to a conclusion on this subject . . . that these are rights guaranteed by the Constitution to every citizen, and that every citizen of the United States should have the means by which to enforce them."[27] Senator George Edmunds of Vermont, responding to a proposal to allow separate but equal facilities, declared: "If there is anything in the fourteenth amendment it is exactly opposite to that."[28]

Other opponents of the legislation argued not that segregation was consistent with equality, but that the bill sought to impose "social equality" rather than the "civil equality" commanded by the amendment.[29] Senator Saulsbury of Delaware, for example, claimed that the intent of the bill was "to enforce familiarity, association, and companionship between the races."[30] Senator Blair of Missouri called the bill an attempt "to impose upon the whites of the community the necessity of a close association in all matters with the negroes."[31] Supporters of the bill responded that it applied only within public institutions—public schools and licensed facilities required by common law to be open to all persons without discrimination. Sumner stated that each person "is always free to choose who shall be his friend, his associate, his guest," but that when he "walks the streets . . . he is subject to the prevailing law of Equality."[32] Representative Chester Darrall of Louisiana tellingly quoted Confederate general P. G. T. Beauregard, commander at Fort Sumter, to the effect that

> It would not be denied that in traveling and at places of public resort we often share these privileges in common with thieves, prostitutes, gamblers, and others who have worse sins to answer for than the accident of color; but no one ever supposed that we thereby assented to the social equality of these people with ourselves. I therefore say that participation in these public privileges involves no question of social equality.[33]

The constitutionality of segregation under the newly enacted Fourteenth Amendment was thus squarely at issue in the debates over the Sumner-Butler bill. Throughout these debates, supporters of the Fourteenth Amendment, with few exceptions, argued that de jure segregation of public schools is unconstitutional. On ten recorded votes in the Senate and eight recorded votes in the House of Representatives, a majority voted to prohibit de jure school segregation.[34] Margins of victory were as high as 29-16 in the Senate[35] and 141-72 on a procedural vote in the House.[36] There were three recorded votes in the Senate and one in the House on motions to permit separate but equal facilities. All failed, by votes of 23-30, 21-26, and 16-28 in the Senate,[37] and by a vote of 91-114 in the House.[38] The only reason school desegregation legislation was not enacted is that, because of procedural problems and Democratic filibustering, a two-thirds vote was required at key junctures, and support for the measure fell just short of two-thirds.[39]

In the end, in 1875, Congress voted to bar segregation in common carriers and places of public accommodation, and to remain silent on the issue of schools.[40] For a variety of reasons, school desegregation was more controversial than desegregation of railroads or inns, and there were some legal doubts about whether access to the benefits of public spending (including publicly funded schools) was a matter of constitutional right. Segregation, however, was roundly rejected. A large majority, even at the end, voted against a separate-but-equal provision for schools. Despite its practical advantages to black students who often were relegated to inferior facilities, the majority believed that a separate-but-equal provision would "recognize a distinction in color which we ought not to recognize by any legislation of the Congress of the United States."[41] James Monroe, an Ohio Republican, stated that legislation authorizing racial segregation would set a "dangerous precedent." Julius Burrows, a Michigan Republican, stated that "[i]f you cannot legislate free schools, I prefer that the bill should be altogether silent upon the question until other times and other men can do the subject justice."[42] Black citizens, according to Monroe, "think their chances for good schools will be better under the Constitution with the protection of the courts than under a bill containing [a separate-but-equal clause]."[43]

The debate and votes on the Sumner-Butler bill demonstrate that segregated facilities were deemed inherently unequal, in violation of the Fourteenth Amendment. While Congress failed to enact section 5 legislation embodying that view, the opinions of legislators regarding the meaning of the amendment, expressed so soon after its enactment, are entitled to great weight by this Court. I therefore concur in the judgment of the Court that the assignment of pupils to separate schools or classrooms on account of their race is in violation of the Fourteenth Amendment.

It has been argued that, whatever the original meaning of the Fourteenth Amendment might be, segregation has been sanctioned by prior decisions of this Court, and that we are bound by principles of stare decisis to adhere to those precedents. We cannot accept that argument. The prior decisions of this Court are entitled to great respect, on account of the learning and attention that they bring to bear on the issues presented. The nine members of this Court at any given time should not lightly presume that our understanding of the Constitution exceeds that of our predecessors. But when we are convinced that an earlier decision is in error, we cannot perpetuate the error merely because it is embodied in the *U.S. Reports*. The legitimacy of constitutional judicial review rests on the supremacy of the Constitution, not the supremacy of this Court.

II.

One of the cases presented today, no. 8, *Bolling v. Sharpe*, presents a different constitutional question. Like the other respondent school boards, the school board in *Bolling* assigns pupils to separate schools on the basis of race. Unlike the other school boards, however, the respondent in *Bolling* is not an instrumentality of a state. It is an agency established by Congress pursuant to Art. I, §8, cl. 17, to govern the public schools of the District of Columbia. As such, it is not subject to the restrictions placed on "States" by the Fourteenth Amendment. In particular, it is not subject to the Equal Protection or Privileges or Immunities Clauses, which, we have held today, prohibit de jure segregation of public schoolchildren.

The suggestion that the Due Process Clause of the Fifth Amendment prohibits segregation of public facilities is without foundation. Even the most avid and creative opponents of segregation never made such an argument, and for good reason. The Due Process Clause is fundamentally a guarantee of procedural regularity: government may not deprive individuals of vested legal rights without proper legal authorization and nonarbitrary process in accordance with the established laws of the land. If the clause could be expanded to cover the case now before us, it would lose any determinate meaning. Lest the clause be converted into an all-purpose authorization for courts to second-guess any legislation of which they disapprove, it must be confined to its literal and traditional meaning.

Nor does the Privileges or Immunities Clause avail petitioners. Even assuming that there are certain rights that pertain to Americans as citizens, the plain language of the clause begins: "No State shall make or enforce any law. . . ." There is no provision of the Constitution preventing Congress from making or enforcing laws that abridge the privileges or immunities of citizens, except insofar as they are enumerated in the Bill of Rights or deducible from other provisions of the Constitution.

It has been argued that this Court should disregard the absence of pertinent constitutional text on the ground that it would be "unthinkable" that the same Constitution would impose a lesser duty on the federal than on the state governments. But having based our decision in *Brown* on the determination that the terms "equal protection of the laws" or "privileges or immunities of citizens" prohibit segregation, it would be passing strange to hold that the absence of those terms is without consequence here. The Constitution contains many limitations that apply only to the states,[44] or only to the federal government,[45] and this Court is not free to disregard those aspects of the constitutional design.

The decision of the framers of the Fourteenth Amendment to impose its limitations only on the states, far from being "unthinkable," reflects their understanding of the institutional capacities of various units of government within our system. From the beginnings of this nation, the states have been understood as the principal repositories of popular will, and hence of republican government, precisely because of their relatively small size and the closeness that can exist between the people and their elected leaders. The federal government, while less immediately responsive to the popular will, encompasses a broader and more diverse set of interests, beliefs, groups, and loyalties—what Madison called a "multiplicity of factions." See *The Federalist*, no. 10. By virtue of this greater diversity, the federal government is less likely to countenance the systematic oppression of minority groups within our midst. The experience of the framers of the Fourteenth Amendment, during both the Civil War and Reconstruction, confirmed this understanding. Congress, they believed, was the institution least likely to engage in oppression of minorities, and most likely to serve as an effective guarantor of the equal protection of the laws and the privileges and immunities of citizens. Accordingly, they did not consider it necessary to impose judicially enforceable constitutional constraints on Congress in this regard.

Moreover, the framers of the Fourteenth Amendment might well have believed that imposition of such constraints on Congress would be counterproductive. What constitutes "equal protection of the laws" or the "privileges or immunities of citizens" is not always obvious. It was the experience of the framers of the Fourteenth Amendment that this Court, in particular, was able to subvert basic freedoms in the name of enforcing them. For example, this Court protected slavery against legitimate congressional limitation by an expansive interpretation of the Due Process Clause. It was no accident that the framers of the Fourteenth Amendment assigned the task of enforcing the Fourteenth Amendment to Congress, and not to this Court.[46] It is not difficult to imagine future conflicts in which Congress might determine that particular practices or laws—for example, favoring members of previously oppressed minorities, or protecting the free exercise of religion against formally neutral laws—are needed to fulfill the broader purposes of the Fourteenth Amendment, while this Court might hold that they violate the Amendment. The framers of the Fourteenth Amendment evidently made the judgment that in such a conflict, the decisions of Congress are more likely to reflect a proper balancing of interests than the decisions of this Court. In any event, this Court must exercise particular self-restraint when the question presented is the scope of our own authority over Congress. Such authority cannot arise by inference—let alone in the teeth of the constitutional text.

In this case, however, it is not necessary to reach the constitutional argument. No act of Congress has ever authorized or required that the schools of the District of Columbia be segregated. The structural logic that explains the decision of the framers not to impose the strictures of the Equal Protection Clause or the Privileges or Immunities Clause on Congress does not extend to subordinate federal agencies. They do not represent diverse constituencies, and might well indulge the impulse to oppress those for whom they lack political affinity. As a matter of statutory interpretation, therefore, federal courts should interpret the silences and ambiguities of federal legislation so as to avoid anomalous conflicts between the rights of citizens within the federal sphere and the rights of citizens elsewhere. Federal courts should not presume that Congress has delegated the authority to depart from general principles of equal protection of the laws to subordinate agencies without a clear statement to that effect.

I concur in the judgment in *Bolling* on the ground that respondent school board of the District of Columbia lacks statutory authority to segregate the children in its schools by race.

III.

Finally, it is necessary to address the question of remedy. While the details of injunctive relief must be left to the district courts in each case, it is appropriate to offer general guidance.

First, there is no warrant for delay in desegregation. Compliance with the dictates of the Constitution may well be emotionally disruptive to people long accustomed to racially segregated public facilities. But delay can only exacerbate the transition. In much of the affected region, there is little residential segregation; accordingly, desegregation can be accomplished through simple adoption of neighborhood schools. To delay implementation might invite flight to segregated communities, which will make genuine desegregation far more complicated. It would be ironic if the courts stayed implementation of desegregation now, when it would be relatively straightforward, only to find—a decade or more from now—that ending de jure segregation would have little practical effect.

Second, the constitutional command is that states may not treat citizens differently according to their race. It has been suggested that actual integrated *results*—mixed schools—are needed in order to eradicate prejudice and accustom young Americans to living as equals with members of other races. That may well be a worthy objective; but it is not required by the Constitution. So long as the state employs racially neutral pupil assignment policies, the Constitution is satisfied. As Representative John Lynch, a black congressman from Mississippi, put the point during the debate over the Sumner-Butler bill:

> The colored people in asking the passage of this bill just as it passed the Senate do not thereby admit that their children can be better educated in white than in colored schools; nor that white teachers because they are white are better qualified to teach than colored ones. But they recognize the fact that the distinction when made and tolerated by law is an unjust and odious proscription; that you make their color a ground of objection, and consequently a crime. This is what we most earnestly protest against.

The problem, he said, is "legislative compulsion."[47]

Third, courts must scrutinize pupil assignment policies to ensure that ostensibly neutral policies have not been crafted as a subterfuge to produce segregation. For example, genuine freedom of choice plans, such as magnet school programs, are facially permissible and may even have integrative effects. But if a school district were to assign students by default to schools with children of their own race, this would not satisfy the Constitution, even if students were given the legal right to transfer to the other school. Similarly, neighborhood school policies are facially permissible and can serve many community-building purposes. But if a school district were to gerrymander attendance boundaries to produce artificially segregated schools, this would not satisfy the Constitution. The question in every case is whether the state has classified or segregated pupils according to race, or employed ostensibly neutral criteria for the purpose of classifying or segregating pupils according to race.

The Fourteenth Amendment's promise of equality before the law has been long in coming to fulfillment. Lacking effectual political support, civil rights enforcement waned after 1876. Social Darwinism and "scientific" racism took hold among the academic and legal elite. The legal climate changed dramatically in the last two decades of the nineteenth century. Black citizens were progressively disenfranchised, through more and more brazen stratagems. Even as northern and western states brought their schools into compliance with equality dictates under their own constitutions and laws, southern states boldly began to write segregation into their statutes and state constitutions. Common carriers and places of public accommodation, which were officially desegregated during Reconstruction, became increasingly segregated in the decades following 1876. As of 1875, not a single state required common carriers to segregate their facilities. The segregation law upheld in *Plessy* was enacted in 1890; the first such law in the land was passed only in 1887. After this Court gave its approval to segregation in *Plessy* and to disenfranchisement in *Giles* and other cases, these innovative policies swept the southern states, to the point that today they seem as traditional as hoopskirts and juleps.

In a constitutional system, it is incumbent upon us to evaluate the practices and prejudices of our day against the higher law of the Constitution—to determine whether we are keeping faith with the commitments that "We, the People" made to ourselves. For many decades, those commitments have been breached. It is time to set the clock back.

NOTES

1. 60 U.S. 393 (1857).
2. 163 U.S. 537 (1896).
3. 175 U.S. 528 (1899).
4. 211 U.S. 45 (1908).
5. 189 U.S. 475 (1903).
6. Future courts will no doubt wish to use this quotation.
7. 83 U.S. (16 Wall.) 36 (1873).
8. There were factual findings to that effect in the Kansas, South Carolina, Virginia, and Delaware cases. See 98 F. Supp. 797, 798; 103 F. Supp. 920, 921; 103 F. Supp. 337, 341; 91 A.2d 137, 149.
9. See, for example, this colloquy between Senator Oliver Morton of Indiana and Senator Augustus Merrimon of North Carolina:

> *Mr. MORTON.* If I understand the scope of the Senator's question he now admits, in effect, . . . that if the State law excludes the colored

children from the schools entirely, that is a violation of the four-teenth amendment.

Mr. MERRIMON. I admit that with all its force. But the point I make is this, that it is competent for the State to make a distinction on account of race or color if it shall make the same provision for the black race that it makes for the white race.

2 *Cong. Rec.* app. 359 (1874)

10. See, e.g., *Cong. Globe*, 42d Cong., 2d Sess. 3189–90 (1872) (Sen. Trumbull); id. at app. 5 (Sen. L. Morrill); 2 *Cong. Rec.* 453 (1874) (Rep. Atkins); id. at 419 (Rep. Herndon); id. at 405 (Rep. Durham).

11. See *Cong. Globe*, 42d Cong., 2d Sess. 3191 (1872) (Sen. Trumbull).

12. It is significant to note that the Bill of Rights originally applied only to the federal government, at a time when the enumerated powers of Congress were understood as quite limited. Application of the Bill of Rights to the states, and to a federal government of broad regulatory and spending power, presents issues that this Court has not successfully engaged. For example, the Court's recent decision in *Everson v. Board of Education*, 330 U.S. 1 (1947), is an apt illustration. When the state decides to extend a benefit, such as school transportation, to a broad class of beneficiaries on a neutral basis, it may not (let alone need not) exclude those whose education includes a religious component. The fallacy in the dissenting opinion is to treat the generally available benefits under positive law as different in principle from "matters of common right" such as police protection.

13. *Cong. Globe*, 39th Cong., 1st Sess. 500 (1866) (Sen. Cowan); id. at 1268 (Rep. Kerr); id at 1121 (Rep. Rogers); id. at app. 183 (Sen. Davis).

14. E.g., id. at 1157 (Rep. Thornton); id. at 1291 (Rep. Bingham); id. at 476 (colloquy between Sen. Trumbull and Sen. McDougall); id. at 477 (statement of Sen. W. Saulsbury).

15. Id. at 1366 (Rep. Wilson); id. at 1366–67 (vote on striking the provision).

16. *Railroad Co. v. Brown*, 84 U.S. (17 Wall.) 445 (1873).

17. The legislation did not explicitly refer to segregation, but entitled "all persons" to "the full and equal enjoyment of the accommodations, advantages, and privileges" of covered institutions, including public schools. See 2 *Cong. Rec.* 3451 (1874). Nonetheless, its application to segregation is indisputable. The Senate spokesman for the bill after Sumner's death, Frederick Frelinghuysen, stated unequivocally that under the bill "a colored child has a right to go to a white school, or a white child to a colored school." 2 *Cong. Rec.* 4168 (1874). The leader of the Democratic opposition, Senator Allen Thurman of Ohio, con-curred: "I know that the first section of the bill may to a careless reader seem ambiguous," he stated, "but I do not think there is one member of the majority of the Judiciary Committee who will not say, if the question is put directly to him, that the meaning of the section is that there shall be mixed schools." Id. at

4088. Proposals to amend the bill to permit separate but equal schools were voted down. Id. at 4167, 4171.

18. See, e.g., 2 *Cong. Rec.* 416 (1874) (Rep. Walls); id. at 457 (Rep. Butler); id. at 4081 (Sen. Pratt). An opponent commented: "It has been the assertion of those who support this bill with regard to the schools that compelling the separation of the races into different buildings was a violation of the fourteenth amendment." *Cong. Globe*, 42d Cong., 2d Sess. 3257 (1872) (Sen. Ferry).

19. See, e.g., *Cong. Globe*, 42d Cong., 2d Sess. 3261 (1872) (Sen. Casserly); id. at app. 41–42 (Sen. Vickers); id. at 242 (Sen. Hill).

20. Id. at 3190.

21. Id. at 241.

22. 2 *Cong. Rec.* app. 359 (1874).

23. *Cong. Globe*, 42d Cong., 2d Sess. 242 (1872).

24. 3 *Cong. Rec.* 945 (1875).

25. Id. at 1000 (Rep. Burrows); 2 *Cong. Rec.* 407 (1874) (Rep. Elliott); *Cong. Globe*, 42d Cong., 3d Sess. 383 (Sen. Sumner).

26. 2 *Cong. Rec.* 3452 (1874).

27. Id. at 457.

28. Id. at 4171.

29. See, e.g., id. at 555 (1874) (Rep. Vance); id. at 428 (Rep. Buckner); id. at 411 (Rep. Blount); *Cong. Globe*, 42d Cong., 2d Sess. 3251 (1872) (Sen. Blair); id. at 819 (Sen. Norwood); id. at app. 9 (Sen. Saulsbury); id. at 242 (1872) (Sen. Hill).

30. 2 *Cong. Rec.* 4158 (1874).

31. *Cong. Globe*, 42d Cong., 2d Sess. 3251 (1872).

32. Id. at 382.

33. 2 *Cong. Rec.* app. 479 (1874).

34. *Cong. Globe*, 42d Cong., 2d Sess. 274 (1871); id. at 919 (1872); id. at 1117; id. at 1956; id. at 2074; id. at 2270; id. at 3258; id. at 3264–65; id. at 3268; ibid.; id. at 3735; id. at 2727–38; 2 *Cong. Rec.* 4170 (1874); id. at 4176; id. at 4242–43; id. at 4439; id. at 4691; 3 *Cong. Rec.* 1010–11 (1875).

35. 2 *Cong. Rec.* 4179 (1874).

36. Id. at 4439.

37. *Cong. Globe*, 42d Cong., 2d Sess. 3262 (1872); 2 *Cong. Rec.* 4167 (1874); id. at 4175.

38. 3 *Cong. Rec.* 1010 (1875).

39. It would be incorrect to infer that less than two-thirds of Congress interpreted the Fourteenth Amendment as requiring desegregation. Many of the votes against the Sumner-Butler bill were cast by members of Congress who opposed the amendment and any serious enforcement of it. See, e.g., *Cong. Globe*, 42d Cong., 2d Sess. app. 9 (1872) (Sen. Saulsbury); 2 *Cong. Rec.* 900 (1874) (Rep. Robbins); id. at 419 (Rep. Herndon). Among supporters of the Fourteenth Amendment, the desegregation bill carried by lopsided majorities.

40. 3 *Cong. Rec.* 1011 (1875) (House); id. at 1870 (Senate); see Civil Rights Act of 1875, ch. 114, 18 Stat. 335 (1875).

41. 3 *Cong. Rec.* 997 (1875) (Rep. Kellogg).

42. Id. at 1000.

43. Id. at 998.

44. See Art. I, §10.

45. See Art. I, §9.

46. See *Cong. Globe,* 42d Cong., 2d Sess. 525 (1872) (Sen. Morton) ("the remedy for the violation of the fourteenth and fifteenth amendments was expressly not left to the courts. The remedy was legislative").

47. 3 *Cong. Rec.* 945 (1875).

SUNSTEIN, J., concurring in the judgment.

While I agree with his conclusion, I cannot join the opinion of the Chief Justice, which, like those of several other members of this Court, seems to me to decide too many complex questions, many of them not properly presented here. Rather than embarking in new directions, or offering adventurous interpretations of constitutional provisions on which the parties do not rely, I would emphasize the continuity of our decision today with the whole fabric of existing law. Indeed, the result in this case is nearly foreordained by our precedents, and the ruling of *Plessy v. Ferguson* has become an extraordinary anomaly in our jurisprudence, one that deserves immediate burial. I write separately to explain what I believe are the key holdings in these cases, and to offer a rationale that is necessary to explain those holdings.

I.

Invoking what they see as basic constitutional principle, plaintiffs contend that the Equal Protection Clause forbids separate but equal schooling. Invoking what they see as long-standing understandings and traditions, defendants contend that it does not. Of course we are not writing on a clean slate. In several cases involving racial discrimination, this Court has held that the Constitution raises severe doubts about any system of racial discrimination that has the purpose or effect of subordinating Negroes or other groups likely to be subject to prejudice.[1] And in a series of more recent cases involving school segregation in particular, we have suggested that any system of segregation in education faces an extremely heavy burden of justification. These cases do not resolve this one, which we have been careful to leave undecided and indeed expressly reserved. But taken as a whole, they raise substantial doubts about the defendants' position here.

A.

For well over fifty years, the Court has made clear that the Constitution disfavors explicit racial classifications having the purpose or effect of subordinating, stigmatizing, or humiliating any class of citizens. In *Strauder v. West Virginia*, 100 U.S. 303 (1880), decided not long after the ratification of the Fourteenth Amendment, the Court invalidated a West Virginia statute limiting jury service to "white male persons." In that case, we offered an extensive analysis of the historical background. We understood the Fourteenth Amendment "as one of a series of constitutional provisions having a common purpose: namely, securing to a race recently emancipated, a race that through many generations had been held in slavery, all the civil rights which the superior race enjoy." We noted that when these amendments were added to the Constitution, "it required little knowledge of human nature to anticipate that those who had long been regarded as an inferior and subject race would, when suddenly raised to the rank of citizenship, be looked upon with jealousy and positive dislike, and that State laws might be enacted or enforced to perpetuate the distinctions that had before existed." We found that the Fourteenth Amendment contains "a necessary implication of a positive immunity, or right, most valuable to the colored race,—the right to exemption from unfriendly legislation against them distinctively as colored—exemption from legal discriminations, implying inferiority in civil society, lessening the security of their enjoyment of the rights which others enjoy, discriminations which are steps towards reducing them to the condition of a subject race." We said that the West Virginia barrier was "practically a brand upon them, affixed by law, an assertion of their inferiority, and a stimulant to that race prejudice which is inimical to securing to individuals of the race that equal justice which the law aims to secure to all others." The Court's opinion in *Strauder* makes clear that legislation may not impose second-class citizenship on Negroes, in particular via legal "brands" that serve to stimulate racial prejudice.

In *Korematsu v. United States*, 323 U.S. 214 (1944), the Court emphasized the heavy burden that must be met by anyone attempting to defend racial discrimination. To be sure, in the extraordinary circumstances of an international war and a threat to the very survival of the nation, this Court was willing to uphold a form of racial discrimination. But we made clear "that all legal restrictions which curtail the civil rights of a single racial group are immediately suspect. . . . [C]ourts must subject them to the most rigid scrutiny. Pressing public necessity may sometimes justify the existence of such restrictions; racial antagonism never can." In that case, involving the Due Process Clause rather than the Equal Protection Clause, the Court was willing to uphold a form of discrimination only after finding a "pressing public necessity" for it.

B.

In the last fifteen years, this Court has been presented with a large number of challenges to racial segregation in education. In *Missouri ex rel. Gaines v. Canada*, 305 U.S. 337 (1938), we invalidated a Missouri statute arranging for Negroes to attend school in neighboring states when no in-state equivalent was available. We said that by "the operation of the laws of Missouri a privilege has been created for white law students which is denied to negroes by reason of their race." We thought it irrelevant that, in a sense, schools in the neighboring states might be "equal." In *Sipuel v. Board of Regents*, 332 U.S. 631 (1948), decided a decade later, we reaffirmed *Gaines* and held that the state could not deny the plaintiff admission to the only state law school. In *Sweatt v. Painter*, 339 U.S. 629 (1950), we went further and required admission of a Negro student to an all-white school, the University of Texas Law School. A key part of our rationale was that a separate facility for Negro law students was not substantially equal to the University of Texas Law School. In a passage of particular relevance to the issue presented here, we stressed not only objective factors distinguishing the institutions but added: "What is more important, the University of Texas Law School possesses to a far greater degree those qualities which are incapable of objective measurement but which make for greatness in a law school." In our view, the mere fact of segregation was by itself highly relevant: "The law school, the proving ground for legal learning and practice, cannot be effective in isolation from the individuals and institutions with which the law interacts. . . . With such a substantial and significant segment of society excluded, we cannot conclude that the education offered petitioner is substantially equal."

On the very same day we invalidated a practice of requiring a Negro student to be segregated through special seating arrangements in an otherwise all-white school. *McLaurin v. Oklahoma State Regents*, 339 U.S.

627 (1950). We did not deny that the physical facilities were equal. Nor did we deny that in a technical sense, the situation might be said to have provided for a form of "separate but equal" education. But we said that the restrictions adversely affected McLaurin's "ability to study, to engage in discussions and exchange views with other students, and, in general, to learn his profession."

Taken as a whole, these cases raise serious doubts about the proposition that the states may segregate white children and Negro children, and deprive the latter of the opportunities provided to the former, even if the facilities are technically "equal" (as they generally are not, under a doctrine that courts have been ill equipped to implement, in light of the many empirical complexities involved). *Strauder* makes clear that law will not be permitted to stimulate racial prejudice by drawing racial lines intended to promote second-class citizenship. *Korematsu* demonstrates that a "pressing public necessity" must be invoked on behalf of any discriminatory legislation. *Sweatt* and *McLaurin* demonstrate that educational equality will not be measured in terms of facilities alone, and that efforts to isolate and separate members of one group will be taken as a deprivation of equality. As a technical matter, none of these cases disposes of the particular issue raised in this case; we have been careful to reserve that issue until it was squarely presented. But they impose a singularly heavy burden of justification on the defendants. It is to their arguments that we now turn.

II.

The defendants make three basic claims in defense of racially segregated education. They contend that the authors and ratifiers of the Fourteenth Amendment did not intend to eliminate racial segregation; they claim that a system of "separate but equal" does not, in fact, run afoul of the principles announced in our previous cases; and they urge that the issue is foreclosed by *Plessy v. Ferguson*, 163 U.S. 537 (1896).

A.

The parties have spent considerable time on the question whether the ratifiers[2] of the Fourteenth Amendment believed that they were outlawing segregation on the basis of race, in school or elsewhere. If the historical record demonstrated that the ratifiers specifically intended to preserve school segregation, immediately after ratification and for the future as well, I would certainly hesitate to rule otherwise. Of course the specific understandings of the ratifiers of constitutional provisions, while relevant, do not always control the future. What governs is what they wrote, not what they specifically intended. This has been demonstrated in many areas of the law, where interpretation is not controlled by specific historical understandings, however relevant they may be. See, e.g., *De Jonge v. Oregon*, 299 U.S. 353 (1937); *Herndon v. Lowry*, 301 U.S. 242 (1937). At the same time, we should ordinarily be reluctant to invalidate practices of elected branches when the ratifiers of the relevant provisions wanted to leave those practices undisturbed.

In these cases, however, we need not venture into the most controversial interpretive territory, for a reading of the historical record shows that the ratifiers sought to include a general principle without binding the future to any specific understanding about the status of segregation. There is simply insufficient evidence to conclude that the ratifiers of the Fourteenth Amendment intended to preserve a system of racial segregation. To be sure, we should not accept Justice McConnell's ambitious and somewhat heroic effort to demonstrate that the Fourteenth Amendment was originally understood to ban segregation. See opinion of McConnell, J. (concurring in the judgment). The unenacted views of legislators—even a majority of them—to the effect that Congress had the *power* to forbid segregation should not be taken to suggest that the ratifiers of the Fourteenth Amendment believed that they had ratified a *self-executing* ban on segregation for immediate judicial enforcement. But Justice McConnell is certainly correct to emphasize that considerable evidence shows that many who supported the amendment believed that segregation was unconstitutional. See id. At the very least, history shows an absence of anything resembling a clear national judgment that the Fourteenth Amendment was consistent with segregation on the basis of race.

Since the time of ratification, moreover, the underlying circumstances have dramatically changed. An important shift has to do with public education, which now has a central status in the creation of citizenship. Even if racial segregation in schooling was believed to be acceptable at the time of ratification—and I do not say that it was—the emergence of public education as an essential formative influence in the development of children, and in the creation of a shared sense of citizenship, makes it hazardous to say that the original belief, formed in and for such different circumstances, is controlling today. I do not say that the Constitution changes when and because circumstances change. But the application of a general constitutional principle necessarily depends on the particular state of the world. Where, as here, the Constitution contains a general principle, there is no paradox in suggesting that whatever may have been the status of school segregation in a very different era, school segregation amounts to a denial of "equal protection of the laws" when public schooling is central to citizenship. Nothing in the historical background of the Fourteenth Amendment forecloses that conclusion.

B.

We have never held that the ban on racial discrimination is absolute. In *Korematsu*, we said, and held, that a "pressing public necessity" would justify such discrimination. In the context of education, the question is whether any such necessity can be identified to support compulsory separation of white and Negro children. Our previous cases involved higher education; but the need for a powerful justification is all the more evident when children are involved, for here the potential consequences of segregation are all the more severe. White children may be spurred to prejudice and to a false and socially corrosive belief in their own superiority. Negro children may come to believe that they are not full citizens, that whites regard them as inferior, and possibly even that they are inferior in the eyes of the law. See *Strauder*, supra. We cannot shut our eyes to the fact that laws that separate whites and Negroes have often been enacted precisely in order to produce these effects.

The arguments offered on behalf of "separate but equal" do not come close to meeting the constitutional standard announced by *Korematsu*. Undoubtedly many people will be inconvenienced, and possibly worse, by any effort to change a well-entrenched system of segregation on the basis of race. Undoubtedly some people's preferences, or tastes, call for the maintenance of that same system. But these arguments are hardly sufficient to justify discrimination on the basis of race. Inconvenience, and inevitable problems of transition, cannot justify an unconstitutional practice. Nor is it acceptable to defend public prejudice by reference to private prejudice. See *Strauder*, supra; *Korematsu*, supra; *McLaurin*, supra. This is especially clear when at least some of the relevant preferences, or tastes, are a product of racial discrimination it-self. Discrimination cannot be justified by preferences or tastes that it has helped to produce.[3] In any case governmental discrimination can-not be justified by the fact, if it is a fact, that some people want govern-ment to discriminate. See *Strauder*, supra; *Korematsu*, supra.

In short, the defendants have not identified a "pressing public ne-cessity," short of racial prejudice, that would justify segregated educa-tion. I am unable to find constitutionally legitimate justifications for this discriminatory practice.

C.

The strongest arguments on behalf of "separate but equal" education do not involve the reasonableness of the practice, let alone the necessity for it. They involve history and institutional concerns. Thus the defen-dants emphasize the long-standing nature of the practice of school seg-regation; indeed they claim that it is a way of life, a set of time-honored practices that this Court has long held are within the power of the states to choose. For obvious reasons, these concerns must be taken extremely seriously.

While we have never squarely held that school segregation is consti-tutionally acceptable, it is true that in *Plessy v. Ferguson*, 163 U.S. 537 (1896), this Court was willing to uphold a practice of public segregation. *Plessy* has been widely understood, now for a period of decades, to sug-gest that racial segregation in general, and racial segregation in schools in particular, are consistent with the constitutional plan. Where a social practice is well entrenched, and where the Court has suggested that it is constitutional, there is especially good reason for us to adhere to the ordinary practice of stare decisis—above all when we are asked to draw legislatively approved practices into question. If this case did not pre-sent the most extraordinary circumstances, we should hesitate long and hard to invoke the Constitution as a barrier to decisions of state legisla-tures. But for three reasons, I believe that this is a sufficiently extraordi-nary occasion.

The first and most important point is that *Plessy v. Ferguson* cannot stand alongside the rest of the law as it has developed over time. It fits extremely poorly with *Strauder* itself, to which it did not refer. What was said in *Plessy v. Ferguson* cannot easily be squared with the reasoning in *Korematsu*.[4] In addition, our recent cases, involving education itself, make application of *Plessy* to the educational setting seem quite absurd. The fact that schoolchildren are involved makes the argument for segregation all the weaker. In several other cases, involving racial classifications in the housing and railroad industries, we have also forbidden states to collaborate in the production of second-class citizenship for Negroes, even when private action and private prejudice are directly involved. See, e.g., *Shelley v. Kraemer*, 334 US 1 (1948). In short, *Plessy* is inconsistent with the whole fabric of our law.

Second, *Plessy* was reasoned far too casually and too cavalierly to stand as the foundation for school segregation today. Of course the case did not involve education at all. Nor did its opinion confront the general purposes of the Fourteenth Amendment and the relationship between those purposes and the practice of racial segregation. And in some of the most crucial and peculiar parts of the opinion, the Court doubted that "social prejudices can be overcome by legislation," contended that equal rights could not be secured "by an enforced commingling of the two races," and said that legislation "is powerless to eradicate racial instincts, or to abolish distinctions based upon physical differences." All this sociological speculation may or may not be correct, but it is quite irrelevant to a constitutional attack on a system of compulsory segregation. At most, these concerns stand as an objection of policy to a system of compulsory integration—an issue not then, or now, before this Court.

I believe that the reasoning of the *Plessy* Court was a departure from the sound principles of *Strauder*. A system of racial segregation in education is hardly a neutral one of respect for "traditions," but stands instead as "a stimulant to . . . race prejudice." The Constitution sets its face against any such system. Whatever may be the status of *Plessy* in other contexts, a question we have no occasion to decide, it has no legitimate place in public education.

III.

The District of Columbia case raises special considerations. The Equal Protection Clause does not apply to the national government, and hence it is contended, with considerable plausibility, that any barriers in the Fourteenth Amendment are inapplicable to the actions of the federal government.

I accept this proposition. The equality guarantees of the Fourteenth Amendment find no clear parallel in the original Bill of Rights, applicable to the federal government. The central question is therefore whether the Due Process Clause of the Fifth Amendment authorizes the national government to impose racial segregation on the public schools. Here too we do not write in a vacuum. In a long series of cases, the Court struck down economic legislation on the ground that it was arbitrary, an illegitimate effort to burden some for the benefit of others. See *Lochner v. New York*, 198 U.S. 45 (1905); *Adkins v. Children's Hospital*, 261 U.S. 525 (1923). These cases are now discredited. See *United States v. Carolene Products Co.*, 304 U.S. 144 (1938); *West Coast Hotel v. Parrish*, 300 U.S. 379 (1937). But it is important to be clear on what, exactly, has been discredited. We held in *West Coast Hotel* that the effort to protect workers with the minimum wage was an acceptable effort to promote "the public interest" insofar as this effort might reasonably be regarded as an effort to protect "the health of women . . . from unscrupulous and over-reaching employers." We said that the "exploitation of a class of workers" could constitutionally be prevented through a system designed to increase wages. We rejected the view that the system of common law ordering, and free market principles, should be taken as a kind of neutral or prepolitical background,[5] against which any legislative action would be viewed with suspicion. But even in so saying, we made clear that the Due Process Clause requires government to justify any measure by showing that it has a reasonable relationship to a legitimate state interest. See *Ferguson v. Skrupa*, 372 U.S. 726, 728 (1963), and id. at 731 (Harlan, J., concurring in the judgment); *West Coast Hotel*; *Carolene Products*. After the demise of *Lochner*-style "substantive due process"—in the very cases that constituted that demise—we continued to require some kind of demonstration that legislation be plausibly connected with the public interest. It is far too late in the day to hold, as Justice McConnell suggests, that the Due Process Clause is purely procedural, however plausible that view may seem as a textual matter.

Korematsu v. United States, supra, was of course a Fifth Amendment case, and it was there that we announced, in the context of a challenge brought under the Due Process Clause, that discriminatory legislation was "immediately suspect." And in *Carolene Products*, the Court went so far as to suggest that judicial presumptions in favor of the democratic process may be weakened in the context of racial discrimination. See 304 U.S. at 152–53 n.4.

But we need not inquire into the difficult issues that might be raised by application of these principles. At a minimum, our decisions make plain that any governmental action, federal as well as state, must be reasonably related to some legitimate state interest. To say the least, this is not a demanding test; on the contrary, it is quite lenient—far more so than the test for racial classifications under the Equal Protection Clause. But in the context at hand, it is a test that a system of racial segregation cannot pass. What is the legitimate interest to which racial segregation of schoolchildren is legitimately related? We are referred to the interest in preventing disruption of settled arrangements; but that argument proves both too little and too much. Settled by whom, and to what end? We are referred to the interest of many people, most of them white, in compelling the separation of whites and Negroes; but that argument is a reference to racial prejudice. Nothing that we have said raises constitutional questions about genuinely voluntary separation of the races. But the interests invoked on behalf of compulsory segregation are impossible to separate from the interests invoked on behalf of white supremacy and a system of racial caste. These interests cannot qualify as constitutionally legitimate. The practice of school segregation in the District of Columbia therefore violates the minimal commandment of the Due Process Clause.[6]

IV.

It is not appropriate here to solve all the remedial issues that will undoubtedly arise in various school districts. Prompt compliance with the commands of the Constitution is contemplated, and violations motivated by disagreement with the Constitution will not be tolerated, here or elsewhere. I am abundantly aware of the many passions and concerns raised by our decision today. In the history of this nation and this Court, members of the public, and state and national governments themselves, have had occasional doubts about constitutional requirements, or about this Court's interpretation of those requirements; but compliance has been the rule, and violations have been deemed unacceptable, both by those concerned with the rule of law and by posterity.

Courts should be guided by equitable principles in fashioning and enforcing appropriate decrees. As a starting point, courts should require that in the beginning of the next school year, the defendants will make an immediate start toward full compliance with our ruling. If additional time is claimed to be necessary—for reasons other than disagreement with the Constitution—the burden should lie on those acting in violation of constitutional commands to establish, first, that such time is indispensable for reasons connected with the public interest and, second, that compliance will occur in good faith and as promptly as possible. Detailed schedules, with clear deadlines, should be introduced in such circumstances. In no event should defendants be permitted an extension of more than one year. Beyond these general principles, I would leave issues of implementation to legislatures and district courts, with the assumption that compliance will occur promptly and in good faith, and with the full assistance of the elected branches of government.

NOTES

1. We have no occasion here to identify those groups.

2. Those who ratified the amendment are those with the authority to change the Constitution, and hence it is their understanding that is most relevant.

3. This point shows a central problem in the *Plessy* opinion, as discussed below.

4. It is true that the *Korematsu* Court referred to "deprivation of civil rights," a somewhat ambiguous phrase. But we believe that the standard announced there applies to all cases of racial discrimination.

5. This error in *Lochner* is closely related to the error in *Plessy*, where the Court also acted as if the system of segregation was prepolitical and neutral. It is no accident, in my view, that *Plessy* and *Lochner* were decided within the same decade. Our decision today has a great deal in common with our decision in *West Coast Hotel*, supra, where we rejected the view that the status quo—there market ordering under the common law, here segregation—need be taken as natural, neutral, or prepolitical.

6. In view of this conclusion, and that in Part I above, there is no occasion for us to deal with the imaginative uses, in several of the concurring opinions, of the Citizenship Clause and the Privileges and Immunities Clause of the Fourteenth Amendment. The underlying issues have not been briefed or raised by the parties.

BELL, J., dissenting.

I dissent today from the majority's decision in these cases because the detestable segregation in the public schools that the majority finds unconstitutional is a manifestation of the evil of racism the depths and pervasiveness of which this Court fails even to acknowledge, much less address and attempt to correct.

For reasons that I will explain in some detail, I cannot join in a decision that, while serving well the nation's foreign policy and domestic concerns, provides petitioners with no more than a semblance of the racial equality that they and theirs have sought for so long. The Court's long-overdue findings that Negroes are harmed by racial segregation is, regrettably, unaccompanied by an understanding of the economic, political, and psychological advantages whites gain because of that harm.

With some difficulty, the Court finds that *Plessy v. Ferguson*, 163 U.S. 537 (1896), cannot now serve as constitutional justification for segregated schools. *Plessy*, though, is only fortuitously a legal precedent. In actuality, it is a judicial affirmation of an unwritten but no less clearly understood social compact that, older than the Constitution, was incorporated into that document, and has been continually affirmed. Chief Justice Roger Taney's observation in *Dred Scott v. Sandford*, 60 U.S. (19 How.) 393, 407 (1857), that Negroes "had no rights that the white man was bound to respect" was excessive even for its time. The essence of the racial compact, however, is that whites, whatever their status, can view themselves as entitled to privileges and priorities over blacks. Indeed, beyond an appropriate pride in ethnic heritage, this racial compact provides the definitive definition of what it means to be white in America.

Without recognizing and attempting to dismantle this racial compact and in particular the indirect promises made to whites and the surrender of opportunities whites made to gain these racial privileges, today's decision, while viewed as a triumph by Negro petitioners and the class they represent, will be condemned by many whites as a breach of the compact. Their predictable outraged resistance will undermine and eventually negate judicial enforcement efforts, while political support for the Court's decision, like virtually every other racial rights measure adopted basically to serve white interests once those interests have been served, will become irrelevant.

I regret that the Court fails to see in these cases the opportunity to lay bare the simplistic hypocrisy of the "separate but equal" standard, not by overturning *Plessy,* but by ordering its strict enforcement. Respondents' counsel, John W. Davis, a highly respected advocate, urges this Court to uphold "separate but equal" as the constitutionally correct measure of racial status because, as he puts it so elegantly, "somewhere, sometime to every principle comes a moment of repose when it has been so often announced, so confidently relied upon, so long continued, that it passes the limits of judicial discretion and disturbance."

Elegance, though, should not be allowed to trample truth. The "separate" in the "separate but equal" standard has been rigorously enforced. The "equal" has served as a total refutation of equality. Counsel for the Negro children have gone to great lengths to prove what must be obvious to every person who gives the matter even cursory attention: with some notable exceptions, schools provided for Negroes in segregated systems are unequal in facilities—often obscenely so. And yet, until today, this Court has averted its gaze and has rejected challenges to state-run schools that were both segregated and ruinously unequal. See, e.g., *Cumming v. Richmond County Board of Education,* 175 U.S. 528 (1899), where this Court refused to order compliance with "separate but equal" at the request of black parents complaining that the school board had closed the black high school while continuing to operate one for whites.[1]

Responding to a series of challenges in recent years, this Court has acknowledged the flouting of the "separate but equal" standard at the graduate school level.[2] Today, it extends those holdings to encompass segregation in literally thousands of school districts. In doing so, the Court speaks eloquently of the damage segregation does to Negro children's hearts and minds, but the equating of constitutional and educational harm without cognizance of the sources of that harm will worsen the plight of black children for decades to come. By its silent assumption that segregation is an obsolete artifact of a bygone age, the Court sets the stage not for compliance, but for levels of defiance that will prove the antithesis of the equal educational opportunity the petitioners' seek.

In their determination to strike down state-mandated segregation, the petitioners ignore the admonishment of W. E. B. DuBois, one of the nation's finest thinkers. "Negro children need neither segregated schools nor mixed schools. What they need is education."[3] The three phases of relief that I will describe below focus attention on what is needed now by the children of both races. It is the only way to avoid a generation or more of strife over an ideal that, while worthwhile, will not achieve the educationally effective education that petitioners' children need and that existing constitutional standards, stripped of their racist understandings, should provide.

The Court has failed to consider three major components of racial segregation that must be addressed in order to provide meaningful relief. They are:

1. Racial segregation furthers societal stability by subordinating Negro Americans, which makes it easier for rich white Americans to dominate poor white Americans.
2. Negro rights are recognized and protected for only so long as they advance the nation's interests.
3. Realistic rather than symbolic relief for segregated schools will require a specific, judicially monitored plan designed primarily to promote educational equity.

I will discuss each of these components in turn:

I.

Racial segregation furthers societal stability by subordinating Negro Americans, which makes it easier for rich white Americans to dominate poor white Americans.

Segregation grew out of a series of unofficial racial compromises between white elites and poorer whites who demanded laws segregating public facilities to insure official recognition of their superior status over Negroes, with whom, save for color, they shared a similar economic plight. Yale historian C. Vann Woodward reports that after at first resisting these demands, southern leaders in the post-Reconstruction era enacted segregation laws mainly at the insistence of poor whites, who, given their precarious social and economic status, demanded these barriers to retain a sense of racial superiority over blacks.[4] He observes that "[i]t took a lot of ritual and Jim Crow to bolster the creed of white supremacy in the bosom of a white man working for a black man's wages."[5]

Professor Woodward's quote describes more than it explains. Why would whites conflate Jim Crow laws with real economic well-being? The full answer is likely to be complex, but whites' confusion of race and self-interest is not a recent phenomenon. It dates back to early colonial times. Historians of slavery have shown how plantation owners convinced working-class whites to support slavery even though they could never compete with those who could afford slaves. Slaveholders appealed to working-class whites by urging that their shared whiteness compelled the two groups to unite against the threat of slave revolts or escapes. The strategy worked. In their poverty, whites vented their frustrations by hating the slaves rather than their masters, who held both black slave and free white in economic bondage. When slavery ended, the economic disjuncture, camouflaged by racial division, continued unabated.

We must not forget that in a country that views property ownership as a measure of worth, there are a great many whites with relatively little property of a traditional kind—money, securities, land—who come to view their whiteness as a property right.[6] In ways so closely tied to an individual's sense of self that it may not be apparent, the set of assumptions, privileges, and benefits that accompany the status of being white can become a valuable asset that whites seek to protect. Segregation in virtually every aspect of public life became a physical manifestation of this property right, one the law enforced.

For Negroes, the withdrawal of Union troops from the South under the Hayes-Tilden compromise of 1877 presaged the destruction through intimidation and terror of economic and political gains some blacks had made during the Reconstruction years. Jim Crow laws that eventually segregated Negroes in every aspect of public life also rendered them vulnerable to physical violence, including literally thousands of lynchings by white mobs whose hate likely had its roots in an unconscious realization that their property right in whiteness had real meaning only as they terrorized and murdered defenseless Negroes.

A much-neglected history requires the admission that *Plessy v. Ferguson* provided legal confirmation to more than a century of political compromises that diminished the citizenship rights of blacks to the point of invisibility to resolve conflicts among differing groups of whites or further interests deemed important to the nation. Three examples will illustrate the perhaps unconscious but no less pernicious policy.

1. In drafting the Constitution, the framers confronted the already well-established patterns of slavery. While insuring that the foundation of our basic law would recognize rights to life and liberty for every citizen, they knew that America had systematically denied those rights to those of African descent. For the better part of two centuries, the colonies and then the United States developed the country on the labor of literally millions of human beings kidnapped by force from their native Africa and transported under inhuman conditions. The survivors and their progeny were held in a particularly vicious form of human slavery. The war for independence was financed in substantial part out of the profits of slavery.

Among the framers were some who abhorred the "peculiar institution," and many others who viewed slaves as their most important property. Aware that the southern delegates would never agree to a document that jeopardized the enslaved source of their wealth, the framers offered no answer to the admonishment that property in slaves should not be exposed to danger under a government instituted for the protection of property. In at least ten provisions, the framers turned aside the many petitions from slaves and abolitionists of both races urging them to abolish slavery. Instead, they agreed to language that both gave legitimacy to slavery and provided for its protection.[7] For the first but sadly far from the last time, the rights of black people were sacrificed to facilitate compromises between whites with conflicting views.

2. Over time, the friction between free and slave states grew, sparked by scores of lawsuits seeking to utilize the judicial forums of free states to win freedom for slaves who were brought or escaped from slave states. In *Dred Scott v. Sandford*, Chief Justice Roger Taney, as reviled as the framers are revered, attempted to do what they had done. By again refusing to recognize rights for Negroes—whether slave or free—the Court could settle the increasingly divisive slavery issue. The *Dred Scott* decision had the opposite effect, and according to many historians helped precipitate the Civil War.

3. When, hardly a decade after enactment of the Civil War Amendments, it appeared that renewed hostilities might break out following

the close and bitterly disputed presidential election of 1876, a congressional commission appointed to resolve the dispute did so through what became known as the Hayes-Tilden compromise. It provided that the Republican, Rutherford B. Hayes, would be deemed to have won the election. For their part of the bargain, southern Democrats received a number of concessions including the promise—devastating to those so recently freed—to withdraw federal troops and leave their fate to the far from tender mercies of those who deemed Negroes fit only for slavery and subjugation.

These illustrations provide a foundation for understanding how the state-mandated racial segregation that is the subject of this litigation did not suddenly appear like a bad weed in an otherwise beautiful racial garden, a weed the majority seeks to eradicate with a single swing of its judicial hoe. It illustrates as well how segregation provided whites with a sense of belonging based on neither economic nor political well-being, but simply on an identification based on race with the ruling class and a state-supported belief that, as whites, they were superior to blacks.

American racism, though, is not simply a "taint" or "bias." It is the dominant interpretive framework for rendering bodies intelligible. That is to say, racism organizes the American garden's very configuration. Jim Crow was not merely an oppressive legal regime; it consolidated the imaginative lens through which Americans would view race going forward in the future. Jim Crow reaffirmed the binary system through which we (Americans) tend to think of race—i.e., "black" and "white." Jim Crow unceremoniously erased intermediate categories through the biologically ridiculous but politically necessary notion that "one drop" of black blood rendered an individual black. America has not recognized "mulatto," certainly not since post-Reconstruction. The "one drop" concept highlights the rigidity of American racism, and, by virtue of the conceptual currency it continues to enjoy, it makes clear the extent to which Jim Crow segregation was not just a "bad weed." When racism is positioned as a thinking problem (rather than just a "bad weed"), the Court majority's pronouncement can be seen as more a racial provocation than a remedy.

Rather than a now obsolete obstacle to racial equality in the public schools, *Plessy* functioned as a confirmation of myriad racist compromises. Reconstruction precipitated the vastest expansion of federal power since the nation's inception, an expansion for which there would be no match until the New Deal. *Plessy* functioned as a final announcement (to the extent that it was not already clear when Union troops were withdrawn from the South under the terms of the Hayes-Tilden compromise) that the federal government had abdicated any role in restraining state-sponsored racism. As such, the decision normalized post-Reconstruction's racist retrenchment and, concomitantly, the rigid binary structure that racist retrenchment inaugurated. The majority's decision in the present case, of course, does not even begin to address these dimensions of *Plessy*.

By again confirming the historic status of Negroes as the hated and despised "other," *Plessy* marked a transformation in the politics of otherness: the genesis of a new imperative to rigidly fix black people as black. This renewed politics of otherness not only allowed entire categories of poor whites to develop a powerful sense of racial belonging, but allowed entire categories of erstwhile nonwhite immigrants (the Irish are the most prominent example) to become white. The vociferous articulation of rigidly expansive notions of blackness created an entire range of racial opportunities for "would-be" whites.

Consider that during the latter half of the nineteenth century, a shared feeling of superiority to Negroes was one of the few things that united a nation of immigrants from Europe, themselves horribly exploited by the mine and factory owners for whom they toiled long hours under brutal conditions for subsistence wages. These immigrants were far more recent arrivals than the Negroes they mocked. The blackfaced and racially derogatory minstrel shows of that period helped immigrants acculturate and assimilate by inculcating a nationalism whose common theme was the disparagement and disadvantaging of blacks. Thus, policies of racial segregation simultaneously subordinated Negroes while providing whites with a comforting sense of their position in society. Racism's stabilizing force was not limited to poorer whites. Even for wealthier whites, their identities were unstable because intrinsically dependent upon an "other." White racist antipathy belied the extent to which white people desperately needed and—as I fear the majority's decision will show—still need Negroes in a subordinate status in order to sustain the myriad fictions of white racial integrity.

Ideologically, then, the statement "I am not black" has functioned as a kind of border, a psychic demarcation that allows "American" to be quickly (perhaps even thoughtlessly) distinguished from "not American." America has been able to define itself as a white country by marking blacks as that which does not constitute it. The law has served to rationalize racial boundaries with fictions that, in fact, conceal exploitation and marginalization of individuals on both sides of the color line.

Consider how legal fictions adopted by this Court in *Plessy v. Ferguson* in 1896 and *Lochner v. New York* in 1905,[8] served to disadvantage both whites and blacks. In *Lochner*, the fiction was that both employer and worker were each equally free to bargain on an employment contract. In *Plessy*, the fiction was that separate but equal actually provided equality of treatment. Both decisions protected existing property arrangements at the expense of powerless groups—exploited workers in *Lochner* and degraded blacks in *Plessy*. Wage and race oppression were mutually reinforcing. Whites applauded—even insisted on the subordination of blacks as a self-distracting mechanism for a system that transformed them into wage slaves.

Tom Watson, a Populist leader, in 1892 as a staunch advocate of a union between Negro and white farmers tried unsuccessfully to convince poor whites of the adverse economic effects of segregation. "You are kept apart that you may be separately fleeced of your earnings. You are made to hate each other because upon that hatred is rested the keystone of the arch of financial despotism which enslaves you both. You are deceived and blinded that you may not see how this race antagonism perpetuates a monetary system which beggars you both."[9]

Watson's arguments failed, and his subsequent race baiting won him election to the U.S. Senate from Georgia. While it is certainly not the Court majority's intent, its rhetoric reaffirms America's whiteness by opening the narrative and visual possibilities of aestheticizing integration. An integrated world is an ideal (read: beautiful) world. The Court categorically equates "equality" with "integration," where integration entails securing some sort of proximal relationship to white bodies in the same school or class. This integration ethic centralizes whiteness. White bodies are represented as somehow exuding an intrinsic value that percolates into the "hearts and minds" of black children.[10] The *Brown* majority subtly braids proximal situatedness with becoming a good citizen—i.e., a good American.[11] The Court very deliberately seems to avoid staging any sort of elaborate substantive due process analysis.[12] This seems significant because under the rubric of substantive due process the Court might have more easily engaged the question of equalization without hinging black people's rights upon being proximally situated to white people.

Petitioners, viewing integration with whites as the only means of overthrowing "separate but equal," urge an end to state-mandated racial segregation. Whites, of course, resist any change in the "separate but equal" standard they view as a vested property right. Resistance under these circumstances is a manifestation of white victimization, willing, it is true, but victimization nevertheless. The question for this Court then is not the obvious one of whether racially segregated schools violate the Equal Protection Clause of the Fourteenth Amendment, but how can this Court grant racial relief desired by Negroes, resisted by whites, and needed by both? As important, how can the relief granted break out of the reform-retrenchment mold that has doomed earlier racial reforms?

II.

Negro rights are recognized and protected for only so long as they advance the nation's interests.

This Court's decision will replicate a familiar pattern of relief for racial injustices. A semblance of justice for Negroes serves as the vehicle for furthering interests of the nation. Examining the history of civil rights policies, we find that even the most serious injustices suffered by Negroes, including slavery, segregation, and patterns of murderous violence, are not sufficient to gain real relief from any branch of government. Rather, relief from racial discrimination, when it comes, requires that policy makers perceive that the relief will provide a clear benefit for the nation. While it is nowhere mentioned in the majority's opinion, it is quite clear that a major motivation for the Court to outlaw racial segregation now when it declined to do so in the past is the major boost this decision will provide in our competition with communist governments abroad and our fight to uproot subversive elements at home.

A few examples are illustrative:

The Emancipation Proclamation. Even though he was reluctant to arbitrarily deprive even the rebellious Southerners of their property without due process or compensation, President Lincoln finally issued the document on January 1, 1863, because it would disrupt the labor force in the South and open the way for the enlistment of thousands of former slaves who had left their plantations and were following the union armies. In addition, his declaration that the Civil

War was intended to end slavery would serve to mobilize abolitionists in England and France who would prevent their governments from entering the war on the side of the Confederacy. By its terms, of course, the executive order actually freed no slaves for it excluded all slave-owning territories on the Union side and had no legal effect on slavery within the Confederacy.

The Civil War Amendments. The Republicans recognized that unless some action was taken to legitimate the freedmen's status, Southerners would utilize violence to force blacks into slavery, thereby renewing the economic dispute that had led to the Civil War. To avoid this "win the war but lose the peace" result, the Fourteenth and Fifteenth Amendments and Civil Rights Acts of 1870–75 were enacted. They were the work of the Radical Reconstructionists, some of whom were deeply committed to securing the rights of citizenship for the freedmen. For most Republicans, however, a more general motivation was the desire to maintain Republican Party control in the southern states and in Congress.

The Fourteenth Amendment, unpassable as a specific protection for black rights, was enacted finally as a general guarantee of life, liberty, and property of all "persons." Corporations, following a period of ambivalence,[13] were deemed persons under the Fourteenth Amendment,[14] and for several generations received far more protection from the Courts than did Negroes, much of it under a doctrine of "substantive due process" not clearly contained in the amendment's language.[15]

Indeed, Negroes became victims of judicial interpretations of the Fourteenth and Fifteenth Amendments and legislation based on them so narrow as to render the promised protection meaningless in virtually all situations.[16] This Court in the *Civil Rights Cases*, 109 U.S. 3 (1883), found the amendment inadequate to protect Negroes' entitlement to nondiscriminatory service in public facilities. More egregiously, in *Giles v. Harris*, 189 U.S. 475 (1903), the Court rejected a petition by blacks asserting that the voter registration scheme in Alabama was designed to bar blacks from the ballot. Speaking for the Court's majority, Justice Holmes said that if the conspiracy to prevent blacks from voting was as widespread as the petitioners claimed, then there was nothing the Court could do to restore these political rights.

We may regret the pattern in which self-interest is the apparent major motivant in racial remediation policies that are then abandoned when the nation's interest has been served, but we should not ignore this self-interest phenomenon, particularly as it is functioning in the cases now before us. In petitioners' briefs and more particularly in the amicus briefs filed by the Justice Department, the "separate but equal" precedent of *Plessy* is challenged as not only unjust to blacks, but also bad for the country's image, a barrier to development in the South, and harmful to its foreign policy. To make the latter point, the government's brief quoted at some length Secretary of State Dean Acheson, who reported:

> [D]uring the past six years, the damage to our foreign relations attributable to [race discrimination] has become progressively greater. The United States is under constant attack in the foreign press, over the foreign radio, and in such international bodies as the United Nations because of various practices of discrimination against minority groups in this country. . . . [t]he undeniable existence of racial discrimination gives unfriendly governments the most effective kind of ammunition for their propaganda warfare. . . . [s]chool segregation, in particular, has been singled out for hostile foreign comment in the United Nations and elsewhere. . . . [R]acial discrimination in the United States remains a source of constant embarrassment to this government in the day-to-day conduct of its foreign relations; and it jeopardizes the effective maintenance of our moral leadership of the free and democratic nations of the world.[17]

In addition, this Court is not unaware of the nation's need to protect its national security against those who would exploit our internal difficulties for the benefit of external forces. Justice Frankfurter, while concurring in *Dennis v. United States*,[18] wrote that the Court "may take judicial notice that the communist doctrines which these defendants have conspired to advocate are in the ascendency in powerful nations who cannot be acquitted of unfriendliness to the institutions of this country."

It is likely that not since the Civil War has the need to remedy racial injustice been so firmly aligned with the country's vital interests at home and abroad. The majority's ringing statement will provide a symbolic victory to petitioners and the class of Negroes they represent while, in fact, giving a new, improved face to the nation's foreign policy and responding to charges of blatant racial bias at home, thus furnishing a fresh example of the historic attraction to granting recognition and promising reform of racial injustice when such action converges with the nation's interests.

I do not ignore the potential value of this Court's simply recognizing the evil of segregation, an evil Negroes have experienced firsthand for too long. There is, I also agree, a place for symbols in law for a people abandoned by law for much of the nation's history. I recognize and hail the impressive manner in which Negroes have made symbolic gains and given them meaning by the sheer force of their belief. Is it not precisely because of their unstinting faith in this country's ideals that they deserve better than an expression of benign paternalism, no matter how well intended? It will serve as a sad substitute for the needed empathy of action called for when a history of racial subordination is to be undone.

The racial reform-retrenchment pattern so evident here indicates that when the tides of white resentment rise and again swamp the expectations of Negroes in a flood of racial hostility, this Court and likely the country will vacillate. Then, as with the Emancipation Proclamation and the Civil War Amendments, it will rationalize its inability and—let us be honest—its unwillingness to give real meaning to the rights we declare so readily and so willingly sacrifice when our interests turn to new issues, more pressing concerns.

III.

Realistic rather than symbolic relief for segregated schools will require a specific, judicially monitored plan designed primarily to promote educational equity.

While declaring racial segregation harmful to black children, the majority treats these policies as though they descended unwanted from the skies and can now be mopped up like a heavy rainfall and flushed away. The fact is that, as my brief review of the nation's racial history makes clear, a great many white as well as Negro children have been harmed by segregation. Segregation requires school systems to operate duplicate sets of schools that are as educationally inefficient as their gross incompliance with the "separate but equal" *Plessy* mandate makes them constitutionally deficient.

Pressured by this litigation, the school boards assure this Court that they are taking steps to equalize facilities in Negro schools. More important than striking down *Plessy v. Ferguson* is the need to reveal its hypocritical underpinnings by requiring its full enforcement for all children, white as well as black. Full enforcement requires more than either equalizing facilities or, in the case of Delaware because of the inadequacy of the Negro schools, ordering plaintiffs admitted into the white schools. As a primary step toward the disestablishment of the dual school system, I would order relief that must be provided all children in racially segregated districts in three phases:

Phase 1: Equalization. (1) Effective immediately on receipt of this Court's mandate, school officials of the respondent school districts must ascertain through appropriate measures the academic standing of each school district as compared with nationwide norms for school systems of comparable size and financial resources. This data will be published and made available to all patrons of the district. (2) All schools within the district must be fully equalized in physical facilities, teacher training, experience, and salary with the goal that each district as a whole will measure up to national norms within three years.

Phase 2. Representation. The battle cry of those who fought and died to bring this country into existence was "Taxation without representation is tyranny." Effective relief in segregated school districts requires no less than the immediate restructuring of school boards and other policy-making bodies to insure that those formally excluded from representation have persons selected by them in accordance with the percentage of their children in the school system. This restructuring must take effect no later than the start of the 1955–56 school year.

Phase 3. Judicial oversight. To implement these orders efficiently, federal district judges should be instructed to set up three-person monitoring committees, with the Negro and white communities each selecting a monitor and those two agreeing on a third. The monitoring committees will work with school officials to prepare the necessary plans and procedures enabling the school districts to comply with phases 1 and 2. The district courts will oversee compliance and will address firmly any actions intended to subvert or hinder the compliance program.

In my view, the petitioners' goal—the disestablishment of the dual school system—will be more effectively achieved for students, parents, teachers, administrators, and other individuals connected directly or indirectly with the school system by these means than by the majority's ringing order, which I fear will not be effectively enforced and will be vigorously resisted.

In conclusion, I recognize that this dissent comports neither with the hopes of petitioners that we order immediate desegregation nor the pleas of respondent boards that we retain the racial status quo. Our goal, though, should not be to determine winners and losers. It is rather our obligation to unravel the nation's greatest contradiction. Perhaps unwittingly, Justice Harlan, dissenting in *Plessy*, articulated it in definitive fashion when he observed:

> The white race deems itself to be the dominant race in this country. And so it is, in prestige, in achievements, in education, in wealth and in power. So, I doubt not, it will continue to be for all time, if it remains true to its great heritage and holds fast to the principles of constitutional liberty. But in view of the Constitution, in the eye of the law, there is in this country no superior, dominant, ruling class of citizens. There is no caste here. Our Constitution is color-blind, and neither knows nor tolerates classes among citizens.

163 U.S. at 537, 559.

The existence of a dominant white race and the concept of color-blindness are polar opposites that the Equal Protection Clause cannot easily mediate. It has proven barely adequate as a shield against some of the most pernicious modes of social domination. For reasons that my review of its history makes clear, the Equal Protection Clause all too readily lends itself to the staid formalisms that both "separate but equal" and "color blindness" emblematize. The clause's formalist predilection should not be too surprising. After all, equal protection generally seeks to vindicate rights by evaluating the relationships between legally authorized, if not manufactured, categories (rather than squarely addressing the validity of the state's exercise of coercion against an individual or individuals.

The majority's decision to overturn *Plessy* is inadequate because it systematically glosses over the extent to which *Plessy*'s stark formalism participated in the consolidation of American racism. Rather than critically engaging American racism's complexities, the Court substitutes one mantra for another: where "separate" was once equal, "separate" is now categorically unequal. Rewiring the rhetoric of equality (rather than laying bare *Plessy*'s racist underpinnings and consequences) constructs American racism as an eminently fixable aberration. First, by doing nothing more than rewiring the rhetoric of equality, the Court's majority forecloses the possibility of recognizing racism as a broadly shared cultural condition. Imagining racism as a fixable aberration obfuscates the way in which racism functions as an ideological lens through which Americans perceive themselves, their nation, and their nation's Other. Second, the *Brown* majority's vision of racism as an unhappy accident of history immunizes "the law" (as a logical system) from antiracist critique. That is to say, the majority positions the law as that which fixes racism rather than as that which participates in its consolidation. By dismissing *Plessy* without dismantling it, the Court seems to predict if not underwrite eventual failure. Negroes, who despite all are perhaps the nation's most faithful citizens, deserve better.

NOTES

1. The Court then upheld segregation laws in *Berea College v. Kentucky*, 211 U.S. 45 (1908) (statute subjected to a heavy fine a private college that admitted both white and Negro students); and *Gong Lum v. Rice*, 275 U.S. 78 (1927) (rejecting challenge of Chinese parent whose child was assigned to a Negro school).

2. *Missouri ex rel. Gaines v. Canada*, 305 U.S. 337; *Sipuel v. Oklahoma*, 332 U.S. 631; *Sweatt v. Painter*, 339 U.S. 629; *McLaurin v. Oklahoma State Regents*, 339 U.S. 637.

3. W. E. B. Du Bois, "Does the Negro Need Separate Schools?" 4 *J. Negro Educ.* 328 (1935). He warned that "[a] mixed school with poor and unsympathetic teachers, with hostile public opinion, and no teaching of truth concerning black folk, is bad." He added though that "[a] segregated school with ignorant placeholders, inadequate equipment, poor salaries, and wretched housing, is equally bad." He conceded that "[o]ther things being equal, the mixed school is the broader, more natural basis for the education of all youth. It gives wider contacts; it inspires greater self-confidence; and suppresses the inferiority complex. But other things seldom are equal, and in that case, Sympathy, Knowledge, and Truth, outweigh all that the mixed school can offer."

4. C. Vann Woodward, *Origins of the New South 1877–1913*, 211–12 (1951).

5. C. Vann Woodward, *Reunion and Reaction* (1951).

6. See *Plessy v. Ferguson*, 163 U.S. 537, 549 (1896).

7. The original Constitution included up to ten slave clauses, including U.S. Const. art. I, § 2, cl. 3 (apportioning congressional representatives among states based on population, determined by all free persons and three-fifths of the slaves); U.S. Const. Art. I, § 8, cl. 15 (vesting power in Congress to suppress insurrections, including those by slaves); U.S. Const. Art. IV, § 2, cl. 3 (prohibiting states from freeing runaway slaves); and U.S. Const. Art. IV, § 4 (obligating federal government to protect states from domestic violence, including slave insurrections)).

8. 198 U.S. 45 (1905).

9. Thomas E. Watson, "The Negro Question in the South," 6 Arena 540 (1892).

10. See id.

11. See id. at 493. The logical braid occurs as follows: a solid education is the foundation for inculcating "cultural values" and producing good citizens. A solid education is necessarily an integrated one.

12. Ostensibly the Court stages just such an analysis in *Bolling v. Sharpe*, 347 U.S. 497 (1953) (holding that the Fifth Amendment prohibited segregation in D.C. public schools). The substantive due process analysis in *Bolling*, however, is a truncated one (filling barely two reporter pages)—it functions more as an apology for the fact that the Fourteenth Amendment does not apply to the federal government than a robust discussion of substantive due process.

13. *Slaughterhouse Cases*, 83 U.S. (16 Wall.) 36 (1873).

14. *Santa Clara County v. Southern Pac. R.R.*, 118 U.S. 394 (1866).

15. See, e.g., *Allgeyer v. Louisiana*, 165 U.S. 578 (1897); *Lochner v. New York*, 198 U.S. 45 (1905); *Adkins v. Children's Hospital*, 261 U.S. 525 (1923).

16. Usually in cases of more symbolic than substantive value, the Court did recognize the Civil War Amendments' protection against exclusion of Negroes from juries, *Strauder v. West Virginia*, 100 U.S. 303 (1880); *Ex parte Virginia*, 100 U.S. 339 (1880). During the first few decades of the twentieth century, the Court found that Negro rights had been violated in *Bailey v. Alabama*, 219 U.S. 219 (1911) (striking down state peonage laws that coerced primarily black labor); *United States v. Reynolds*, 235 U.S. 133 (1914) (invalidating an Alabama law criminalizing breach of surety agreements whereby private parties paid the fines to liberate convicted criminals from jail in exchange for promises to labor for a specific time); *McCabe v. Atchinson, T. & S.F.R. Co.*, 235 U.S. 151 (1914) (striking down a state law permitting railroads to exclude blacks from first-class service rather than offer separate but equal accommodations); *Guinn v. United States*, 238 U.S. 347 (1915) (invalidating Oklahoma's "grandfather clause" under the Fifteenth Amendment), and *Buchanan v. Warley*, 245 U.S. 60 (1917).

17. Brief for the United States as Amicus Curiae, p. 43–44 (footnotes 43 and 44) *Brown v. Board of Education*.

18. 341 U.S. 494, 547 (1951).

Comments from the Contributors

The contributors to this book were asked to give a short account of why they wrote their *Brown* opinion as they did, and what goals they were trying to accomplish. They were also invited to give credit where it was due for sources written after 1954, which they could not quote directly in their opinions. Here are their responses:

Bruce Ackerman

Brown is typically viewed as the shining example of a Court playing the part of moral revolutionary—proclaiming a new and better law of equal protection for the country, blazing a path toward racial redemption.

I take a different line. The true visionaries were not the Justices of the Warren Court but the Republicans of the Reconstruction Congress. Speaking for the men and women who stood by the Union during the Civil War, these Republican leaders were not sedate conservatives but revolutionary statesmen determined to set the nation on a new and sounder foundation. The Court's first task is to recapture the revolutionary character of their historical achievement and redeem its claim to enduring constitutional significance.

This would not be too tough if the world had stood still since 1868, but it has not. When the Reconstruction generation rewrote the Constitution, their brave new words gained meaning by reference to a vast set of constitutional understandings that were themselves profoundly revised over the course of the next century. In our particular case, the framers of the Fourteenth Amendment decisively sought to establish the primacy of national citizenship in our constitutional arrangements, but in doing so, they had not the slightest inkling of what American government would become over the course of the twentieth century. The Justices in *Brown* were in a very different situation: the Court's jurisprudence had virtually forgotten the meaning of national citizenship, but the Justices were all entirely aware of the vast reorganization of national government elaborated by the American people during the New Deal and Second World War.

Rewriting *Brown*, then, poses a twofold challenge. The first is to realign the legal interpretation of Reconstruction with the one adopted by serious historians of the period. All scholars, regardless of their political persuasion, agree that the Citizenship Clauses were at the absolute center of the original understanding of the Reconstruction Constitution; if the Court is to do justice to the historical achievement of the 1860s, its opinion must begin by restoring these clauses to a central place in constitutional interpretation.

In interpreting the "privileges" of American citizenship, however, it is not enough to place them against the background of nineteenth-century understandings of national government. The Court must confront the fundamental ways in which the *Brown* generation redefined the aims of American government in the cauldron of economic depression and world war. In undertaking this second task, there is no need to write on a clean slate. Instead, my opinion builds on the effort by the Roosevelt Court to rethink the relationship of national and state governments in the regulation of economic life. My aim is to undertake an analogous reconceptualization of federal relationships in the sphere of citizenship.

I hope my opinion provides a useful contrast with two more familiar ways of confronting the great ruptures in constitutional law that occurred between 1868 and 1954. *Legal moralists* use this rupture as an excuse for lifting the language of the Fourteenth Amendment out of all historical context and reading it as a warrant for their favored interpretation of contemporary political morality. (Ronald Dworkin can serve as a paradigm here.) *Original intentionalists* try to ignore the fact of rupture by treating the Reconstruction Constitution as if it were merely a set of narrow rules addressed to particular problems. Any problem beyond the horizon of 1868 remains forever beyond the scope of the Fourteenth Amendment principle. (Professor McConnell's opinion in this volume provides a revealing example, as he struggles to convince us, contrary to fact, that the Reconstruction generation really did intend to eliminate segregated schools.) In contrast, I view the Reconstruction Constitution as a great historical statement of principle, whose proper interpretation must take into account other historical efforts by the American people to rework their constitutional identity. For more on this methodology, see my *We the People* (Cambridge: Harvard University Press, 1991), 86–104, 131–62.

Turning from method to substance, the opinion lays the foundation for the constitutional protection of positive freedoms, and not only negative liberties. Every American has the constitutional right to demand the affirmative state provision of all the privileges of national citizenship. There is no reason to suppose that primary and secondary education will turn out to be the only consequential "privilege" warranting constitutional status. The opinion sketches a methodology for identifying "privileges," but much is left for further development and refinement by subsequent courts.

Jack M. Balkin

Before writing my opinion, I spent some time studying Warren's original opinions in *Brown I*, *Brown II*, and *Bolling*. The more I read them, the more I came to admire Warren and the economy and simplicity of his style. Warren is generally regarded as one of the greatest of America's Chief Justices, particularly in terms of his temperament and moral leadership. But he also knew how to write an opinion that could speak directly to Americans. Although my opinion is much longer and tries to address more issues than his, I borrowed a few phrases from him that I thought were particularly fine.

Several of my goals in writing the opinion should be fairly clear from the introductory chapters. I wanted to establish that the antidiscrimination principle is not simply a concern with prohibited classifications, but is also concerned with the historical subordination of groups and the achievement of equal citizenship for all members of our political community. Like Frank Michelman, I am indebted to the many legal scholars who developed the antisubordination/equal citizenship approach in the years after *Brown* was written, including Charles Black, Kenneth Karst, Owen Fiss, Charles Lawrence, and Catharine MacKinnon.

At several points in the opinion I note that the people who wrote the Fourteenth Amendment were hardly racial egalitarians. Full equality worried them, and many of them were quite complacent about the superiority of whites. Often the words of a Constitution are far wiser and more just than their framers' concrete intentions. Interpreting the Constitution involves interpreting promises that are yet to be fulfilled. That is why constitutional interpretation is not and should not be merely an exercise in hero worship of a founding generation. That is particularly so where race is concerned. Rather, constitutional interpretation should be part of an ongoing process of our country's redemption. We must try to fulfill the Constitution's promises of liberty and equality in our own time.

The Supreme Court has often been a mediocre steward of the Constitution it has been entrusted with. *Plessy* and *Dred Scott* are the most famous examples where the Court let the country down, but there are many others, which are perhaps less horrifying but no less shortsighted. One of the Court's worst recent decisions was *San Antonio Independent School District v. Rodriguez*, 411 U.S. 1 (1973), which held that the Constitution permitted vast disparities in educational opportunity for rich and poor. Today it is obvious to every parent that without genuine educational opportunity their children will be severely disadvantaged, and since 1973 many states have found rights to education in their state constitutions. The problems that minority children faced after *Brown* concerned both race and class. The focus on racial balance in the Supreme Court's opinions ultimately diverted attention away from issues of poverty and educational opportunity; they left courts powerless to remedy the increasing isolation of minority children in substandard schools.

For these reasons, my opinion finds two constitutional violations: of racial equality and of equal educational opportunity. I harbor no illusions that this would necessarily have made an enormous difference, and surely giving real content to an equal opportunity guarantee would take much more work than what I say in the opinion. Judicial opinions by themselves often cannot produce great changes without political will and popular support; but they can sometimes help shape an agenda for the future. *Brown* did not create the civil rights movement, but it had symbolic importance because it put the authority of the Constitution on the side of people fighting for racial equality. If courts had created a constitutional discourse of equal educational opportunity in addition to a discourse of racial equality, they might have strengthened the hands of people pushing for equal educational opportunity in the political world. The idea that the Constitution could demand changes in inequitable local systems of school finance (as it already does for un-

equal local voting districts after *Reynolds v. Sims*, 377 U.S. 533 (1964))
might not have sounded so strange, and America might be better off
today. The country would be better off not because courts ordered
change on their own, but because courts played their appropriate role
in a larger political system.

Derrick A. Bell

The lyric of an old rhythm and blues song asserts with resigned confi-
dence: "I may not be the one you want, but I sure am the one you need."
While the song speaks of frustrated love, it describes as well my reluctant conclusion about the value to black people of the Supreme Court's
decision, close to a half century old, in *Brown v. Board of Education*. For
after giving the matter a great deal of thought, I have concluded that
had I been on the Court and unable to convince its members of my
views, I would have filed this dissent.

On May 17, 1954, I was on a troopship heading home from a year's
military duty in Korea. I entered law school that fall and, after the first
year, began submitting so much writing on racial issues that the faculty
advisor to the law review warned me—only half in jest—that I was trying to turn the publication into the University of Pittsburgh Civil Rights
Journal. At that point, like many, I assumed that the *Brown* decision
marked the beginning of the end of Jim Crow in all its myriad forms and
that for black Americans for too long burdened by our subordinate status there was, to paraphrase the spiritual, "a great day a-coming."

After graduation, I joined the U.S. Department of Justice and served
for several months in the newly formed Civil Rights Division. Later,
Thurgood Marshall, then director counsel of the NAACP Legal Defense
Fund, invited me to join the staff where, from 1960 until 1965, I handled
and supervised most of the southern school litigation that at one point
reached three hundred cases. Rejoining the government in 1965, I
helped supervise enforcement of Title VI of the 1964 Civil Rights Act,
authorizing the termination of federal funds to school districts that
were found in noncompliance with the *Brown* mandate.

Joining a law faculty in 1969, I gained a broader perspective on the
campaign, by then a quarter century long, to desegregate the public
schools. In an article, "Serving Two Masters: Integration Ideals and
Client Interests in School Desegregation Litigation," 85 *Yale L.J.* 470

(1976), I argued that we were misguided in requiring racial balance of the school's student population as the measure of compliance. I urged that educational equity rather than integrated idealism was the appropriate goal. A later piece, Comment, "*Brown v. Board of Education* and the Interest-Convergence Dilemma," 93 *Harv. L. Rev.* 518 (1980), suggested the major role of fortuity in civil rights gains and why those gains tend to be fleeting even when enunciated in terms of permanence. Even so, I viewed *Brown* as basically a positive decision. As the years passed, though, my doubts have grown.

I view my dissent in this project less as a rather controversial intellectual exercise than as a guide for future race initiatives. At this late date in racial justice efforts, we know what does not work, or does not work for long. We need a new policy compass, one that recognizes and incorporates the fact that many whites are all too ready to sacrifice their economic and political interests in causes they view as protecting their entitlement to what so many assume is a vested property right in whiteness. At bottom, of course, whites need what blacks seek. The challenge is to assert petitions for racial justice in forms that whites will realize serve their interests as well as those of blacks.

My thanks to Professor Jack Balkin, Owen Jordan, and Nirej Sekhorn for their suggestions. Thanks also to the members of NYU's Africana Studies "Cultures and Testimonies" Seminar, and to Tricia Rose, its chair.

Several references could not be included in the opinion because they involved materials published after 1954, although they refer to historical matters that occurred prior to the Brown decision.

P. 188. On "historians of slavery," see Edmund Morgan, *American Slavery, American Freedom* (1975). On the idea of whiteness as a property right, see Cheryl Harris, "Whiteness as Property," 106 *Harv. L. Rev.* 1707 (1993).

P. 189. The list of the ten original slavery clauses in the Constitution that appears in fn. 8 is taken from William M. Wiecek, *The Sources of Antislavery Constitutionalism in America, 1760–1848*, at 62–105 (1977).

P. 191. On the "politics of otherness" and the "rigidly expansive notions of blackness," see, e.g., David R. Roediger, *The Wages of Whiteness: Race and the Making of the American Working Class* (1999); Howard Winant, *Racial Conditions: Politics, Theory, Comparisons* (1994); Noel Ignatiev, *How the Irish Became White* (1995). On nationalism and the politics of minstrel shows, see, e.g., Ken Emerson, *Doo Dah: Stephen Foster and the Rise of American Popular Culture* (1997).

P. 191. On the relation between not being black and being American, see Jamaica Kincaid, "The Little Revenge from the Periphery," *Transition*, Issue 73 at 68, 73 (1998).

P. 192. On the equation of "equality" with "integration," see *Brown v. Board of Education*, 347 U.S. 483, 494 (1954) ("To separate them from others of similar age and qualifications [namely white children] solely because of their race generates a feeling of inferiority as to their status in the community that may affect their hearts and minds in a way unlikely ever to be undone.")

P. 195. On the Supreme Court's motivations for outlawing segregation, see Mary Dudziak, *Cold War Civil Rights: Race and the Image of American Democracy* (2000).

Drew S. Days III

Segregation in public schools was not, as a naive reading of the *Brown* and *Bolling* decisions might suggest, an isolated example of invidious racial discrimination. It was, instead, only one manifestation of a pervasive system of racial subjugation, segregation, and discrimination that had dominated life in southern and border states for almost a century. What I tried to do in my concurrence was, unlike the *Brown* Court, to lay bare the interconnections between school segregation, on the one hand, and other elements of America's racial caste system (in housing, voting, employment, transportation, and public accommodations), on the other. In my concurrence I attempted to capture the sense of moral outrage at persistent racism and the "tell it like it is" format that I associate with the opinions of Justice William O. Douglas, particularly his concurrence in *Heart of Atlanta Motel v. United States*, 379 U.S. 241 (1964) (with *Katzenbach v. McClung*, 379 U.S. 294 (1964)) and his opinion in *Bell v. Maryland*, 378 U.S. 226 (1964). I also had the following more specific objectives in mind as I wrote my concurrence:

1. To raise general questions about the sources and reliability of judicial knowledge, the appropriate role of such knowledge in constitutional adjudication, and the limitations of traditional notions of judicial self-restraint;

2. To underscore the weak historical and jurisprudential underpinnings of *Plessy* and of the early-twentieth-century school desegregation decisions that the Court glossed over in *Brown*;

3. To criticize specifically *Brown*'s failure to overrule *Plessy* outright;

4. To caution that the Court's emphasis on the right to a racially non-segregated public education might suggest that other separate-but-equal arrangements would somehow survive the ruling in *Brown;*

5. To agree with several of my colleagues that the strict scrutiny/compelling interest approach would have provided a more secure constitutional footing. In so doing, moreover, the Court would have supplied a much-needed logical predicate for its rather inscrutable per curiam orders, issued shortly after *Brown*, declaring unconstitutional segregated public beaches, *Mayor of Baltimore v. Dawson*, 350 U.S. 877 (1955); golf courses, *Holmes v. Atlanta*, 350 U.S. 879 (1955); and buses, *Gayle v. Browder*, 352 U.S. 903 (1956), practices having nothing to do with public education;

6. To express my agreement with Bruce Ackerman's position that the first sentence of section 1 of the Fourteenth Amendment provides an ample basis for the Court's ruling in *Bolling* but also to share Michael McConnell's view that there is nothing "unthinkable," at least from a historical standpoint, about viewing the Fifth Amendment's Due Process Clause and the Fourteenth Amendment's Equal Protection Clause as dictating different results with respect to racial segregation in public education; and

7. To emphasize the right of individual blacks to a timely, effective remedy for the constitutional injuries they suffered, a consideration that seems to have been progressively ignored in the subsequent nearly half century of school desegregation litigation.

John Hart Ely

My opinion was written before any of the others, and thus had little to react against. In addition, although I clerked many years ago, every opinion I wrote in that capacity—aside from one lonely dissent—became the Opinion of the Court. I thus suspect that, preposterous as any such conscious attempt would have been given this cast of characters, I must on some unconscious level have reverted to law clerk mode and tried to write an Opinion of the Court, which accounts for the relatively spare treatment and avoidance of significant excursions into theories with which I personally am identified. In short, I was writing an opinion rather than an article.

I hold a view unusual for legal academics, that in general Supreme Court Justices do about as good a job as we do with the problems they face, and thus, more than most of my colleagues, made a point of retaining some of the language of the original *Brown* opinion, in particular the memorable "hearts and minds" passage, which has always seemed to me both eloquent and entirely to the point.

Of course there are important changes as well. The Court's controversial footnote 11, citing various social scientists to prove that segregation hurts black children, is omitted. Not on the inane ground often heard at the time, that it was not "law": if you want to know whether two groups are being treated equally, social psychology would obviously be more on point than "law" (whatever that is even supposed to mean in this context). The problem was rather that the studies the Court cited either went entirely to a different point, irrelevant to this litigation, that black schools were almost invariably tangibly inferior to white schools, or were methodologically unsound on their face—this point is annotated in detail in John Hart Ely, "If at First You Don't Succeed, Ignore the Question Next Time? Group Harm in *Brown v. Board of Education* and *Loving v. Virginia*," 15 *Const. Commentary* 215, 217–18 n.9 (1998)—thus rendering the more commonsensical ("get real") approach used here, as indeed it was elsewhere in Warren's opinion, vastly more effective. See also Charles L. Black Jr., "The Lawfulness of the Segregation Decisions," 69 *Yale L.J.* 421 (1960).

My approach to the District of Columbia ("*Bolling*") issue—one we all seem to agree the Court handled unconvincingly—briefly adumbrated in footnote 10 of my opinion, is defended at length in chapter 4 of John Hart Ely, *Democracy and Distrust: A Theory of Judicial Review* (1980).

I was frankly surprised to find myself so much more aggressive on the timing issue than my colleagues, but this is one respecting which I would have thought the intervening forty-five years had provided very clear lessons. The most vitriolic and politically opportunistic opposition to *Brown* did not develop until several years after it was handed down, thereby increasing the possibility (and reality) of violence and ensuring that "all deliberate speed" would stretch out to a seeming eternity. I simply cannot imagine that the usual requirement of immediate compliance with constitutional commands—in this case inescapably leavened (as of May 17, 1954) by a one-school-year grace period—would have done worse by the black and working-class white children we put on the front lines here than the agonizingly gradualist approach we actually followed did.

Catharine A. MacKinnon

My main concern in writing this opinion—a mere forty-five years too late—was to build a substantive rather than abstract approach to equality into the Fourteenth Amendment, so that it would stand against, rather than be incapacitated by, the realities of social inequality. Avoiding dismissal of this effort as ahistorical required a grounding in the contemporaneous sources and the record. I learned that the Justices could have done this then.

At the foundation of a substantive *Brown* is a theory of the harm of segregation. It always bothered me that the Supreme Court in *Brown* implied that the harm was in the children's heads and never said that the Black children were the white children's intellectual equals, although the opinion mostly treated them as if they were. I also wanted to make the world safer for historically Black colleges, which promote equality but are threatened by the mainstream equality paradigm, and to form a basis for continuity rather than distinction between sex- and race-based discrimination.

Because *Brown* challenged facial discrimination, it was difficult to address in advance what we now know was coming: the so-called de-facto discrimination dodge, in which housing, job, and educational discrimination connect circularly so that the pea of discrimination is always under another shell. Without overreaching factually and temporally, as well as doctrinally, all I felt I could do about this was ensure that, if my approach had been taken, the distinction between facial and impact discrimination would be as largely inconsequential legally as it is in the real world. I wish I could have figured out how to preclude a decision like *San Antonio Independent School District v. Rodriguez*, 411 U.S. 1 (1973), in which poor children attending schools financed by a low tax base were found not discriminated against in education. The approach outlined here would have been adaptable to economic class-based discrimination, as well as to the ethnicity that was largely its proxy in *Rodriguez*, but would not have ensured the right result.

The Supreme Court of Canada embraced substantive equality when it was argued in *Andrew v. Law Society*, (1989) 1 SCR 513. It is also being used in South Africa under its new constitution. The substantive analysis has, however, never been explicitly argued in the United States. The key language in my *Brown* opinion, that the state must promote equality to be consistent with the Fourteenth Amendment, is drawn from Justice Thurgood Marshall's opinion in *California Savings and Loan v. Guerra*, 479 U.S. 272 (1987), a statutory ruling in which the Court took a position, in upholding the legality of the Pregnancy Discrimination Act, that was argued by no brief filed in the case. The civil rights litigation community in the United States has failed to take on the "similarly situated" test and all that flows from it, including the way this country's equality rule builds social inequality in. This insult becomes injury daily as inequality continues, and steps to alter it, like affirmative action, are repeatedly needed, severed from ordinary nondiscrimination, and under constant threat of elimination. The substantive equality approach of this opinion would have changed—and would change—that.

This opinion is dedicated to a certain twelve-year-old girl.

Michael W. McConnell

This opinion is based on historical research I completed several years ago on the original understanding of the Fourteenth Amendment. It was published as Michael W. McConnell, "Originalism and the Desegregation Decisions," 81 *Va. L. Rev.* 947 (1995). Comments by constitutional historians on the work can be found in Vol. 81, No. 7 of the *Virginia Law Review* (Oct. 1995) and Vol. 13, No. 3 of *Constitutional Commentary* (winter 1996).

Frank I. Michelman

I add a few short notes.

1. Under the rules, I could not cite authorities that postdate the decisions. Who knows whether the reasoning in my opinion, or the similar reasoning in some of my colleagues' opinions, would have occurred to us, or would have whatever force it has for us today, but for intervening commentary? I think especially of Charles L. Black Jr., "The Lawfulness of the Segregation Decisions," 69 *Yale L. J.* 421 (1960), Charles R. Lawrence III, "The Id, the Ego, and Equal Protection: Reckoning with

Unconscious Racism," 39 *Stan. L. Rev.* 317 (1987), and Kenneth L. Karst, *Belonging to America: Equal Citizenship and the Constitution* (1989), but there are many other contributors.

2. Footnote 7, prompted by a question from T. Alexander Aleinikoff at the AALS session where drafts of these opinions were read, looks ahead to *Plyler v. Doe*, 457 U.S. 202 (1982), and Proposition 187—matters and events that I doubt would have occurred to a judge at work in 1954–55.

3. I am aware of the apparent unrealism of my concluding call to the states, localities, and Congress for constructive involvement. It nevertheless seems to me the right and appropriate thing to do. First, I think it is right in principle. Second, a line of this kind on the Court's part might, against the odds, have helped open a process, undoubtedly protracted, difficult, and painful, that could have left us with better long-term results. Third, such an immediate call by the Court for a democratic assumption of responsibility could have laid the grounds for further remedies along the lines of those charted in Professor Bell's opinion, by which I am strongly drawn.

Cass R. Sunstein

The major challenge in *Brown* is to keep two things in sight: the right substantive principle; and the right conception of the judicial role. Warren's opinion was imperfect on both counts. Most important, I sought to get the right substantive principle, by pointing the way toward an anticaste principle as the basic foundation for the outcome. At the same time, I sought to get the right conception of the judicial role, above all by indicating the continuity of the outcome with the rest of the law's fabric, and also by not ruling more broadly than necessary. These are important because any particular Court might after all be wrong, and disciplining devices of this kind help to minimize the potential damage from judicial overreaching.

Here the substantive conception and the judicial role are happily and closely related: the anticaste principle emerges nicely from history and precedent. Ours is not a static constitution (and in *Brown* that had to be acknowledged); but it changes as a result of incremental processes that impose the discipline on judges that is rightly sought by many people through inferior means, including originalists. The presumption in favor of incrementalism also had to be affirmed. By 1954, the Court had earned the right to speak relatively ambitiously and in terms of opposition to caste.

The issue under the federal Constitution is very hard. But due process rationality review, in a not entirely unconventional form, seems to me sufficient to resolve the District of Columbia case. No legitimate interest could justify segregation on the basis of race. On the remedy issue, we benefit from hindsight. I think I would have agreed with Warren at the time, but in retrospect a firmer signal would have been better. In the 1980s, Justice Marshall liked to say, "After all these years, I've finally figured out what 'all deliberate speed' really means: S-l-o-w." One problem with "slow" is that it gives continuing hope to those seeking to resist the Court's decision. I'm not sure, but I think "fast" might have better served all of the interests relevant to remedy selection, including judicial legitimacy, social stability, and racial equality.

The Supreme Court's Original Opinions in
Brown I, Bolling, and *Brown II*

BROWN et al.

v.

BOARD OF EDUCATION OF TOPEKA, SHAWNEE
COUNTY, KAN., et al.

BRIGGS et al.

v.

ELLIOTT et al.

DAVIS et al.

v.

COUNTY SCHOOL BOARD OF PRINCE EDWARD
COUNTY, VA., et al.

GEBHART et al.

v.

BELTON et al.

Nos. 1, 2, 4, 10.

Supreme Court of the United States
Reargued Dec. 7, 8, 9, 1953.
Decided May 17, 1954.
347 U.S. 483 (1954)

MR. CHIEF JUSTICE WARREN delivered the opinion of the Court.

These cases come to us from the States of Kansas, South Carolina, Virginia, and Delaware. They are premised on different facts and different local conditions, but a common legal question justifies their consideration together in this consolidated opinion.[1]

In each of the cases, minors of the Negro race, through their legal representatives, seek the aid of the courts in obtaining admission to the public schools of their community on a nonsegregated basis. In each instance, they have been denied admission to schools attended by white children under laws requiring or permitting segregation according to race. This segregation was alleged to deprive the plaintiffs of the equal protection of the laws under the Fourteenth Amendment. In each of the cases other than the Delaware case, a three-judge federal district court denied relief to the plaintiffs on the so-called "separate but equal" doctrine announced by this Court in *Plessy v. Ferguson,* 163 U.S. 537, 16 S.Ct. 1138, 41 L.Ed. 256. Under that doctrine, equality of treatment is accorded when the races are provided substantially equal facilities, even though these facilities be separate. In the Delaware case, the Supreme Court of Delaware adhered to that doctrine, but ordered that the plaintiffs be admitted to the white schools because of their superiority to the Negro schools.

The plaintiffs contend that segregated public schools are not "equal" and cannot be made "equal," and that hence they are deprived of the equal protection of the laws. Because of the obvious importance of the question presented, the Court took jurisdiction.[2] Argument was heard in the 1952 Term, and reargument was heard this Term on certain questions propounded by the Court.[3]

Reargument was largely devoted to the circumstances surrounding the adoption of the Fourteenth Amendment in 1868. It covered exhaustively consideration of the Amendment in Congress, ratification by the states, then existing practices in racial segregation, and the views of proponents and opponents of the Amendment. This discussion and our own investigation convince us that, although these sources cast some light, it is not enough to resolve the problem with which we are faced. At best, they are inconclusive. The most avid proponents of the post-War Amendments undoubtedly intended them to remove all legal distinctions among "all persons born or naturalized in the United States." Their opponents, just as certainly, were antagonistic to both the letter and the spirit of the Amendments and wished them to have the most limited effect. What others in Congress and the state legislatures had in mind cannot be determined with any degree of certainty.

An additional reason for the inconclusive nature of the Amendment's history, with respect to segregated schools, is the status of public education at that time.[4] In the South, the movement toward free common schools, supported by general taxation, had not yet taken hold. Education of white children was largely in the hands of private groups. Education of Negroes was almost nonexistent, and practically all of the race were illiterate. In fact, any education of Negroes was forbidden by law in some states. Today, in contrast, many Negroes have achieved outstanding success in the arts and sciences as well as in the business and professional world. It is true that public school education at the time of the Amendment had advanced further in the North, but the effect of the Amendment on Northern States was generally ignored in the congressional debates. Even in the North, the conditions of public education did not approximate those existing today. The curriculum was usually rudimentary; ungraded schools were common in rural areas; the school term was but three months a year in many states; and compulsory school attendance was virtually unknown. As a consequence, it is not surprising that there should be so little in the history of the Fourteenth Amendment relating to its intended effect on public education.

In the first cases in this Court construing the Fourteenth Amendment, decided shortly after its adoption, the Court interpreted it as proscribing all state-imposed discriminations against the Negro race.[5] The doctrine of "separate but equal" did not make its appearance in this court until 1896 in the case of *Plessy v. Ferguson,* supra, involving not education but transportation.[6] American courts have since labored with the doctrine for over half a century. In this Court, there have been six cases involving the "separate but equal" doctrine in the field of public education.[7] In *Cumming v. Board of Education of Richmond County,* 175 U.S. 528, 20 S.Ct. 197, 44 L.Ed. 262, and *Gong Lum v. Rice,* 275 U.S. 78, 48 S.Ct. 91, 72 L.Ed. 172, the validity of the doctrine itself was not challenged.[8] In more recent cases, all on the graduate school level, inequality was found in that specific benefits enjoyed by white students were denied to Negro students of the same educational qualifications. *State of Missouri ex rel. Gaines v. Canada,* 305 U.S. 337, 59 S.Ct. 232, 83 L.Ed. 208; *Sipuel v. Board of Regents of University of Oklahoma,* 332 U.S. 631, 68 S.Ct. 299, 92 L.Ed. 247; *Sweatt v. Painter,* 339 U.S. 629, 70 S.Ct. 848, 94 L.Ed. 1114; *McLaurin v. Oklahoma State Regents,* 339 U.S. 637, 70 S.Ct. 851, 94 L.Ed. 1149. In none of these cases was it necessary to re-examine the doctrine to grant relief to the Negro plaintiff. And in *Sweatt v. Painter, supra,* the Court expressly reserved decision on the question whether *Plessy v. Ferguson* should be held inapplicable to public education.

In the instant cases, that question is directly presented. Here, unlike *Sweatt v. Painter,* there are findings below that the Negro and white schools involved have been equalized, or are being equalized, with respect to buildings, curricula, qualifications and salaries of teachers, and other "tangible" factors.[9] Our decision, therefore, cannot turn on merely a comparison of these tangible factors in the Negro and white schools involved in each of the cases. We must look instead to the effect of segregation itself on public education.

In approaching this problem, we cannot turn the clock back to 1868 when the Amendment was adopted, or even to 1896 when *Plessy v. Ferguson* was written. We must consider public education in the light of its full development and its present place in American life throughout the Nation. Only in this way can it be determined if segregation in public schools deprives these plaintiffs of the equal protection of the laws.

Today, education is perhaps the most important function of state and local governments. Compulsory school attendance laws and the great expenditures for education both demonstrate our recognition of the importance of education to our democratic society. It is required in the performance of our most basic public responsibilities, even service in the armed forces. It is the very foundation of good citizenship. Today it is a principal instrument in awakening the child to cultural values, in preparing him for later professional training, and in helping him to adjust normally to his environment. In these days, it is doubtful that any child may reasonably be expected to succeed in life if he is denied the opportunity of an education. Such an opportunity, where the state has undertaken to provide it, is a right which must be made available to all on equal terms.

We come then to the question presented: Does segregation of children in public schools solely on the basis of race, even though the physical facilities and other "tangible" factors may be equal, deprive the children of the minority group of equal educational opportunities? We believe that it does.

In *Sweatt v. Painter, supra* (339 U.S. 629, 70 S.Ct. 850), in finding that a segregated law school for Negroes could not provide them equal educational opportunities, this Court relied in large part on "those qualities which are incapable of objective measurement but which make for greatness in a law school." In *McLaurin v. Oklahoma State Regents, supra* (339 U.S. 637, 70 S.Ct. 853), the Court, in requiring that a Negro admitted to a white graduate school be treated like all other students, again resorted to intangible considerations: ". . . his ability to study, to engage in discussions and exchange views with other students, and, in general, to learn his profession." Such considerations apply with added force to children in grade and high schools. To separate them from others of similar age and qualifications solely because of their race generates a feeling of inferiority as to their status in the community that may affect their hearts and minds in a way unlikely ever to be undone. The effect of this separation on their educational opportunities was well stated by a finding in the Kansas case by a court which nevertheless felt compelled to rule against the Negro plaintiffs:

> Segregation of white and colored children in public schools has a detrimental effect upon the colored children. The impact is greater when it has the sanction of the law; for the policy of separating the races is usually interpreted as denoting the inferiority of the negro group. A sense of inferiority affects the motivation of a child to learn. Segregation with the sanction of law, therefore, has a tendency to [retard] the educational and mental development of Negro children and to deprive them of some of the benefits they would receive in a racial[ly] integrated school system.[10]

Whatever may have been the extent of psychological knowledge at the time of *Plessy v. Ferguson,* this finding is amply supported by modern authority.[11] Any language in *Plessy v. Ferguson* contrary to this finding is rejected.

We conclude that in the field of public education the doctrine of "separate but equal" has no place. Separate educational facilities are inherently unequal. Therefore, we hold that the plaintiffs and others similarly situated for whom the actions have been brought are, by reason of the segregation complained of, deprived of the equal protection of the laws guaranteed by the Fourteenth Amendment. This disposition makes unnecessary any discussion whether such segregation also violates the Due Process Clause of the Fourteenth Amendment.[12]

Because these are class actions, because of the wide applicability of this decision, and because of the great variety of local conditions, the formulation of decrees in these cases presents problems of considerable complexity. On reargument, the consideration of appropriate relief was necessarily subordinated to the primary question—the constitutionality of segregation in public education. We have now announced that such segregation is a denial of the equal protection of the laws. In order that we may have the full assistance of the parties in formulating decrees, the cases will be restored to the docket, and the parties are requested to present further argument on Questions 4 and 5 previously propounded by the Court for the reargument this Term.[13] The Attorney General of the United States is again invited to participate. The Attorneys General of the states requiring or permitting segregation in public education will also be permitted to appear as amici curiae upon request to do so by September 15, 1954, and submission of briefs by October 1, 1954.[14]

It is so ordered.

Cases ordered restored to docket for further argument on question of appropriate decrees.

NOTES TO BROWN I

1. In the Kansas case, *Brown v. Board of Education,* the plaintiffs are Negro children of elementary school age residing in Topeka. They brought this action in the United States District Court for the District of Kansas to enjoin enforcement of a Kansas statute which permits, but does not require, cities of more than 15,000 population to maintain separate school facilities for Negro and white students. Kan.Gen.Stat.1949, s 72—1724. Pursuant to that authority, the Topeka Board of Education elected to establish segregated elementary schools. Other public schools in the community, however, are operated on a nonsegregated basis. The three-judge District Court, convened under 28 U.S.C. ss 2281 and 2284, 28 U.S.C.A. ss 2281, 2284, found that segregation in public education has a detrimental effect upon Negro children, but denied relief on the ground that the Negro and white schools were substantially equal with respect to buildings, transportation, curricula, and educational qualifications of teachers. 98 F.Supp. 797. The case is here on direct appeal under 28 U.S.C. s 1253, 28 U.S.C.A. s 1253. In the South Carolina case, *Briggs v. Elliott,* the plaintiffs are Negro children of both elementary and high school age residing in Clarendon County. They brought this action in the United States District Court for the Eastern District of South Carolina to enjoin enforcement of provisions in the state constitution and statutory code which require the segregation of Negroes and whites in public schools. S.C.Const. Art. XI, s 7; S.C.Code 1942, s 5377. The three-judge District Court, convened under 28 U.S.C. ss 2281 and 2284, 28 U.S.C.A. ss 2281, 2284, denied the requested relief. The court found that the Negro schools were inferior to the white schools and ordered the defendants to begin immediately to equalize the facilities. But the court sustained the validity of the contested provisions and denied the plaintiffs admission to the white schools during the equalization program. 98 F.Supp. 529. This Court vacated the District Court's judgment and

remanded the case for the purpose of obtaining the court's views on a report filed by the defendants concerning the progress made in the equalization program. 342 U.S. 350, 72 S.Ct. 327, 96 L.Ed. 392. On remand, the District Court found that substantial equality had been achieved except for buildings and that the defendants were proceeding to rectify this inequality as well. 103 F.Supp. 920. The case is again here on direct appeal under 28 U.S.C. s 1253, 28 U.S.C.A. s 1253. In the Virginia case, *Davis v. County School Board,* the plaintiffs are Negro children of high school age residing in Prince Edward County. They brought this action in the United States District Court for the Eastern District of Virginia to enjoin enforcement of provisions in the state constitution and statutory code which require the segregation of Negroes and whites in public schools. Va.Const. s 140; Va.Code 1950, s 22—221. The three-judge District Court, convened under 28 U.S.C. ss 2281 and 2284, 28 U.S.C.A. ss 2281, 2284, denied the requested relief. The court found the Negro school inferior in physical plant, curricula, and transportation, and ordered the defendants forthwith to provide substantially equal curricula and transportation and to "proceed with all reasonable diligence and dispatch to remove" the inequality in physical plant. But, as in the South Carolina case, the court sustained the validity of the contested provisions and denied the plaintiffs admission to the white schools during the equalization program. 103 F.Supp. 337. The case is here on direct appeal under 28 U.S.C. s 1253, 28 U.S.C.A. s 1253.

2. 344 U.S. 1, 73 S.Ct. 1, 97 L.Ed. 3, Id., 344 U.S. 141, 73 S.Ct. 124, 97 L.Ed. 152, *Gebhart v. Belton,* 344 U.S. 891, 73 S.Ct. 213, 97 L.Ed. 689.

3. 345 U.S. 972, 73 S.Ct. 1118, 97 L.Ed. 1388. The Attorney General of the United States participated both Terms as amicus curiae.

4. For a general study of the development of public education prior to the Amendment, see Butts and Cremin, A History of Education in American Culture (1953), Pts. I, II: Cubberley, Public Education in the United States (1934 ed.), cc. II–XII. School practices current at the time of the adoption of the Fourteenth Amendment are described in Butts and Cremin, *supra,* at 269–275; Cubberley, *supra,* at 288–339, 408–431; Knight, Public Education in the South (1922), cc. VIII, IX. See also H. Ex. Doc. No. 315, 41st Cong., 2d Sess. (1871). Although the demand for free public schools followed substantially the same pattern in both the North and the South, the development in the South did not begin to gain momentum until about 1850, some twenty years after that in the North. The reasons for the somewhat slower development in the South (e.g., the rural character of the South and the different regional attitudes toward state assistance) are well explained in Cubberley, *supra,* at 408–423. In the country as a whole, but particularly in the South, the War virtually stopped all progress in public education. Id., at 427–428. The low status of Negro education in all sections of the country, both before and immediately after the War, is described in Beale, A History of Freedom of Teaching in American Schools (1941), 112–132, 175–195.

Compulsory school attendance laws were not generally adopted until after the ratification of the Fourteenth Amendment, and it was not until 1918 that such laws were in force in all the states. Cubberley, supra, at 563–565.

5. *In re Slaughter-House Cases,* 1873, 16 Wall. 36, 67–72, 21 L.Ed. 394; *Strauder v. West Virginia,* 1880, 100 U.S. 303, 307–308, 25 L.Ed. 664.

It ordains that no State shall deprive any person of life, liberty, or property, without due process of law, or deny to any person within its jurisdiction the equal protection of the laws. What is this but declaring that the law in the States shall be the same for the black as for the white; that all persons, whether colored or white, shall stand equal before the laws of the States, and, in regard to the colored race, for whose protection the amendment was primarily designed, that no discrimination shall be made against them by law because of their color? The words of the amendment, it is true, are prohibitory, but they contain a necessary implication of a positive immunity, or right, most valuable to the colored race,—the right to exemption from unfriendly legislation against them distinctively as colored,—exemption from legal discriminations, implying inferiority in civil society, lessening the security of their enjoyment of the rights which others enjoy, and discriminations which are steps towards reducing them to the condition of a subject race.

6. The doctrine apparently originated in *Roberts v. City of Boston,* 1850, 5 Cush. 198, 59 Mass. 198, 206, upholding school segregation against attack as being violative of a state constitutional guarantee of equality. Segregation in Boston public schools was eliminated in 1855. Mass. Acts 1855, c. 256. But elsewhere in the North segregation in public education has persisted in some communities until recent years. It is apparent that such segregation has long been a nationwide problem, not merely one of sectional concern.

7. See also *Berea College v. Kentucky,* 1908, 211 U.S. 45, 29 S.Ct. 33, 53 L.Ed. 81.

8. In the *Cumming* case, Negro taxpayers sought an injunction requiring the defendant school board to discontinue the operation of a high school for white children until the board resumed operation of a high school for Negro children. Similarly, in the *Gong Lum* case, the plaintiff, a child of Chinese descent, contended only that state authorities had misapplied the doctrine by classifying him with Negro children and requiring him to attend a Negro school.

9. In the Kansas case, the court below found substantial equality as to all such factors. 98 F.Supp. 797, 798. In the South Carolina case, the court below found that the defendants were proceeding "promptly and in good faith to comply with the court's decree." 103 F.Supp. 920, 921. In the Virginia case, the court below noted that the equalization program was already "afoot and progressing," 103 F.Supp. 337, 341; since then, we have been advised, in the Virginia Attorney General's brief on reargument, that the program has now been

completed. In the Delaware case, the court below similarly noted that the state's equalization program was well under way. 91 A.2d 137, 139.

10. A similar finding was made in the Delaware case: "I conclude from the testimony that in our Delaware society, State-imposed segregation in education itself results in the Negro children, as a class, receiving educational opportunities which are substantially inferior to those available to white children otherwise similarly situated." 87 A.2d 862, 865.

11. K. B. Clark, Effect of Prejudice and Discrimination on Personality Development (Midcentury White House Conference on Children and Youth, 1950); Witmer and Kotinsky, Personality in the Making (1952), c. VI; Deutscher and Chein, The Psychological Effects of Enforced Segregation: A Survey of Social Science Opinion, 26 J.Psychol. 259 (1948); Chein, What Are the Psychological Effects of Segregation Under Conditions of Equal Facilities?, 3 Int. J. Opinion and Attitude Res. 229 (1949); Brameld, Educational Costs, in Discrimination and National Welfare (MacIver, ed., 1949), 44–48; Frazier, The Negro in the United States (1949), 674–681. And see generally Myrdal, An American Dilemma (1944).

12. See *Bolling v. Sharpe*, 347 U.S. 497, 74 S.Ct. 693, concerning the Due Process Clause of the Fifth Amendment.

13.

4. Assuming it is decided that segregation in public schools violates the Fourteenth Amendment

  (a) would a decree necessarily follow providing that, within the limits set by normal geographic school districting, Negro children should forthwith be admitted to schools of their choice, or

  (b) may this Court, in the exercise of its equity powers, permit an effective gradual adjustment to be brought about from existing segregated systems to a system not based on color distinctions?

5. On the assumption on which questions 4(a) and (b) are based, and assuming further that this Court will exercise its equity powers to the end described in question 4(b),

  (a) should this Court formulate detailed decrees in these cases;

  (b) if so, what specific issues should the decrees reach;

  (c) should this Court appoint a special master to hear evidence with a view to recommending specific terms for such decrees;

  (d) should this Court remand to the courts of first instance with directions to frame decrees in these cases, and if so what general directions should the decrees of this Court include and what procedures should the courts of first instance follow in arriving at the specific terms of more detailed decrees?'

14. See Rule 42, Revised Rules of this Court, effective July 1, 1954, 28 U.S.C.A.

BOLLING et al.

v.

SHARPE et al.

No. 8.

Supreme Court of the United States
Reargued Dec. 8, 9, 1953.
Decided May 17, 1954.
347 U.S. 497 (1954)

MR. CHIEF JUSTICE WARREN delivered the opinion of the Court.

This case challenges the validity of segregation in the public schools of the District of Columbia. The petitioners, minors of the Negro race, allege that such segregation deprives them of due process of law under the Fifth Amendment. They were refused admission to a public school attended by white children solely because of their race. They sought the aid of the District Court for the District of Columbia in obtaining admission. That court dismissed their complaint. The Court granted a writ of certiorari before judgment in the Court of Appeals because of the importance of the constitutional question presented. 344 U.S. 873, 73 S.Ct. 173, 97 L.Ed. 676.

We have this day held that the Equal Protection Clause of the Fourteenth Amendment prohibits the states from maintaining racially segregated public schools.[1] The legal problem in the District of Columbia is somewhat different, however. The Fifth Amendment, which is applicable in the District of Columbia, does not contain an equal protection clause as does the Fourteenth Amendment which applies only to the states. But the concepts of equal protection and due process, both stemming from our American ideal of fairness, are not mutually exclusive. The "equal protection of the laws" is a more explicit safeguard of prohibited unfairness than "due process of law," and, therefore, we do not imply that the two are always interchangeable phrases. But, as this Court has recognized, discrimination may be so unjustifiable as to be violative of due process.[2]

Classifications based solely upon race must be scrutinized with particular care, since they are contrary to our traditions and hence constitutionally suspect.[3] As long ago as 1896, this Court declared the principle "that the constitution of the United States, in its present form, forbids, so far as civil and political rights are concerned, discrimination by the general government, or by the states, against any citizen because of his race."[4] And in *Buchanan v. Warley,* 245 U.S. 60, 38 S.Ct. 16, 62 L.Ed. 149, the Court held that a statute which limited the right of a property owner to convey his property to a person of another race was, as an unreasonable discrimination, a denial of due process of law.

Although the Court has not assumed to define 'liberty' with any great precision, that term is not confined to mere freedom from bodily restraint. Liberty under law extends to the full range of conduct which the individual is free to pursue, and it cannot be restricted except for a proper governmental objective. Segregation in public education is not reasonably related to any proper governmental objective, and thus it imposes on Negro children of the District of Columbia a burden that constitutes an arbitrary deprivation of their liberty in violation of the Due Process Clause.

In view of our decision that the Constitution prohibits the states from maintaining racially segregated public schools, it would be unthinkable that the same Constitution would impose a lesser duty on the Federal Government.[5] We hold that racial segregation in the public schools of the District of Columbia is a denial of the due process of law guaranteed by the Fifth Amendment to the Constitution.

For the reasons set out in *Brown v. Board of Education,* this case will be restored to the docket for reargument on Questions 4 and 5 previously propounded by the Court. 345 U.S. 972, 73 S.Ct. 1114, 97 L.Ed. 1388.

It is so ordered.

Case restored to docket for reargument on question of appropriate decree.

NOTES TO BOLLING V. SHARPE

1. *Brown v. Board of Education,* 347 U.S. 483, 74 S.Ct. 686.

2. *Detroit Bank v. United States,* 317 U.S. 329, 63 S.Ct. 297, 87 L.Ed. 304; *Currin v. Wallace,* 306 U.S. 1, 13–14, 59 S.Ct. 379, 386, 83 L.Ed. 441; *Steward Machine Co. v. Davis,* 301 U.S. 548, 585, 57 S.Ct. 883, 890, 81 L.Ed. 1279.

3. *Korematsu v. United States,* 323 U.S. 214, 216, 65 S.Ct. 193, 194, 89 L.Ed. 194; *Hirabayashi v. United States,* 320 U.S. 81, 100, 63 S.Ct. 1375, 1385, 87 L.Ed. 1774.

4. *Gibson v. Mississippi,* 162 U.S. 565, 591, 16 S.Ct. 904, 910, 40 L.Ed. 1075. Cf. *Steele v. Louisville & Nashville R. Co.,* 323 U.S. 192, 198–199, 65 S.Ct. 226, 230, 89 L.Ed. 173.

5. Cf. *Hurd v. Hodge,* 334 U.S. 24, 68 S.Ct. 847, 92 L.Ed. 1187.

Oliver BROWN, et al., Appellants,

v.

BOARD OF EDUCATION OF TOPEKA, Shawnee County,
KANSAS, et al.

Harry BRIGGS, Jr., et al., Appellants,

v.

R. W. ELLIOTT, et al.

Dorothy E. DAVIS, et al., Appellants,

v.

COUNTY SCHOOL BOARD OF PRINCE EDWARD COUNTY,
VIRGINIA, et al.

Spottswood Thomas BOLLING, et al., Petitioners,

v.

C. Melvin SHARPE, et al.

Francis B. GEBHART, et al., Petitioners,

v.

Ethel Louise BELTON, et al.

Nos. 1 to 5.

Supreme Court of the United States
Argued April 11, 12, 13 and 14, 1955.
Decided May 31, 1955.
349 U.S. 294 (1955)

Mr. Chief Justice Warren delivered the opinion of the Court.

These cases were decided on May 17, 1954. The opinions of that date,[1]
declaring the fundamental principle that racial discrimination in public

education is unconstitutional, are incorporated herein by reference. All provisions of federal, state, or local law requiring or permitting such discrimination must yield to this principle. There remains for consideration the manner in which relief is to be accorded.

Because these cases arose under different local conditions and their disposition will involve a variety of local problems, we requested further argument on the question of relief.[2] In view of the nationwide importance of the decision, we invited the Attorney General of the United States and the Attorneys General of all states requiring or permitting racial discrimination in public education to present their views on that question. The parties, the United States, and the States of Florida, North Carolina, Arkansas, Oklahoma, Maryland, and Texas filed briefs and participated in the oral argument.

These presentations were informative and helpful to the Court in its consideration of the complexities arising from the transition to a system of public education freed of racial discrimination. The presentations also demonstrated that substantial steps to eliminate racial discrimination in public schools have already been taken, not only in some of the communities in which these cases arose, but in some of the states appearing as amici curiae, and in other states as well. Substantial progress has been made in the District of Columbia and in the communities in Kansas and Delaware involved in this litigation. The defendants in the cases coming to us from South Carolina and Virginia are awaiting the decision of this Court concerning relief.

Full implementation of these constitutional principles may require solution of varied local school problems. School authorities have the primary responsibility for elucidating, assessing, and solving these problems; courts will have to consider whether the action of school authorities constitutes good faith implementation of the governing constitutional principles. Because of their proximity to local conditions and the possible need for further hearings, the courts which originally heard these cases can best perform this judicial appraisal. Accordingly, we believe it appropriate to remand the cases to those courts.[3]

In fashioning and effectuating the decrees, the courts will be guided by equitable principles. Traditionally, equity has been characterized by a practical flexibility in shaping its remedies[4] and by a facility for adjusting and reconciling public and private needs.[5] These cases call for the exercise of these traditional attributes of equity power. At stake is the personal interest of the plaintiffs in admission to public schools as soon as practicable on a nondiscriminatory basis. To effectuate this interest may call for elimination of a variety of obstacles in making the transition to school systems operated in accordance with the constitutional principles set forth in our May 17, 1954, decision. Courts of equity may properly take into account the public interest in the elimination of such obstacles in a systematic and effective manner. But it should go without saying that the vitality of these constitutional principles cannot be allowed to yield simply because of disagreement with them.

While giving weight to these public and private considerations, the courts will require that the defendants make a prompt and reasonable start toward full compliance with our May 17, 1954, ruling. Once such a start has been made, the courts may find that additional time is necessary to carry out the ruling in an effective manner. The burden rests upon the defendants to establish that such time is necessary in the public interest and is consistent with good faith compliance at the earliest practicable date. To that end, the courts may consider problems related to administration, arising from the physical condition of the school plant, the school transportation system, personnel, revision of school districts and attendance areas into compact units to achieve a system of determining admission to the public schools on a nonracial basis, and revision of local laws and regulations which may be necessary in solving the foregoing problems. They will also consider the adequacy of any plans the defendants may propose to meet these problems and to effectuate a transition to a racially nondiscriminatory school system. During this period of transition, the courts will retain jurisdiction of these cases.

The judgments below, except that in the Delaware case, are accordingly reversed and the cases are remanded to the District Courts to take such proceedings and enter such orders and decrees consistent with this opinion as are necessary and proper to admit to public schools on a racially nondiscriminatory basis with all deliberate speed the parties to these cases. The judgment in the Delaware case—ordering the immediate admission of the plaintiffs to schools previously attended only by white children—is affirmed on the basis of the principles stated in our May 17, 1954, opinion, but the case is remanded to the Supreme Court of Delaware for such further proceedings as that Court may deem necessary in light of this opinion.

It is so ordered.

Judgments, except that in case No. 5, reversed and cases remanded with directions; judgment in case No. 5 affirmed and case remanded with directions.

NOTES TO BROWN II

1. 347 U.S. 483, 74 S.Ct. 686, 98 L.Ed. 873, 347 U.S. 497, 74 S.Ct. 693, 98 L.Ed. 884.

2. Further argument was requested on the following questions, 347 U.S. 483, 495–496, note 13, 74 S.Ct. 686, 692, 98 L.Ed. 873, previously propounded by the Court:

4. Assuming it is decided that segregation in public schools violates the Fourteenth Amendment

(a) would a decree necessarily follow providing that, within the limits set by normal geographic school districting, Negro children should forthwith be admitted to schools of their choice, or

(b) may this Court, in the exercise of its equity powers, permit an effective gradual adjustment to be brought about from existing segregated systems to a system not based on color distinctions?

5. On the assumption on which questions 4(a) and (b) are based, and assuming further that this Court will exercise its equity powers to the end described in question 4(b),

(a) should this Court formulate detailed decrees in these cases;

(b) if so, what specific issues should the decrees reach;

(c) should this Court appoint a special master to hear evidence with a view to recommending specific terms for such decrees;

(d) should this Court remand to the courts of first instance with directions to frame decrees in these cases, and if so what general directions should the decrees of this Court include and what procedures should the courts of first instance follow in arriving at the specific terms of more detailed decrees?

3. The cases coming to us from Kansas, South Carolina, and Virginia were originally heard by three-judge District Courts convened under 28 U.S.C. ss 2281 and 2284, 28 U.S.C.A. ss 2281, 2284. These cases will accordingly be remanded to those three-judge courts. See *Briggs v. Elliott,* 342 U.S. 350, 72 S.Ct. 327, 96 L.Ed. 392.

4. See *Alexander v. Hillman,* 296 U.S. 222, 239, 56 S.Ct. 204, 209, 80 L.Ed. 192.

5. See *Hecht Co. v. Bowles,* 321 U.S. 321, 329–330, 64 S.Ct. 587, 591, 592, 88 L.Ed. 754.

The Constitution of the United States of America
Selected Provisions

Amendment V (1791)

No person shall be held to answer for a capital, or otherwise infamous crime, unless on a presentment or indictment of a Grand Jury, except in cases arising in the land or naval forces, or in the Militia, when in actual service in time of War or public danger; nor shall any person be subject for the same offense to be twice put in jeopardy of life or limb; nor shall be compelled in any criminal case to be a witness against himself, nor be deprived of life, liberty, or property, without due process of law; nor shall private property be taken for public use without just compensation.

Amendment XIII (1865)

1. Neither slavery nor involuntary servitude, except as a punishment for a crime whereof the party shall have been duly convicted, shall exist within the United States, or any place subject to their jurisdiction.

2. Congress shall have power to enforce this article by appropriate legislation.

Amendment XIV (1868)

1. All persons born or naturalized in the United States, and subject to the jurisdiction thereof, are citizens of the United States and of the State

wherein they reside. No State shall make or enforce any law which shall abridge the privileges or immunities of citizens of the United States; nor shall any State deprive any person of life, liberty, or property, without due process of law; nor deny to any person within its jurisdiction the equal protection of the laws.

2. Representatives shall be apportioned among the several States according to their respective numbers, counting the whole number of persons in each State, excluding Indians not taxed. But when the right to vote at any election for the choice of electors for President and Vice-President of the United States, Representatives in Congress, the Executive and Judicial officers of a State, or the members of the Legislature thereof, is denied to any of the male inhabitants of such State, being twenty-one years of age, and citizens of the United States, or in any way abridged, except for participation in rebellion, or other crime, the basis of representation therein shall be reduced in the proportion which the number of such male citizens shall bear to the whole number of male citizens twenty-one years of age in such State.

3. No person shall be a Senator or Representative in Congress, or elector of President and Vice-President, or hold any office, civil or military, under the United States, or under any State, who, having previously taken an oath, as a member of Congress, or as an officer of the United States, or as a member of any State legislature, or as an executive or judicial officer of any State, to support the Constitution of the United States, shall have engaged in insurrection or rebellion against the same, or given aid or comfort to the enemies thereof. But Congress may by a vote of two-thirds of each House, remove such disability.

4. The validity of the public debt of the United States, authorized by law, including debts incurred for payment of pensions and bounties for services in suppressing insurrection or rebellion, shall not be questioned. But neither the United States nor any State shall assume or pay any debt or obligation incurred in aid of insurrection or rebellion against the United States, or any claim for the loss or emancipation of any slave; but all such debts, obligations and claims shall be held illegal and void.

5. The Congress shall have the power to enforce, by appropriate legislation, the provisions of this article.

Amendment XV (1870)

1. The right of citizens of the United States to vote shall not be denied or abridged by the United States or by any State on account of race, color, or previous condition of servitude.

2. The Congress shall have the power to enforce this article by appropriate legislation.

Brown v. Board of Education:
A Selected Bibliography

Brown v. Board of Education is one of the most written about opinions in American history. A comprehensive bibliography would take many pages. Instead, I offer a list of works consulted in preparing this book, plus a basic list of works (1) on *Brown* itself, (2) on the civil rights movement, (3) on race relations, (4) on educational policy, (5) on theories of constitutional equality, and (6) on constitutional interpretation generally.

Ackerman, Bruce A. "Beyond *Carolene* Products." 98 *Harv. L. Rev.* 713 (1985).

———, 1 and 2 *We the People: Transformations.* Cambridge: Harvard University Press, 1991, 1998.

Amar, Akhil Reed. *The Bill of Rights: Creation and Reconstruction.* New Haven: Yale University Press, 1998.

Armor, David J. *Forced Justice: School Desegregation and the Law.* New York: Oxford University Press, 1995.

Balkin, J. M. "The Constitution of Status." 107 *Yale L.J.* 2313 (1997).

Ball, Howard. *A Defiant Life: Thurgood Marshall and the Persistence of Racism in America.* New York: Crown Publishers, 1998.

Bell, Derrick A. *And We Are Not Saved: The Elusive Quest for Racial Justice.* New York: Basic Books, 1987.

———. "*Brown v. Board of Education* and the Interest-Convergence Dilemma," 93 *Harv. L. Rev.* 518 (1980).

———. *Faces at the Bottom of the Well: The Permanence of Racism.* New York: Basic Books, 1992.

———. *Race, Racism, and American Law.* 4th ed. Boston: Little Brown, 2000.

———. "Serving Two Masters: Integration Ideals and Client Interests in School Desegregation Litigation." 85 *Yale L.J.* 470 (1976).

Berger, Raoul. *Government by Judiciary: The Transformation of the Fourteenth Amendment.* Cambridge: Harvard University Press, 1977.

Bickel, Alexander M. *The Least Dangerous Branch: The Supreme Court at the Bar of Politics.* New Haven: Yale University Press, 1962.

———. "The Original Understanding and the Segregation Decision," 69 *Harv. L. Rev.* 1 (1955).

Black, Charles L., Jr. "The Lawfulness of the Segregation Decisions." 69 *Yale L.J.* 421 (1960).

Bork, Robert H. *The Tempting of America: The Political Seduction of the Law.* New York: Free Press, 1990.

Branch, Taylor. *Parting the Waters: America in the King Years, 1954–1963.* New York: Simon & Schuster, 1988.

Brauer, Carl M. *John F. Kennedy and the Second Reconstruction.* New York: Columbia University Press, 1977.

Brest, Paul. "The Supreme Court, 1975 Term—Foreword: In Defense of the Antidiscrimination Principle." 90 *Harv. L. Rev.* 1 (1976).

Brest, Paul; Levinson, Sanford; Balkin, J. M.; and Amar, Akhil Reed. *Processes of Constitutional Decisionmaking: Cases and Materials.* 4th ed. New York: Aspen Publishers, 2000.

Brown, Kevin. "Do African-Americans Need Immersion Schools? The Paradoxes Created by Legal Conceptualization of Race and Public Education." 78 *Iowa L. Rev.* 813 (1993).

———. "Has the Supreme Court Allowed the Cure for De Jure Segregation to Replicate the Disease?" 78 *Cornell L. Rev.* 1 (1992).

Butts, R. Freeman, and Cremin, Lawrence A. *A History of Education in American Culture.* New York: Holt, Rinehart and Winston, 1963.

Carter, Dan T. *The Politics of Rage: George Wallace, the Origins of the New Conservatism, and the Transformation of American Politics.* New York: Simon & Schuster, 1995.

Cremin, Lawrence A. *American Education: The National Experience 1783–1876.* New York: Harper and Row, 1980.

———. *Traditions of American Education.* New York: Basic Books, 1977.

Crenshaw, Kimberle Williams. "Race, Reform, and Retrenchment: Transformation and Legitimation in Antidiscrimination Law," 101 *Harv. L. Rev.* 1331 (1988).

Dahl, Robert. "Decision-Making in a Democracy: The Supreme Court as a National Policy-Maker," 6 *J. Pub. L.* 279 (1957).

Days, Drew S., III. "Brown Blues: Rethinking the Integrative Ideal." 34 *Wm. & Mary L. Rev.* 53 (1992).

———. "Fullilove." 96 *Yale L.J.* 453 (1987).

———. "School Desegregation Law in the 1980's: Why Isn't Anybody Laughing?" 95 *Yale L.J.* 1737 (1986).

Dimond, Paul R. "The Anti-Caste Principle—Toward a Constitutional Standard for Review of Race Cases." 30 *Wayne L. Rev.* 1 (1983).

———. *Beyond Busing: Inside the Challenge to Urban Segregation.* Ann Arbor: University of Michigan Press, 1985.

Dudziak, Mary L. "Desegregation as a Cold War Imperative." 41 *Stan. L. Rev.* 61 (1988).

Dunne, Finley Peter. *Mr. Dooley at His Best*. Elmer Ellis ed. New York: C. Scribner's Sons, 1938.

Ely, John Hart. *Democracy and Distrust: A Theory of Judicial Review*. Cambridge: Harvard University Press, 1980.

Fairclough, Adam. *To Redeem the Soul of America: The Southern Christian Leadership Conference and Martin Luther King, Jr.* Athens: University of Georgia Press, 1987.

Fava, Eileen M. "Desegregation and Parental Control in Public Schooling." 11 *B.C. Third World L.J.* 83 (1991).

Fiss, Owen M. "Groups and the Equal Protection Clause." 5 *Phil. & Pub. Aff.* 107 (1976).

———. "A Life Lived Twice." 100 *Yale L.J.* 1117 (1991).

———. "The Supreme Court, 1978 Term—Foreword: The Forms of Justice." 93 *Harv. L. Rev.* 1 (1979).

Foner, Eric. *Free Soil, Free Labor, Free Men: The Ideology of the Republican Party before the Civil War*. New York: Oxford University Press, 1995.

———. *Reconstruction: America's Unfinished Revolution, 1863–1877*. New York: Harper & Row, 1988.

Franklin, John Hope, and Moss, Alfred A., Jr. *From Slavery to Freedom: A History of Negro Americans*. 7th ed. New York: Alfred A. Knopf, 1994.

Freeman, Alan. "Legitimating Racial Discrimination through Antidiscrimination Law: A Critical Review of Supreme Court Doctrine." 62 *Minn. L. Rev.* 1049 (1978).

Friedman, Leon, ed. *Argument: The Oral Argument before the Supreme Court in Brown v. Board of Education of Topeka, 1952–55*. New York: Chelsea House Publishers, 1969.

Garrow, David J. *Bearing the Cross: Martin Luther King, Jr., and the Southern Christian Leadership Conference*. New York: William Morrow, 1986.

Graham, Hugh Davis. *The Civil Rights Era: Origins and Development of National Policy, 1960–1972*. New York: Oxford University Press, 1990.

Haney-López, Ian F. *White by Law: The Legal Construction of Race*. New York: New York University Press, 1996.

Henry, A'lelia Robinson. "Perpetuating Inequality: *Plessy v. Ferguson* and the Dilemma of Black Access to Public and Higher Education." 27 *J. of Law and Education* 47 (1998).

Higginbotham, A. Leon, Jr. *In the Matter of Color: Race and the American Legal Process*. New York: Oxford University Press, 1978.

———. *Shades of Freedom: Racial Politics and Presumptions of the American Legal Process*. New York: Oxford University Press, 1996.

Hutchinson, Dennis J. "Unanimity and Desegregation: Decisionmaking in the Supreme Court, 1948–1958." 68 *Geo. L.J.* 1 (1979).

Johnson, Alex M., Jr. "Bid Whist, Tonk, and *United States v. Fordice*: Why

Integrationism Fails African-Americans Again." 81 *Calif. L. Rev.* 1401 (1993).

Joondeph, Bradley W. "A Second Redemption?" 56 *Wash. & Lee L. Rev.* 169 (1999).

Karst, Kenneth L. *Belonging to America: Equal Citizenship and the Constitution.* New Haven: Yale University Press, 1989.

———. "The Supreme Court 1976 Term—Foreword: Equal Citizenship under the Fourteenth Amendment." 91 *Harv. L. Rev.* 1 (1977).

Kelly, Alfred. "The School Desegregation Case." In *Quarrels That Have Shaped the Constitution,* John Garraty ed. New York, Harper & Row, 1964.

Kirp, David L. *Just Schools: The Idea of Racial Equality in American Education.* Berkeley: University of California Press, 1982.

Klarman, Michael J. "*Brown,* Originalism, and Constitutional Theory: A Response to Professor McConnell." 81 *Va. L. Rev.* 1881 (1995).

———. "*Brown,* Racial Change, and the Civil Rights Movement." 80. *Va. L. Rev.* 7 (1994).

———. "The *Plessy* Era." 1998 *Sup. Ct. Rev.* 303 (1998).

———. "The Puzzling Resistance to Political Process Theory." 77 *Va. L. Rev.* 747 (1991).

———. "Rethinking the Civil Rights and Civil Liberties Revolutions." 82 *Va. L. Rev.* 1 (1996).

Klinkner, Philip A., and Smith, Rogers M. *The Unsteady March: The Rise and Decline of Racial Equality in America.* Chicago: University of Chicago Press, 1999.

Kluger, Richard. *Simple Justice: The History of* Brown v. Board of Education *and Black America's Search for Equality.* New York: Alfred A. Knopf, 1976.

Kolchin, Peter. *American Slavery, 1619–1877.* New York: Hill and Wang, 1993.

Lagemann, Ellen Condliffe, and Miller, LaMar P., eds. Brown v. Board of Education: *The Challenge for Today's Schools,* New York: Teachers College Press, 1996.

Lawrence, Charles R. III. "The Id, the Ego, and Equal Protection: Reckoning with Unconscious Racism." 39 *Stan. L. Rev.* 317 (1987).

Levin, Betsy, and Hawley, Willis D., eds. *The Courts, Social Science, and School Desegregation.* Piscataway, N.J.: Transaction Publishers, 1976.

Lomotey, Kofi, and Teddlie, Charles, eds. *Forty Years after the* Brown *Decision: Implications of School Desegregation for U.S. Education.* New York: AMS Press, 1996.

MacKinnon, Catharine A. *Feminism Unmodified: Discourses on Life and Law.* Cambridge: Harvard University Press, 1987.

McConnell, Michael W. "Originalism and the Desegregation Decisions." 81 *Va. L. Rev.* 947 (1995).

———. "The Originalist Case for *Brown v. Board of Education.*" 19 *Harv. J.L. & Pub. Pol'y* 457 (1996).

————. "The Originalist Justification for *Brown*: A Reply to Professor Klarman." 81 *Va. L. Rev.* 1937 (1995).

————. "Segregation and the Original Understanding: A Reply to Professor Maltz." 13 *Const. Commentary* 233 (1996).

Michelman, Frank I. *Brennan and Democracy*. Princeton: Princeton University Press, 1999.

Morris, Aldon B. *The Origins of the Civil Rights Movement: Black Communities Organizing for Change*. New York: Free Press, 1984.

Nelson, William E. *The Fourteenth Amendment: From Political Principle to Judicial Doctrine*. Cambridge: Harvard University Press, 1988.

Nomination of Robert H. Bork to Be Associate Justice of the Supreme Court of the United States. Hearings before the Committee on the Judiciary, United States Senate (1987).

Orfield, Gary A. *The Reconstruction of Southern Education: The Schools and the 1964 Civil Rights Act*. New York: Wiley-Interscience, 1969.

Orfield, Gary A.; Bachmeier, Mark D.; James, David R.; and Eitle, Tamela. "Deepening Segregation in American Public Schools." Harvard Project on School Desegregation (April 5, 1997).

Orfield, Gary A., and Eaton, Susan E. *Dismantling Desegregation: The Quiet Reversal of* Brown v. Board of Education. New York: New Press, 1996.

Orfield, Gary A., and Yun, John T. "Resegregation in American Schools" (June 1999). available at <http://www.law.harvard.edu/groups/civilrights/publications/ resegregation99.html> (last visited September 5, 2000).

Patterson, James T. *Grand Expectations: The United States, 1945–1974*. New York: Oxford University Press, 1996.

Powe, Lucas A., Jr. *The Warren Court and American Politics*. Cambridge: Harvard University Press, 2000.

Rosenberg, Gerald. *The Hollow Hope: Can Courts Bring About Social Change?* Chicago: University of Chicago Press, 1991.

Rossell, Christine H., and Hawley, Willis D., eds. *The Consequences of School Desegregation*. Philadelphia: Temple University Press, 1983.

Ryan, James E. "Schools, Race, and Money." 109 *Yale L.J.* 249 (1999).

Sarat, Austin, ed. *Race, Law, and Culture: Reflections on* Brown v. Board of Education. New York: Oxford University Press, 1997.

Schwartz, Bernard. *Super Chief*. New York: New York University Press, 1983.

Shapiro, Martin. *Freedom of Speech: The Supreme Court and Judicial Review*. Englewood Cliffs, N.J.: Prentice-Hall, 1966.

Siegel, Reva. "Why Equal Protection No Longer Protects: The Evolving Forms of Status-Protecting State Action." 49 *Stan. L. Rev.* IIII (1997).

Strauss, David. "Discriminatory Intent and the Taming of *Brown*," 56 *U. Chi. L. Rev.* 935 (1989).

————. "The Myth of Colorblindness." 1986 *Sup. Ct. Rev.* 99 (1986).

Sunstein, Cass R. "The Anticaste Principle." 92 *Mich. L. Rev.* 2410 (1994).

———. *One Case at a Time: Judicial Minimalism on the Supreme Court.* Cambridge: Harvard University Press, 1999.

"Symposium: *Brown v. Board of Education.*" 20 *S. Ill. U. L.J.* 1 (1995)(also containing a series of revised opinions to *Brown*).

Thomas, Bettye Collier, and Franklin, V. P. *My Soul is a Witness: A Chronology of the Civil Rights Era, 1954–1965.* New York: Henry Holt and Company, 2000.

Tushnet, Mark V. *Making Civil Rights Law: Thurgood Marshall and the Supreme Court, 1936–1961.* New York: Oxford University Press, 1994.

———. *The NAACP's Legal Strategy against Segregated Education, 1925–50.* Chapel Hill: University of North Carolina Press, 1987.

———. *Taking the Constitution Away from the Courts.* Princeton: Princeton University Press, 1999.

Tushnet, Mark, and Lezin, Katya. "What Really Happened in *Brown v. Board of Education.*" 91 *Colum. L. Rev.* 1867 (1991).

Urofsky, Melvin I., ed. *The Supreme Court Justices: A Biographical Dictionary.* New York: Garland Publishing, 1994.

Warren, Earl. *The Memoirs of Earl Warren.* New York: Doubleday & Co., 1977.

Washington, James M., ed. *A Testament of Hope: The Essential Writings of Martin Luther King, Jr.* New York: Harper & Row, 1986.

Wechsler, Herbert. "Toward Neutral Principles of Constitutional Law." 73 *Harv. L. Rev.* 1 (1959).

Wexler, Sanford. *The Civil Rights Movement: An Eyewitness History.* New York: Facts on File, 1993.

White, G. Edward. *Earl Warren: A Public Life.* New York: Oxford University Press, 1982.

Wilkinson, J. Harvie, III. *From* Brown *to* Bakke: *The Supreme Court and School Integration, 1954–1978.* New York: Oxford University Press, 1979.

Williams, Juan. *Eyes on the Prize: America's Civil Rights Years, 1954–1965.* New York: Viking Press, 1987.

———. *Thurgood Marshall: American Revolutionary.* New York: Times Books, 1998.

Wilson, William Julius. *The Bridge over the Racial Divide: Rising Inequality and Coalition Politics.* Berkeley: University of California Press, 1999.

———. *The Truly Disadvantaged: The Inner City, the Underclass, and Public Policy.* Chicago: University of Chicago Press, 1987.

Woodward, C. Vann. *The Strange Career of Jim Crow.* New York: Oxford University Press, 1955.

X, Malcolm. *By Any Means Necessary: Speeches, Interviews, and a Letter.* G. Breitman ed. New York: Pathfinder Press, 1970.

About the Contributors

Bruce Ackerman is Sterling Professor of Law and Political Science at Yale University. His major works include *Social Justice in the Liberal State* (1980) and *We the People*, vol. 1 (1991), vol. 2 (1998). He has also written many books on practical problems ranging from housing policy to environmental law to welfare policy to international relations—including, most recently, *The Stakeholder Society* (with Anne Alstott, 1999). He is a member of the American Law Institute and the American Academy of Arts and Sciences.

Jack M. Balkin is Knight Professor of Constitutional Law and the First Amendment at Yale Law School and the founder and director of Yale's Information Society Project, an interdisciplinary center devoted to the study of law and the new information technologies. Professor Balkin writes in the areas of constitutional law, jurisprudence, and social and cultural theory. He is the author of *Cultural Software: A Theory of Ideology* (1998), and *Processes of Constitutional Decisionmaking* (with Paul Brest, Sanford Levinson, and Akhil Reed Amar, 4th ed. 2000).

Derrick A. Bell is Visiting Professor of Law at NYU Law School. A law teacher for more than thirty years, he is the author of *Race, Racism, and American Law* (4th ed., 2000); *Afrolantica Legacies* (1998); *Constitutional Conflicts* (1997); *Gospel Choirs: Psalms of Survival in an Alien Land Called Home* (1996); *Confronting Authority: Reflections of an Ardent Protester* (1994); *Faces at the Bottom of the Well: The Permanence of Racism* (1992); and *And We Are Not Saved: The Elusive Quest for Racial Justice* (1987).

Drew S. Days III is Alfred M. Rankin Professor at Yale Law School. Professor Days served on the staff of the NAACP Legal Defense Fund from 1969 to 1977. From 1977 to 1980, he was the Assistant Attorney General for Civil Rights in the Carter Administration. Professor Days has been a member of the Yale Law Faculty since 1981, with the exception of a three-year stint (1993–96) as the Solicitor General of the United States in the first Clinton Administration.

John Hart Ely is Richard A. Hausler Professor of Law at the University of Miami. He has served in the United States Army's Military Police Corps; on the staff of the Warren Commission investigating President Kennedy's assassination; as Chief Justice Warren's law clerk; as a criminal trial lawyer with Defenders, Inc., in San Diego; as General Counsel (the third-ranking official) of the U.S. Department of Transportation; and as a Professor of Law at Yale, Harvard (where he was the Tyler Professor of Constitutional Law), and Stanford (where he served as Dean from 1982 to 1987). He is a fellow of the American Academy of Arts and Sciences and the Council on Foreign Relations; has been awarded honorary doctor of laws degrees by the University of San Diego and the Illinois Institute of Technology; and is the author of *On Constitutional Ground* (1996), *War and Responsibility* (1993), and *Democracy and Distrust* (1980), which won the Order of the Coif award as the best book about law published in 1980–82 and is the most frequently cited book about law published in the twentieth century.

Catharine A. MacKinnon is Elizabeth A. Long Professor of Law at the University of Michigan Law School and long-term Visiting Professor of Law at the University of Chicago Law School. Her work has centered on the theory and practice of sex equality under law and in society, domestically and internationally. She pioneered the legal claim for sexual harassment and, with Andrea Dworkin, the recognition of civil rights for those violated in and through pornography. Over the last decade, she has represented Muslim and Croat women survivors of sexual atrocities in the Serb-led genocide in Croatia and Bosnia-Herzegovina seeking international justice. She is the author of *Sex Equality* (2001), a legal casebook that situates U.S. case law in theoretical, social, and international context and aims to promote the equality of the sexes.

Michael W. McConnell, now Presidential Professor at the University of Utah College of Law and formerly William B. Graham Professor at the University of Chicago Law School, specializes in constitutional law and has written widely on such subjects as freedom of religion, segregation, unenumerated rights, and constitutional theory. He served as law clerk to Chief Judge J. Skelly Wright on the United States Court of Appeals for the D.C. Circuit and for Associate Justice William J. Brennan Jr. on the United States Supreme Court, as Assistant General Counsel of the Office of Management and Budget, and as Assistant to the Solicitor General of the United States. He has argued eleven cases in the Supreme Court, most recently *Mitchell v. Helms*, No. 98-1648, involving aid to religious schools. He has served as Chair of the Constitutional Law Section of the Association of American Law Schools, Co-Chair of the Emergency Committee to Defend the First Amendment, and member of the President's Intelligence Oversight Board. In 1996, he was elected a Fellow of the American Academy of Arts and Sciences.

Frank I. Michelman is Robert Walmsley University Professor at Harvard University, where he has taught since 1963. He is the author *Brennan and Democracy* (1999) and has published widely in the fields of constitutional law and theory, property law and theory, local government law, and jurisprudence. He was the 2000 Storrs Lecturer at Yale University, where he spoke on "Constitutional Essentialism: On the Idea of the Constitution in the Liberal Justification of Politics." Professor Michelman is immediate past President of the American Society for Political and Legal Philosophy and a fellow of the American Academy of Arts and Sciences. In recent years, he has consulted on matters of constitutionalism in South Africa.

Cass R. Sunstein is Karl N. Llewellyn Distinguished Service Professor at the University of Chicago Law School and Department of Political Science. His books include *Republic.com* (2001), *Designing Democracy: What Constitutions Do* (forthcoming 2001), *One Case at a Time* (1999), *Legal Reasoning and Political Conflict* (1996), and *The Partial Constitution* (1993).

Table of Cases

Index

For references to specific cases, please also see the Table of Cases